The
Disappearing
American Voter

The Disappearing American Voter

Ruy A. Teixeira

The Brookings Institution
Washington, D.C.

Copyright © 1992 by
THE BROOKINGS INSTITUTION
1775 Massachusetts Avenue, N.W., Washington, D.C. 20036

Library of Congress Cataloging-in-Publication Data:

Teixeira, Ruy A.
    The disappearing American voter / Ruy A. Teixeira.
        p.   cm.
    Includes bibliographical references and index.
    ISBN 0-8157-8302-7 —ISBN 0-8157-8303-5 (pbk.)
    1. Voting—United States—Abstention.   2. United States—Politics
    and government—1945–1989.   I. Title
JK1987.T45   1992
324.973'092—dc20   92-26059
                                                                CIP

9 8 7 6 5 4 3 2 1

The paper used in this publication meets the minimum requirements of the American National Standard for Information Sci-
ences—Permanence of Paper for Printed Library Materials, ANSI
Z39.48-1984

Foreword

The rate of voter turnout in U.S. national elections has been falling almost uninterruptedly for thirty years. In the 1988 election half the voting-age population—more than 91 million Americans—did not bother to go to the polls. What are the consequences for American democracy of this low and declining rate of voter participation? And what, if anything, can be done to reverse this disturbing trend?

Ruy A. Teixeira, visiting fellow in the Brookings Governmental Studies program, starts from the premise that Americans must have a clear, empirically based understanding of the problem before they can develop effective means of solving it. He analyzes the phenomenon of low and declining turnout and assesses the likely impact of various cures. Along the way he dispells a number of myths about who is voting and who is not and how low turnout might bias American politics. The analysis concludes with practical suggestions for increasing turnout by making registering and voting easier and improving people's motivation to go to the polls.

Support for this project was partly provided by grants from the Joyce Foundation and the Deer Creek Foundation.

National Election Study and Bureau of the Census data were provided by the Inter-University Consortium for Political and Social Research. Other data were provided by Knight-Ridder Newspapers, Christopher Wlezien of the University of Florida, Henry Brady of the University of California, Berkeley, People for the American Way, the Republican National Committee, Times-Mirror Center for the People, Press and Politics, and the Markle Foundation.

The manuscript benefited from the comments of anonymous reviewers and of Steven Bennet, Curtis Gans, Thomas Mann, Warren Miller, and Raymond Wolfinger. Elizabeth Greenberg provided excellent research assistance. Eric Messick, an intern on the project, helped with library and clerical tasks. Leslie Albin edited the manuscript, Alison M. Rimsky and Lisa Pace verified its factual content, and Susan J. Thompson and Elizabeth O. Toy typed the final text. Susan Woollen prepared it for typesetting, James R. Schneider directed the final stages of editing and production, and Celeste Newbrough indexed it.

The views expressed in this book are those of the author and should not be ascribed to the trustees, officers, or other staff members of the Brookings Institution.

BRUCE K. MACLAURY
President

September 1992
Washington, D.C.

Contents

Tables

Figures

Introduction

After a small increase in 1984, the rate of voter turnout in America has resumed its steady deterioration. With the 3-percentage-point decline in the 1988 election, voter turnout has fallen 13 points since 1960. It is now barely half (50.2 percent) of the voting-age population, a figure below the low mark reached by the 1948 Dewey-Truman election and the lowest level since 1924. The sheer magnitude of nonvoting is staggering—more than 91 million Americans did not bother to go to the polls in 1988.

This is obviously a dismal situation that has occasioned much comment. And the same questions keep being debated, frequently generating more heat than light. Why are American voter turnout rates generally so low? Why have levels of turnout been dropping steadily for the past three decades? Do these low and falling rates significantly bias American politics? And what, if anything, can be done to increase anemic levels of voter participation?

In this book I address each of these questions in detail. My intent in doing so is the result of what I have observed in the public domain: to generate more light than heat. Thus I analyze each of the questions *empirically*, to the extent existing data allow. Where data do not allow empirical analysis or where certain assumptions are necessary to conduct a data-driven analysis, I clearly say so. And where analysis indicates that results are uncertain or can only be specified within a certain range, I try to make this clear as well.

Such an approach is intended to specify where there is much room for debate and where there is relatively little. In this way I hope the debate on the causes and cures of low voter turnout can be narrowed down to those issues about which reasonable people may disagree, rather than being focused, as is now so often the case, on issues about which there is little factual basis for dispute. If this narrowing down can be accomplished, both policymakers and the public will have a clearer view of the problem and what can be done to solve it.

The analysis is presented in five chapters. The first examines the reasons for generally low U.S. voter turnout, comparing U.S. levels with those of other countries and of earlier periods in U.S. history and analyzing the factors responsible. The second chapter analyzes the phenomenon of falling turnout since 1960. Here the main factors leading to this decline are identified and the responsibility for it allocated among them. The third chapter investigates the extent to which low turnout may be warping U.S. politics. It considers two questions. First, what are the demographic biases in voting rates and how have they been changing? Second, what difference, if any, does nonvoting make to electoral and policy outcomes?

The last two chapters discuss how voter turnout in the United States can be increased. Chapter 4 examines one possible approach: decreasing citizens' average costs of voting. The chapter includes an extensive discussion of registration reform and its probable effect on voter turnout and on American politics in general. Chapter 5 examines the other possible approach: increasing voter motivation. The chapter explains why confronting the lack of voter motivation is a necessary component of efforts to achieve higher turnout and a more responsive democracy. It goes on to outline some possible methods for strengthening motivation through legislative and institutional change.

In these discussions the reader may encounter some surprises. For example, many people believe that nonvoters have completely rejected "the system," that they are all poor, that low turnout rates mean that many conservatives are elected, and that nonvoting allows the policy preferences of the affluent to dominate the government—in short, that low and declining turnout indicates the political system is biased and fundamentally rotten. The evidence presented here does not support these allegations. Indeed it suggests that these problems are less severe than generally supposed and would not, by themselves, constitute compelling reasons to call for higher voter turnout.

The reasons we should try to achieve higher turnout must be found instead in less dramatic but still vital concerns about the type of democracy we wish to have. These concerns are rooted in the link between those governing and those governed, between policymakers and citizens. In particular, low and declining turnout attenuates this link in two ways.

First is the problem of democratic legitimacy. As fewer and fewer people vote, the extent to which government truly rests on the consent of the governed is eroded. As a result, elected officials may believe they do not have sufficient legitimacy to pursue desired policies, and citizens may believe that government is not legitimate enough to merit support. The result of this lack of confidence could be anything from widespread social and political disorganization to the reinforcment of some of the milder social pathologies we already see: gridlocked government and a political culture that turns talented people away from careers in public service.

Second is the problem of agenda setting. In a democracy, policy alternatives presented to the public should ideally reflect the needs and interests of the people as a whole. If they do not, some segments of the population may be disadvantaged by these alternatives, even if their specific preferences about them differ little from those of the rest of the population. Low and declining voter turnout may contribute to this problem of an unrepresentative policy agenda because nonvoters and voters do differ from one another in attributes that reflect individual needs and interests, such as income, even if their specific policy preferences generally do not. As a result, policy decisions of officials may accurately reflect people's immediate preferences, but in the long run the policy agenda may only poorly represent the segments of the population that vote the least.

Such a situation seems especially worrisome, given that the behavior of political activists—contacting officials, getting involved in community organizations, giving to campaigns, and so on—may have more impact on policymakers, and that the needs and interests of these activists differ ever more sharply from those of the rest of the population. Thus participating in elections, which should act as a democratic counterweight to high-impact activism, exposing policymakers to a wider array of needs and interests, may fail to play that role effectively when nonvoting is widespread. As a result the democratic link between the needs of the populace and the agenda set by policymakers may erode over time.

This problem may be accentuated by the well-publicized activities of organized groups lobbying for particularized agendas (so-called special interests). These activities should be thought of as a form of political participation by such groups—participation that has become increasingly widespread. And because this form of activity has a relatively high impact, attempting as it does to influence public policy directly through extensive personal contacts and the dispensation of favors, the need for a democratic counterweight to special interest participation seems crucial. Widespread nonvoting makes it less likely that electoral participation by ordinary citizens will be that counterweight.

Of course, other reasons could be advanced in favor of increasing turnout. For example, participation by itself may help people develop personally, so more participation is good for that reason. Or somewhat more abstractly, real democracy may call for participation, so more participation must mean more democracy, which is good.

But I believe these reasons are subordinate to concerns about the quality of the link between policymakers and citizens. Low and declining voter turnout threatens this link and compromises the type of democracy the United States is today and will become in the future. Provided the costs of reform are not too great, these concerns should be enough to merit action to increase voter turnout without invoking either the specter of a rotting political system in which the affluent dictate election outcomes or the utopian vision of a democracy in which all citizens participate all the time.

I am convinced therefore that increased voter turnout would indeed be a social good. But in the pages that follow, I seek to separate fact from fiction so that efforts to attain this goal will proceed clear-eyed and without pretense.

1

Why Is American Voter Turnout So Low?

Voter turnout levels are now quite low in the United States compared both with those of other advanced industrial democracies and with those of earlier periods in U.S. history. Here I analyze the main reasons that lie behind the phenomenon of generally low U.S. voter turnout. First, the extent to which U.S. voter turnout lags behind international and historical standards is described. Second, the main factors that appear to underlie relatively low U.S. voter turnout, both cross-nationally and historically, are discussed. Finally, responsibility for generally low U.S. voter turnout is partitioned among several sets of factors uncovered by these analyses.

How Low Is American Voter Turnout?

Table 1-1 shows voter turnout in the United States in the last three decades, both for on-year (presidential) and off-year elections. The first thing that jumps out from these data is that turnout has been going down steadily over three decades.[1] But the second striking feature of these data is that turnout levels were not high at any time in this period. For example, the high-water mark of presidential turnout in these three decades was 62.8 percent in 1960. That is barely more than three-fifths

---

1. Local election turnout has apparently declined in a similar manner (see Leighley 1992). On the other hand turnout in presidential primaries has remained fairly stable (Committee for the Study of the American Electorate 1992; Rothenberg and Brody 1988), whereas participation in certain political activities outside of voting (such as contributing money and contacting officials) has actually gone *up* (Brady and others 1988).

TABLE 1-1. *Turnout in U.S. National Elections, 1960–90*[a]
Percent

	Presidential election			Off-year[b]	
Year	U.S. total	South[c]	Non-South	Year	U.S. total
1960	62.8	42.9	69.8	1962	47.5
1964	61.9	47.0	67.3	1966	48.4
1968	60.9	51.6	64.3	1970	46.8
1972	55.2	44.9	59.1	1974	38.3
1976	53.6	46.8	56.2	1978	37.3
1980	52.8	47.0	54.9	1982	40.5
1984	53.1	48.3	55.2	1986	36.3
1988	50.2	44.9	52.5	1990	36.4

SOURCE: Committee for the Study of the American Electorate 1989, 1990.
a. Based on the voting-age population.
b. Based on highest statewide turnout—that is, turnout in a given state was set equal to the highest turnout for a statewide office in that year (or to the summed congressional turnout if there was not a statewide race).
c. Includes Alabama, Arkansas, Florida, Georgia, Kentucky, Louisiana, Mississippi, North Carolina, South Carolina, Tennessee, Texas, Virginia, and West Virginia.

of the voting-age population (VAP).[2] Similarly the highest off-year turnout was 48.4 percent in 1966, less than half the electorate.

Now of course levels of turnout are even lower. Turnout was just over one-half the VAP (50.2 percent) in the presidential election of 1988, while turnout in the 1990 off-year election was little more than one-third (36.4 percent). But clearly the United States has not become a low-turnout society simply because of declining turnout. Rather a *low* turnout society (1960s) has been turned into an *even lower* turnout society (1990s) by these trends.

Table 1-1 also provides some important regional detail on this story by breaking down presidential turnout trends between the South and the rest of the country (the non-South). As these data make clear, the overall decline in turnout is really the result of two different trends. Southern turnout went *up* 2 percentage points over the 1960–88 pe-

2. The voting-age population is the standard base (denominator) for estimating turnout rates in the United States. This is both because the voting-age population is a good approximation of the actual number of eligible voters and because adjusting the voting-age population to remove legally ineligible voters (that is, aliens) is a difficult and imprecise process. Furthermore—though this is little known—citizenship is not a constitutional requirement for voting in the United States. Both the time it takes to become a citizen (national) and the actual restriction of suffrage to citizens (state) are matters of legislation. Thus at the most basic level of the system, the voting-age population *is* the eligible population. For all these reasons the term "turnout" in this book generally refers to turnout of the voting-age population.

riod,[3] while nonsouthern turnout declined faster than the national rate (down 17 points).[4] In a sense what has happened is the South has remained a very low turnout area despite a slight increase, while the rest of the country has *become* a very low turnout area as a result of a steep decline.

And just how low is overall U.S. voter turnout at this point? As the data in the table suggest, it depends, to some extent, on whether the on-year or off-year election series is examined. The off-year election figures certainly paint the worst picture, averaging only 37.7 percent in the 1982–90 period. But given the preeminent importance of the presidency in American politics, it would not be fair to measure general U.S. turnout levels by elections that do not include a presidential contest. For this reason, U.S. presidential turnout levels will be used to compare the contemporary United States with other countries and with earlier eras in American history. But presidential elections represent only the upper bound of U.S. voter participation. Beneath these "flagship" elections lurks an entire substratum of much lower turnout off-year and local elections.[5]

U.S. Turnout Compared Internationally

Even when presidential turnout is used as the yardstick, U.S. voting participation is quite low by international standards (table 1-2). Among twenty advanced industrial democracies, the average U.S. turnout rate of 53 percent in the 1980s ranks next to last (only Switzerland has a lower turnout rate).

Moreover, the *size* of the gap between the United States and other democracies is huge. Because the highest ranked democracies (Belgium, Austria, Australia) have turnouts of 90 percent or more, the gap between the United States and these democracies approaches or exceeds 40 percentage points. And even if one compares the U.S. rate

3. Changes in southern turnout are, themselves the result of two different trends among white southerners and black southerners (see chapter 2).

4. It is worth noting that nonsouthern turnout at the beginning of this period was on a par with current national turnout levels in such democracies as the United Kingdom, France, and Canada (see table 1-2). There is a problem with this comparison, however, in that one is comparing only part of the United States (the high-turnout part) with these other nations. Presumably these nations also have relatively high- and relatively low-turnout areas, in which case a fairer comparison would be between the U.S. non-South and the high-turnout parts of these other nations. This comparison is unlikely to be as favorable.

5. A good rule of thumb is that off-year turnout is about 15 percentage points lower than presidential turnout, whereas local turnout is another 15 points lower than off-year turnout (thus the spread between local and presidential turnout is about 30 points).

TABLE 1-2. *Average Turnout in Twenty Democracies, 1980–89*
Percent

Nation	Turnout		Nation	Turnout
Belgium	94		Israel	79
Austria	92		Greece	78
Australia	90		Finland	74
New Zealand	89		United Kingdom	74
Sweden	88		Ireland	73
West Germany	87		Canada	72
Denmark	86		France	70
Italy	84		Japan	68
Netherlands	84		United States	53
Norway	83		Switzerland	49

SOURCE: Duch 1990 cited in Erikson, Luttbeg, and Tedin 1991, table 1-1. Data are from national legislative elections, except in the United States, where data are from presidential elections. The base is the legally eligible electorate.

with the *average* across all twenty democracies (78 percent), the gap is still 25 points. By these data then the contemporary United States is an exceptionally low-turnout society.

U.S. Turnout Compared Historically

Historical comparisons tell a similar story. The United States was a much higher-turnout society throughout much of the nineteenth century than it is today (table 1-3).[6] Between 1840 and 1900, turnout averaged 77.7 percent, about 23 points higher than the 1972–88 average of 54.9 percent and virtually identical[7] to the current average among the twenty industrial democracies listed in table 1-2.

Again these data show the contemporary United States as an unusually low turnout society. The data also show very clearly that low turnout is not just a phenomenon of the last several decades. Through-

6. The data in table 1-3 use the *eligible* electorate as a denominator, rather than the voting-age population. This reflects the fact that meaningful historical comparisons of turnout rates are not possible without taking into account the large proportions of the population that could not vote at different times in U.S. history (for instance, almost all women could not vote before 1920). Thus despite the data problems that bedevil estimates of the eligible electorate, it is preferable to use these estimates, rather than the voting-age population, when making historical comparisons.

Note that because of the differing denominators, turnout rates for elections reported in both tables 1-1 and 1-3 are slightly larger in table 1-3. This reflects the fact that the turnout rates in table 1-3 use the slightly smaller, eligible electorate denominator (for the 1960–90 period, this essentially means the voting-age population minus aliens).

7. Though the international turnout average would be slightly higher if the United States were excluded from that average (this would bring the international average up to 80 percent).

TABLE 1-3. *Turnout in U.S. Presidential Elections, 1824–1988*[a]
Percent

Year	Turnout	Year	Turnout
1824	26.7	1908	65.7
1828	57.3	1912	59.0
1832	56.7	1916	61.8
1836	56.5	1920	49.3
1840	80.3	1924	48.9
1844	79.0	1928	56.9
1848	72.8	1932	57.0
1852	69.5	1936	61.0
1856	79.4	1940	62.5
1860	81.8	1944	55.9
1864	76.3	1948	53.4
1868	80.9	1952	63.8
1872	72.1	1956	61.6
1876	82.6	1960	65.4
1880	80.6	1964	63.3
1884	78.3	1968	62.3
1888	80.5	1972	57.1
1892	75.9	1976	55.2
1896	79.7	1980	54.3
1900	73.7	1984	55.2
1904	65.5	1988	52.8

SOURCES: Burnham 1987, table 5-3; and author's computations.
a. Based on legally eligible electorate (This excludes most blacks before 1870, most women before 1920, and most or all aliens throughout).

out most of the twentieth century, in fact, turnout rates have lagged far behind the standard set by the previous century.

For example, in the New Deal period (1932–44), seemingly an era of high political mobilization, turnout of the eligible electorate averaged only 59 percent. And in the 1952–60 period, the three contiguous elections with the highest average turnout since 1912, the rate of voter participation was just 64 percent—still 14 points less than in 1840–1900.

Are Conventional Turnout Figures Unfair?

The data just summarized indicate that the contemporary United States is a very low turnout society, both by international and historical standards. Some say that U.S. turnout data are fatally flawed, however— that conventional turnout figures unfairly exaggerate the seriousness of the problem.[8] Specifically, turnout rates based on the voting-age pop-

8. Mitofsky and Plissner 1988.

ulation are said to include too many people who cannot vote (aliens, felons, those in mental institutions, those who moved within thirty days of the election) and exclude some people who do vote (those who voted but did not vote for president).

But the data for the 1960—88 presidential elections reported in table 1-3 (where aliens are excluded) generally differ by only about 2 percentage points from the corresponding data in table 1-1 (where aliens are not excluded). As a further check I performed a specific calculation for the 1988 election[9] that removed not only aliens but also felons, mental institution residents, and recent movers from the denominator (Americans abroad were added, however, because they can vote) and then added nonpresidential voters to the numerator. The final result: an estimated turnout for the 1988 election of roughly 54.3 percent, about 4 points higher than the turnout shown in table 1-1. This is a difference but manifestly not enough to take the United States out of the low-turnout category (compare with table 1-2).

Another objection to conventional turnout figures centers on the role of registration. Because only those registered can vote, it is sometimes argued that U.S. turnout should be assessed and compared on the basis of turnout of the registered (which is actually fairly high—current estimates range from 78 to 86 percent in presidential elections).[10] But such an approach ignores the fact that registration in the United States is voluntary, not automatic as in most other democracies. Because of this difference turnout of the registered in the United States amounts to turnout among a self-selected *subset* of the eligible electorate, whereas turnout of the registered in other countries approximates turnout of the entire eligible electorate. Clearly it will not do to compare countries on the basis of a statistic whose meaning fluctuates so dramatically. The best measure of voter participation remains turnout among the eligible electorate, typically approximated by turnout of the voting-age population.

Explaining Cross-National and Historical Variation in Turnout

The data in the previous section have established that the United States is, indeed, a very low-turnout society by cross-national and historical standards. I now investigate why, broadly speaking, this is so.

9. I am indebted to Curtis B. Gans of the Committee for the Study of the American Electorate for showing me his very similar calculation.

10. The issue of turnout of registered voters is covered in detail in chapter 2. See U.S. Bureau of the Census 1989; and Committee for the Study of the American Electorate 1989.

The first step is to develop an analysis of why some people vote and other people do not. Such an analysis provides a theoretical framework for selecting attributes of societies that should logically affect voter turnout. Then if these societal attributes also vary cross-nationally and historically, they should provide at least part of the explanation for observed variation in turnout levels.

Why People Vote

Looked at from one perspective the amazing thing about voting is that everyone does not do it. It is after all a relatively low-cost activity, requiring little more than fulfilling some minor bureaucratic requirements and traveling to the polling place. On the plus side the voter helps determine the policies affecting his or her life by participating in the selection of policymakers. Yet everyone does not vote. Even in 1960, the recent high-water mark of American voter turnout, more than one in three eligible voters did not bother to cast a ballot. And in other democracies, where turnout is typically much higher than in the United States,[11] turnout rates are by no means 100 percent, but vary widely between a little under 70 percent to somewhat over 90 percent (table 1-2).

The perspective sketched above does not tally with the facts for two good reasons. First, voting, while a low-cost activity, is not a zero-cost activity. The costs of registering, finding out where the polling booth is, and taking the time and effort to travel to it on election day are tangible, nonzero ones. In addition, information costs may exist, because not everyone will have easy access to the minimal number of facts necessary to distinguish between candidates. For some people, this set of costs may seem large and not worth the trouble of absorbing.

The second reason has to do with the benefits obtained from balloting. Although the outcome of an election may strongly affect a person's life, the individual citizen does not have to participate in the election to obtain these benefits. The benefits are available to everyone, voter and nonvoter alike.[12] Theorists of voting have therefore pointed out that the worth of a citizen's vote is not equal to the benefits derived

11. Switzerland is an obvious exception. See Lange, Ridout, and Cooney 1978, pp. 93–99, 145–46, and Powell 1982, chapter 6 for discussions of the factors underlying low Swiss voter turnout.
12. This is an example of the problem of provision of "public goods" by large groups (Olson 1965, pp. 9–15), with the outcome of the election as the public good. Nonvoters in this sense become "free riders" on the group of voters participating in the election.

from a given election outcome but to the product obtained by multi-plying the value of these benefits by the probability that the citizen's individual vote will produce that outcome.[13] This "expected value" is the real outcome-related benefit of voting, and in most elections it will be small, because the probability of a lone individual's vote affecting an election outcome is minuscule.

The expected-value factor makes it clearer why everyone does not participate in elections. The costs are not zero, and the benefits, in the expected-value sense, may be so small as to be indistinguishable from zero. By this logic it is surprising that anyone bothers to vote. This problem—the "paradox of voting"—has been duly noted by theorists.[14]

The solution to the problem, at least on a general level, is clear enough. By participating in an election, individual voters must be de-riving benefits that are not dependent on directly influencing the out-come of that election. Such benefits are fundamentally *expressive* and depend on the extent to which a citizen finds his or her vote *meaning-ful* in the context of the election. A wide range of such benefits can be imagined, but they generally fall into two categories.

In the first category a citizen votes in an election to express his or her general commitment to a party, reference group (blacks, women, workers), cause, or even to society as a whole. These expressive ben-efits are primarily *symbolic*[15] because the citizen derives meaning from expressing this general commitment and is relatively detached from the specific issues and dynamics of the election.

In the second category a citizen votes in an election to express his or her specific concern about that election and its relation to govern-ment policy and personnel outcomes. These expressive benefits are basically *instrumental*[16] because they are driven fundamentally by a desire to see certain "real world" outcomes that depend on the election

13. Downs 1957, chap. 14.
14. Riker and Ordeshook 1968; Cyr 1975.
15. Sometimes these symbolic benefits are thought of as the only real expressive benefits relevant to voting (see Lange, Ridout, and Cooney 1978, pp. 164–67; and, to a lesser extent, Conway 1991, pp. 8–11). But clearly given the improbability of directly influencing election outcomes, even votes motivated by concern about the outcome are fundamentally expressive.
16. Sometimes the term "instrumental benefits" of voting is reserved for situations in which the individual casts a vote and receives an immediate benefit from an external source (Wolfinger and Rosenstone 1980, pp. 6–10)—most crudely, money in the pocket or a job; more subtly, approval (or lack of dispproval) from others. This is certainly a defensible use of the term. However because I believe expressive benefits are generally more important to the act of voting, I reserve this term for distinguishing among types of expressive benefits.

result.[17] Of course there is no hard and fast line between symbolic and instrumental expressive benefits. And no doubt individual citizens are typically motivated by a mix of symbolic and instrumental considerations. The basic point remains, however, that without an adequate level of these expressive benefits, however categorized,[18] citizens will not be motivated to participate.

In general then for a citizen to vote, he or she must find these symbolic or instrumental benefits high enough to merit absorbing the costs of participation.[19] Clearly any societal attribute that affects the average level of symbolic or instrumental expressive benefits the electorate can obtain or the average level of costs the electorate must absorb should have an effect on average societal turnout levels. It then follows that, to the extent this attribute varies cross-nationally or historically, it constitutes part of the explanation for observed variation in turnout levels.

Explaining Cross-National Variation in Turnout Levels

One set of relevant attributes that varies cross-nationally is the legal structure of voting. These attributes primarily affect the costs of voting (or nonvoting) by attaching legal obstacles or penalties to the voting process.

The most obvious factor here is the U.S. system of voter registration.[20] This system, based on registration through voluntary, individual initiative, makes it exceptionally difficult by international standards for U.S. citizens to qualify to vote. In most other countries registration is automatic,[21] performed by the state without any individual initia-

---

17. This helps explain how expressive benefits can be "election-specific" and therefore help drive election-to-election variation in turnout. See Aldrich (forthcoming) for more discussion.

18. Or wherever they come from. For arguments that *mobilization*, broadly defined, underlies the realization of expressive benefits in elections, see Rosenstone and Hansen (forthcoming) and Uhlaner 1989. See Knack 1991a for a critique of Uhlaner's strong emphasis on the role of groups.

19. For a more formal treatment of the turnout decision, which is basically consistent with the position sketched here, see Aldrich's excellent review essay (forthcoming) on turnout and rational choice.

20. I have a great deal more to say about the U.S. voter registration system in chapter 4.

21. Technically speaking, Canada and the United Kingdom do not have automatic registration. They build their registration lists through an enumeration process before elections. But since the enumertion process is organized and conducted by the state, registration can be termed automatic in these countries without violating the spirit of the term.

tive.[22] The registration process therefore raises the costs of voting in the United States and should, as a consequence, depress U.S. turnout levels relative to those of other democracies.

Another aspect of the legal structure of voting is compulsory voting laws. Such laws are on the books in several countries, including Italy,[23] Belgium, and Australia.[24] Although by and large these laws appear to be lightly enforced, even the threat of enforcement should act to raise the costs of not voting (which is the same thing as raising the benefits of voting, because cost avoidance is technically a benefit). Hence compulsory voting laws should enhance turnout levels in these countries relative to the levels in other democracies (including the United States).

Several other aspects of the legal structure of voting could potentially have an effect on the costs or benefits[25] of voting and therefore turnout levels. These aspects include the frequency with which the electorate is expected to vote; the ease with which absentee, postal, and other special ballots can be cast; and whether election day is a holiday or rest day or not.[26] These characteristics of the legal structure are usually considered to be of minor significance when compared with registration systems and compulsory voting, a viewpoint that makes good sense theoretically.[27] To the extent these characteristics have an impact, how-

22. An exception is France, where registration is also voluntary. However even here the situation differs in a critical respect from that in the United States. French citizens are required to register in their community and obtain identification cards, a process that tends to promote concommitant voter registration (reflecting this, the French registration rate has averaged over 90 percent in the recent past [Powell 1986, appendix 1]). No such community or other registration requirement exists in the United States, of course.

23. Though in Italy the compulsion to vote is particularly light, being limited to the notation of nonvoting on individuals' documents.

24. See Crewe 1981; Powell 1982, chap. 6; and Jackman 1987 for discussions of different types of compulsory voting laws and levels of enforcement.

25. The ease of special balloting and the election day holiday are clearly cost-related characteristics, whereas election frequency is generally thought of as a benefit-related characteristic. This is because frequent elections are thought to attentuate the meaningfulness of any individual election, especially where balloting for important offices is spread across a number of elections instead of being concentrated in one general election.

26. See Crewe 1981 for a good discussion of these aspects of the voting system and how they vary across countries.

27. For example, the frequency with which elections are held should not have a large effect on turnout for major offices in major elections (such as presidential turnout in the United States) because people can choose to vote only in important elections and ignore the minor ones. Thus the impact of frequently held elections should be felt mostly in high "dropoff" from major to minor elections, rather than in a lack of participation in major elections. (But see Boyd 1981, 1986, 1989 for an argument that election frequency and, more generally, election calendars are of some salience. See also the discussion in chapter 2 of the possible role of changing election calendars in declining turnout.)

The election day holiday is also of problematic value. Will people use the holiday for

ever, systems such as Sweden's, in which election day is a rest day, special balloting arrangements are fairly easy, and elections are infrequent, should have somewhat lower costs and higher benefits, and thus higher turnout, than systems such as that in the United States where election day is a workday, special balloting arrangements are generally difficult, and elections are very frequent.[28]

Another set of relevant attributes that varies cross-nationally is the structure of electoral competition.[29] These attributes primarily affect the instrumental expressive benefits of voting by increasing (or decreasing) the voter's sense that his or her vote will be "represented" in the government.

One such attribute is the extent to which districts are nationally competitive. The idea here is that, where electoral districts are single-member or winner-take-all, voters supporting the minority side in an unbalanced (lopsided) district will have reduced incentives to cast a ballot (as will party organizations to mobilize these voters). This reflects the fact that, as far as the ultimate formation of a government is concerned, the ballots of these voters essentially do not count (for example, Democratic presidential voters in a heavily Republican state in the United States or Labour voters in a heavily Conservative district in the United Kingdom).

In contrast, in an electoral system with a simple direct presidential vote (France) or national election proportional representation (the Netherlands),[30] minority voters in lopsided districts still have an incentive to vote (as do parties to mobilize them). Therefore the benefits of voting should be higher in countries with such systems, leading to, all else equal, higher turnout levels.

Another aspect of the structure of electoral competition is the extent of electoral disproportionality, that is, the amount of disparity between the votes cast for a minor party and the number of seats that party

---

voting or for doing other things (like going out of town) that may preclude voting? And does having more free time available really make the expenditure of time for voting less onerous? The answers to these questions are not obvious.

28. The United States appears to lead the world by a wide margin in this category.

29. See Jackman 1987 for a lucid discussion of the relationship between factors structuring electoral competition and national turnout levels. He discusses each of the factors mentioned here, both theoretically and empirically.

30. Proportional representation (PR) may also permit the existence of a broader range of parties, so that there is a closer match between voters' beliefs and party principles than in non-PR systems. This should also enhance the expressive benefits of voting. However, the entry of multiple parties into coalition governments—also associated with PR—probably *depresses* voter turnout. This potential turnout-depressing effect of multipartyism is discussed later in this section.

receives in the legislature. Where a high degree of disproportionality exists (most common in countries with majority-plurality systems, such as France and the United States[31]), minority-party voters are more likely to consider their votes "wasted." In contrast, where a relatively proportional seat-vote relationship exists (most common in countries with proportional representation systems, such as Denmark and Israel), minority-party voters are less likely to believe their votes do not count. As a result benefits for voters should be higher in countries with little electoral disproportionality, thereby enhancing turnout levels.

Another part of the structure of electoral competition is whether voters vote for one (unicameralism) or two (bicameralism) legislative bodies and, if they vote for two, how much these bodies must compromise to pass legislation. Voters are likely to feel their views most directly represented in a unicameral situation (for example, in Israel or Denmark), in which no interlegislative compromises are necessary, and least directly represented in a strong bicameral system (for example, in Germany or the United States), in which such interlegislative compromises are an essential part of government. Thus benefits for voters should be higher in countries that tend toward the unicameral situation, producing as a result higher turnout levels.

The final relevant aspect of how electoral competition is structured is the extent of multipartyism (that is, the number of parties that enter into forming the national government) where many parties can and do form coalition governments (for example, Finland). In countries with high multipartyism, voters are more likely to feel their votes have been diluted by the necessity to compromise with other parties. In contrast in strong two-party systems like the United States, voters can be assured their votes will not be diluted by coalitional compromise necessary to form a government. Because of this, benefits to voters should be higher—all else equal—in these strong two-party systems, thereby tending to promote higher turnout levels.

Another important attribute that varies cross-nationally is the level of party mobilization—that is, the extent to which parties have direct links to voters through social groups, community institutions, or orga-

---

31. Interestingly enough, the United States fares relatively well among majority/plurality systems in terms of its amount of electoral disproportionality (Lijphart 1984, table 9-1). However Lijphart's measure does not capture the extent to which minority parties simply disappear (or fail to appear at all) because of the exceptional difficulties posed by the U.S. electoral structure. Presumably this feature should contribute to a sense among certain voters that their ballots are wasted.

nizational networks. This attribute primarily affects the expressive benefits of voting—both symbolic and instrumental—through its impact on voters' sense of the meaningfulness of partisan choice.[32]

Party mobilization has a number of different aspects, from the density and penetration of party organizations to the strength of alignment between parties and social groups. All affect turnout in the same basic manner, however. By giving the voter strong, consistent cues—frequently on a personal level—about how to interpret the significance of a given election, party mobilization enhances the benefits of voting in that election. Thus a country like Austria, where party organization is quite strong and parties have sharply defined links to social groups, should have higher turnout, all else equal, than a country like the United States where party organization is very weak (especially at the local level) and party–social group links are relatively blurry.

A wide variety of systemic attributes have been examined that vary cross-nationally and should, through their effects on the costs and benefits of voting, have an impact on turnout levels. A clear pattern is beginning to emerge. On virtually every characteristic examined,[33] the U.S. system is structured in such a way as to *increase the costs* and *decrease the benefits* of voting.

Given this overwhelmingly high-cost, low-benefit system, it seems much less surprising that U.S. turnout levels lag so far behind other democracies. In fact the U.S. environment seems so uncongenial to voter participation, one might wonder why turnout levels are not even lower than they are.

One reason they are not has to do with the individual-level characteristics of U.S. citizens. These characteristics include, surprisingly enough, the general attitudes of individuals about politics. As pointed out in numerous studies,[34] U.S. citizens have relatively high levels of a number of politically oriented characteristics believed to facilitate voter turnout: interest in politics, political efficacy,[35] civic duty, following politics in the media, and party identification. All these characteristics

---

32. Party mobilization may also play a role in reducing the costs of voting. Most directly parties may physically assist voters in geting to the polls. Less directly, party mobilization may reduce information costs by reducing the amount of information the voter has to gather independently to make a voting decision.

33. The one exception is multipartyism.

34. Almond and Verba 1963; Verba, Nie, and Kim 1978; Wolfinger, Glass, and Squire 1985; Powell 1986.

35. Roughly this means a sense that the government is responsive to the wishes of ordinary people.

should serve to enhance expressive benefits for U.S. voters and therefore lead to higher turnout than one might expect strictly on the basis of U.S. systemic attributes.[36]

Similarly U.S. voters are comparatively advantaged by their individual demographic characteristics.[37] Most significantly U.S. voters are on average much more educated than their counterparts in other democracies.[38] Because higher education levels are believed to produce increased capacity to handle election-relevant information, this characteristic of U.S. voters should also serve to make U.S. turnout higher than it otherwise would be.

In summary the U.S. political system is, on virtually all counts, a high-cost, low-benefit system that tends to depress turnout levels. The individual-level characteristics of U.S. citizens, however, serve as a countervailing force (virtually the *only* countervailing force[39]) within this intrinsically low turnout system. As a result U.S. turnout is very low— as would be expected from the systemic influences—but not as low as it probably would be without the favorable attitudinal and demographic profile of the U.S. electorate.

Explaining Historical Variation in Turnout Levels

The examination of cross-national variation in turnout levels provides some clues for understanding historical variation in turnout levels. Specifically this examination implies that if turnout levels have changed

36. Some analysts (Wolfinger, Glass, and Squire 1985) have stated that because low American voter turnout cannot be explained on the basis of a relatively unfavorable ("alienated") attitude structure, attitudinal considerations are not relevant to an explanation of U.S. turnout levels. That seems unreasonable, because the U.S. attitude structure does not have to be offered as an explanation, *in and of itself*, for low U.S. voter turnout. More reasonably, the turnout-enhancing attitudes of U.S. citizens can be viewed as a countervailing force to other turnout-depressing (primarily systemic) influences and, therefore, as *part* of an overall explanation for observed U.S. turnout levels.

37. Powell 1986, pp. 18–20.

38. The critical role of education in voter turnout is discussed in chapter 2. For an extensive and very clear treatment of this relationship, see Wolfinger and Rosenstone 1980.

39. Indeed it may be that some of these characteristics—for example, following politics in the media—are actually adaptations on the part of U.S. voters to the difficulties of voting in a high-cost, low-benefit environment. The U.S. voter after all is not embedded in an electoral system that makes the significance of vote choice obvious, nor enmeshed in a social web of party-based linkages that constantly underlines the significance of that choice. One way of compensating for this lack of structural and collective cues may be for individuals to give themselves their own cues through low-level forms of political involvement.

substantially in U.S. history, it is because of changes in one or more of the turnout-influencing factors just discussed.

As shown in table 1-3, turnout levels have fluctuated throughout U.S. history. Most relevant to the issue of low U.S. voter turnout, however, is the general drop in voter participation from the relatively high levels of the middle and late nineteenth century to the relatively low levels of the twentieth century.[40] This implies that potentially relevant changes should be looked for in the period marking the transition to the twentieth century (that is, in the Progressive era, roughly 1896–1916).

The first set of attributes to be examined is the legal structure of voting. Substantial changes did occur here, the most important of which was the widespread institution of personal registration requirements.[41] The imposition of these requirements must have substantially increased the costs of voting for the average citizen and, therefore, should have affected turnout levels during this period.

The second set of attributes concerns the basic structure of electoral competition. Generally speaking the basic structure of electoral competition did not change in this period in any major way that would have affected turnout levels. The one possible exception was changes in official ballot laws to prevent multiple listings of candidates' names and therefore major-minor-party fusion arrangements. To the extent this reform had an impact, it may have increased electoral disproportionality, and therefore decreased the benefits of voting. But fusionism was probably too specific to certain states and certain elections to make it much of an influence on general turnout levels.

The third attribute to be considered here is party mobilization. The Progressive era did in fact witness a variety of changes that affected the links between parties and voters. To begin with, several legal changes damped down the intense relationship between parties and the electoral process. These included the replacement of party-provided ballots

40. Detailed explanations for many of the more specific turnout fluctuations displayed in table 1-3 may be found in Kleppner 1982, and Burnham 1982. In addition the most recent change in turnout levels—the sharp decline since 1960—is discussed in detail in chapter 2.

41. It is sometimes argued that personal registration and other changes around this time had another important effect on turnout levels—basically by reducing the number of fraudulent ballots cast. By this account, relatively high nineteenth century voter turnouts reflect, to a large extent, the high number of fraudulent ballots cast and are therefore artifactual (Converse 1972). Undoubtedly fraudulent ballots had some effect on recorded turnout levels in the nineteenth century, but Kleppner 1982 and Burnham 1982, 1986, argue persuasively that this effect was relatively minor (see, particularly, Burnham 1986).

with officially provided ballots distributed at polling places; the replacement of party-dominated caucus or convention candidate selection with direct primaries; and the introduction of nonpartisan balloting for many local offices and on referenda.

In addition—and probably related to the legal changes—the alignment between parties and social groups weakened, the level of party competition decreased, and the intensity with which parties organized for elections declined.[42] All these changes served to weaken substantially the links between parties and voters, which had been quite strong during most of the nineteenth century. As a result the benefits of voting must have declined, thereby affecting turnout levels.

A clear pattern has emerged from this examination of various attributes affecting the costs and benefits of voting. On every characteristic examined, historical changes in the U.S. system have acted to *increase the costs* and *decrease the benefits* of voting. Given this secular tendency toward a high-cost, low-benefit system, the question may be not why U.S. turnout is so low but why U.S. turnout is not even lower.

Part of the answer to this puzzle may lie—as it did in the cross-national analysis—with the individual characteristics of U.S. voters. Now admittedly virtually nothing of the *attitudinal* characteristics of citizens in this particular era of American history is known with any certainty, since modern survey data only date back to the 1930s. Thus it cannot be determined whether the attitudes of U.S. voters changed in such a way as to affect turnout—or, if they changed at all.

However something is known about the demographic characteristics of eligible voters and how they changed, primarily from census data. In general most of these demographic changes—chiefly, increasing education levels, but also a somewhat older population—appear to be changes that would have facilitated voting participation.[43] This suggests that changes in the individual-level characteristics, to the extent that they are known, may have served as a countervailing force within a generally turnout-depressing historical trajectory. As a result contemporary U.S. turnout levels are indeed very low, but not as low as they probably would be absent historical changes in the demographic composition of the electorate.

42. Kleppner 1982 and Burnham 1982 cover these changes in detail.
43. It should be noted that Kleppner's data suggest education and age were much weaker predictors of turnout in the nineteenth century than they are today (Kleppner 1982). If true, however, education and age trends could be even *more* of a countervailing force, because both distribution *and* effect changes could act to keep up turnout levels.

Relative Weight of Factors Explaining
Low American Voter Turnout

The preceding section has established that, whether compared cross-nationally or historically, the costs of voting in the United States are exceptionally high and the benefits exceptionally low. Because of this, turnout levels in the United States tend to lag far behind international and historical standards.

A more specific allocation of responsibility for low turnout would be desirable, however. For example, is it mostly the high costs of voting or the low benefits that keep U.S. citizens from the polls? And to the extent benefits are important, is it lack of benefits from party mobilization or from the structure of electoral competition that has the most impact?

One way to answer these questions is to partition U.S. nonvoting into components stemming from different causes. Such an exercise is necessarily rough because of limitations of both data and method.[44] However, available studies do contain much suggestive information, which if treated cautiously allows some limited conclusions to be drawn.

How much U.S. nonvoting has to be accounted for? Based on the last presidential election (1988), about 50 percent of the electorate did not bother to cast a ballot.[45] This compares to nonvoting levels as low as 5 percent in other democracies.

However, the fact that almost any election anywhere (in a genuinely democratic country) has at least 5 percent nonvoting suggests the first category. Probably some component of U.S. nonvoting (say, 5 percent) cannot be eliminated under any circumstances, no matter how low the costs of voting or how high the benefits. This component of nonvoting can be thought of as *frictional* nonvoting—nonvoting that should be ascribed not to the specific costs or benefits of the U.S. system but rather to the inevitable scattering of personal problems or idiosyncrasies among the population that render participation infeasible in a given election (sickness, accidents, insanity, sudden travel, unusual work schedules, and so forth).

A second component of nonvoting may be ascribed to the unusually high costs of voting in the United States. Essentially, this is the effect of

44. For example, most of the cross-national regression analysis of turnout variation uses N's lower than twenty and up to seven variables. With so few cases and so many variables, it is difficult to have complete confidence in the results produced by any particular model.

45. The figure would be slightly less if adjustments are made for aliens who cannot vote.

a personal (United States) versus automatic (most other democracies) registration system. Powell, using cross-national data, estimates this effect at about 14 percentage points—that is, U.S. turnout is 14 points lower than it would otherwise be because of the personal registration system.[46] This can be taken as an upper bound estimate, both because of Powell's methodology[47] and the existence of somewhat lower estimates based on U.S. data alone.[48] Thus even if other, minor aspects of the costs of voting in the United States are taken into account, it seems doubtful that the cost-related component of U.S. nonvoting could be much higher than this 14-point figure. Because 45 points of nonvoting still must be accounted for (50 points total minus 5 points for frictional nonvoting), it can be reasonably estimated that no more than one-third is attributable to relatively high U.S. voting costs.

The other two-thirds (30 points) must logically be attributable to the low benefits of voting in the United States.[49] Even with proper skepticism about the magnitude of this estimate,[50] it seems hard to avoid the conclusion that low benefits, rather than high costs, are the most potent influence on American nonvoting. Better data would no doubt change this estimate somewhat, but the estimate would have to change quite drastically to alter this conclusion.

The question now becomes: What are the most important influences within this benefit-related component of U.S. nonvoting? Here the waters are especially murky, partly because certain attributes have been poorly measured, partly because certain attributes have not been measured at all, and partly because the individual characteristics of U.S. voters are a complicating and countervailing force. The best that I can say is the following.

First, the influence of party mobilization appears to be substantial. Powell's estimate, based solely on the strength of alignment between parties and social groups, was that low party mobilization levels de-

46. Powell 1986.
47. Powell's 14-point estimate is essentially a residual, based on the turnout differential between the United States and the average democracy and the amount of this differential still unexplained when other (that is, nonregistration) factors are taken into account.
48. See Wolfinger and Rosenstone 1980, Burnham 1982, and Committee for the Study of the American Electorate 1987. I have more to say about the probable effect of eliminating personal registration in chapter 4.
49. It is interesting that this one-third–two-thirds cost-benefit split mirrors the split produced by decompositions of early twentieth century turnout decline between registration (cost) and political (benefit) factors (see Kleppner 1982 and Burnham 1982).
50. It is based on assignment of the residual, always a risky, if unavoidable, procedure.

pressed U.S. turnout by 10 percentage points relative to an average democracy.[51] Given that party mobilization also includes such factors as the density and penetration of party organization, it is possible this estimated effect is somewhat low.

Second the influence of the structure of electoral competition also appears to be substantial. Based on Jackman's model,[52] the influence of the U.S. structure of electoral competition (single-member, winner-take-all districts; strong bicameralism; relative electoral disproportionality; the two-party system) appears to be roughly the same as that of low party mobilization: U.S. turnout is depressed almost 10 points relative to the average democracy.

Thus low party mobilization and the U.S. structure of electoral competition together probably account for a good part (as much as two-thirds) of the 30 points of benefit-related U.S. nonvoting. Whether these two factors are truly coequal in influence, and what other factors (if any) are involved here is difficult to say, given the limitations of available data. Despite the limitations, the estimates presented here do give some sense of which influences play major roles in benefit-related nonvoting in the United States.

Conclusion

In this chapter it has been established that U.S. voter turnout is indeed low by international and historical standards. This generally low turnout is attributable to the high costs (primarily personal registration) and low benefits (primarily the turnout-inhibiting structure of electoral competition and weak party mobilization) of voting in the United States. Within this high-cost, low-benefit system, however, the individual characteristics of U.S. voters act somewhat as a countervailing force. Finally, low benefits are apparently more important than high costs in depressing U.S. voter turnout.

---

51. Powell 1986, p. 26.
52. As Jackman 1987 points out, his model does not technically apply to the United States because of the way the model was estimated. Lacking an alternative, I use the model anyway, with appropriate reservations.

2

Why is American Voter Turnout Going Down?

Not only are American voter turnout levels low, but they have been going down steadily for the last three decades. From a high of around 63 percent of the voting-age population in 1960, turnout in presidential elections has declined to just barely half (50.2 percent) of the VAP in 1988 (table 1-1). That figure is below the low-turnout mark set by the 1948 Dewey-Truman election and is the lowest level since 1924.

Here I analyze the basic reasons behind this phenomenon of declining U.S. voter turnout. First the magnitude and extent of U.S. voter turnout decline are described. Second the main factors that appear to lie behind this decline in voter turnout are analyzed and discussed. Finally responsibility for declining voter turnout is allocated among several sets of factors uncovered by these analyses.

How Serious Is the Decline in American Voter Turnout?

Voter turnout in the United States went down 13 percentage points between 1960 and 1988 (table 1-1). Moreover the decline was steady, with the sole exception of 1984, when turnout ticked upward a slight half point (from 52.6 to 53.1 percent). Otherwise, each election has had a lower turnout than the one preceding it. On the face of it the decline seems to reflect a substantial and serious decrease in the will-

24

ingness of citizens to participate in the easiest and most elementary way in their society: by casting a ballot.

Some object, however, that trend data based on the voting-age population are deceptive. These data are not corrected for the large numbers of voting-age individuals who cannot vote because they are not eligible. The implication is that, if these data were "corrected" to reflect the proper base of eligible citizens, turnout trends would look quite different.

This does not prove to be the case. Comparing table 1-1, based on the VAP, with table 1-3, where aliens are removed from the population base, shows the trends are identical. Both tables show a decline in turnout between 1960 and 1988 of 12.6 percentage points (62.8 to 50.2 in table 1-1, 65.4 to 52.8 in table 1-3).[1] The figures suggest that the decline in turnout is quite robust and does not depend on the data source used to examine the trend.[2]

Another objection to standard turnout trend data is it cloaks the real problem: the decline in *registration*. According to this line of analysis, presented most forcefully by Piven and Cloward,[3] the turnout rate of registrants is extremely high and quite stable across elections (that is, once people are registered, they vote). Thus if fewer people are voting over time, this simply reflects the fact that fewer people are registering. The focus therefore should be on registration trends, the real source of the observed decline in turnout levels.

This view is flawed, both logically and empirically. First even if falling registration is the source of falling turnout, it is not clear that turnout data are therefore irrelevant. Because voting is essentially a two-step process in the United States—*first* one registers, *then* one votes—it hardly seems surprising that many of those lacking the motivation to vote would stop at the first step in the process and simply fail to register. By this logic it would be surprising to see falling turnout *without* falling

1. This partially reflects the fact that, although the proportion of aliens has been going up in recent years, the differences in alien concentration between 1988 and 1960 are smaller than generally supposed. This in turn reflects the fact that alien concentration actually *dropped* in the 1960s before it started its trend upward to current levels. See Carson, Huelskamp, and Woodall 1991 for data on alien concentration as proxied by percentage foreign born.

2. Even a comprehensive effort to remove all those ineligible to vote from the denominator (that is, not just aliens, but also felons, those in mental institutions, and those who moved within thirty days of the election) and add all those who voted to the numerator (that is, adding those who voted in the election but not for president) does not change the trend line significantly. The estimated turnout decline is still close to 12 points.

3. Piven and Cloward 1988.

registration. But such a relationship hardly makes data about turnout trends useless or somehow deceptive.

More serious, the assertion that only registration rates have been declining over time is not supported by available data. Although it is true registration rates have been falling since 1960,[4] the turnout rates of those registered to vote *have also been falling* over this same time period.[5] In other words, not only have people become less inclined to register, they have become less inclined to vote once they are registered.

Exactly how much the turnout rate of registrants has been going down is, however, a matter of some dispute, with estimates ranging from 5 to 13 percentage points. The high estimate comes from aggregate data kept by the secretaries of state. These data say that the turnout rate of registrants has declined by about 13 points since 1960 (from 83.4 to 70.5 percent).[6] But as Piven and Cloward have forcefully argued,[7] these statistics are suspect because official registration rolls contain deadwood—that is, voters who have died or moved away, but whose names have not been removed from the rolls. Because of this the number of registrants is overestimated in these data and therefore their turnout rate is underestimated.

But although these figures understate the total turnout rate of registrants *in any given year*, it is by no means clear that the deadwood factor has grown enough over time—that is, through loosened purging procedures—to be responsible for the declining turnout *trend* observed in these data. In fact some states have actually tightened their purging procedures. It appears quite unlikely such mixed procedural change could have produced *increased* inflation of the registration rolls on a large enough scale to account for the very large turnout decline observed.[8] In fact if one assumes a *constant* inflation rate of 10 percent

---

4. According to official statistics kept by the secretaries of state, registration dropped 4.3 percentage points between 1960 and 1988 (Committee for the Study of the American Electorate 1989); according to Bureau of the Census surveys, registration dropped 7.7 points between 1968 and 1988 among the voting-age population and 5.6 points among the citizen-eligible population (U.S. Bureau of the Census 1969, 1989).

5. Note that turnout in North Dakota, where there is no registration at all—so everyone is, in effect, "registered"—has fallen sharply over the 1960–88 period (down 17.4 percentage points).

6. See Committee for the Study of the American Electorate 1989, p. 3.

7. The point was originally made in Squire, Wolfinger, and Glass 1987.

8. It would be quite difficult to be any more precise than this in assessing the net effect of these mixed changes in purging procedures on registration rolls. A precise estimate would have to take into account not only changes in the length of the purging period for nonvoting, but also changes in (1) whether and how much purging is conducted for other reasons (for instance, general address verification to eliminate those

in the registration rolls (that is, at any given point, reported registration has been 10 percent higher than "true" registration), the decline in the turnout rate of registrants is actually slightly larger (down 14 points, from 92.7 to 78.4 percent).[9] All of this suggests that a substantial portion of the 13-point decline in the official statistics is probably real, not just an artifact of the data involved.

The low estimate comes from survey data collected by the Bureau of the Census in November of election years.[10] According to the census data, the turnout rate of registrants has gone down about 5 points since 1968[11] (from 91.3 to 86.2 percent).[12] These data do not suffer from a deadwood problem because they rely on survey respondents' self-reporting of their registration and voting status, not on the official rolls. This, however, creates the problem of *overreporting*,[13] because a substantial number of respondents say they voted—and, therefore, registered—when they actually did not (over 57 percent of respondents claimed to have voted in the 1988 election, compared to the estimated 50 percent who actually voted in that election). This makes the census data overestimate turnout and registration rates.

The extent to which overreporting skews the turnout rate of registrants computed from these data is difficult to say because no one knows how many of the nonvoters who claimed to have voted were registered. However, it can be shown mathematically that the census-based rate could be inflated by as much as 10 points. Moreover, depending on changes over time in the true registration status of these misreporting nonvoters, it is possible this overestimate is getting pro-

---

who have moved, died, and so on); (2) the frequency with which these purges—for nonvoting or otherwise—are conducted; and (3) changes in notification procedures. All of these factors potentially affect the rigor of purging procedures and therefore the amount of deadwood removed. I know of no study that attempts to estimate the effects of these different sets of changes.

9. Committee for the Study of the American Electorate 1989.

10. A basic description of this data source is in appendix A along with descriptions of other surveys used in this study.

11. This is the first year for which data on both registration and turnout are available. Unfortunately this means that the census data cover a shorter time period (twenty years) than the secretaries of state data (twenty-eight years), which makes the comparison between the two data sources somewhat difficult. One way of compensating for this is to extrapolate the rate of decline found in the census data back to 1960, so that the two data sources cover the same period. The result is an additional 2-percentage-point decline in the turnout rate of registrants, for an estimated total decline of 7 points over the 1960–88 period. This narrows, but by no means eliminates, the differences between the two data sources.

12. U.S. Bureau of the Census 1989.

13. Overreporting is discussed in more detail in appendix A.

gressively worse, resulting in an *underestimate* of the decline in the turnout rate of registrants. This is not to say that such an underestimate *does* exist, but simply to suggest that the census data cannot be regarded as the last word on this very complicated subject.

Thus neither the data from secretaries of state nor the census can be reliably said to capture the true turnout rate of registrants.[14] Consequently, neither data source can be said necessarily to capture the true trend line for the last twenty to twenty-eight years. In light of all this, my own view is the turnout rate of registrants has dropped substantially over time, with the exact magnitude of this drop probably falling somewhere in between the official and census figures.[15]

Explaining the Decline in Turnout since 1960

The data in the previous section established that the decline in voter turnout since 1960 is indeed substantial and serious, not just an artifact of the data involved. Nor is the decline in turnout simply a matter of fewer people negotiating the relatively onerous U.S. registration system, because even those registered are showing less of a propensity to vote. Americans, for whatever reasons, are defecting in increasing numbers from the voting process at *both* steps of the two-step process.

The question then becomes: What are these reasons? What factor or set of factors is responsible for the increasing defection of Americans from the voting process? The analytical framework introduced in chapter 1 provides a useful method for approaching this question.

This framework may be summarized as follows. For a citizen to vote, he or she must find the benefits[16] of voting high enough to merit absorbing the costs of participation. Therefore any attribute of U.S. society

14. In fact no one will know the true rate until a large-scale validation study is done on a sample of sufficient size and representativeness, such as the census sample. Until such data are available I am inclined to think that the true rate lies somewhere in between the inflation-adjusted official rate (78 percent) and the census rate (86 percent).

15. This viewpoint is supported by data from the National Election Study (NES), a survey taken in every election year by the Center for Political Studies at the University of Michigan. In contrast to the census survey, the NES has periodically attempted to verify self-reported registration and turnout by consulting election records in local offices. Despite the many problems with the NES sample (small size, possible selection bias) and with the methods used to verify these self-reports (see Traugott 1989 and Presser, Traugott, and Traugott 1990), these data are still worth considering in this context. According to this validated NES data, the turnout rate of registrants fell from 94.9 percent in 1964 (the first year it was done) to 87.3 in 1976, 83.9 in 1980, 85.7 in 1984, and 84.9 percent in 1988, a decline of 10 points from 1964 to 1988 (Bennett 1990b).

16. Defined as the symbolic or instrumental expressive benefits of voting or both. See the discussion in chapter 1.

that affects, first, the average level of benefits the electorate can obtain or, second, the average level of costs the electorate must absorb should have an effect on average U.S. turnout levels. It then follows that, to the extent this attribute has varied since 1960, it may constitute part of the explanation for the observed decline in U.S. voter turnout.

As seen in chapter 1, a variety of characteristics of U.S. society affect the average costs and benefits of voting. If these characteristics have changed in such a way as to increase the costs, decrease the benefits, or both, these changes could provide part or all of an explanation for post-1960 turnout decline. First I consider changes that may have affected the *costs* of voting.

Changes in the Voter Registration System

The chief factor affecting the costs of voting in the United States is the voter registration system. And in fact substantial changes have been made in the voter registration system since 1960. These include: (1) the abolition of poll taxes; (2) the abolition of literacy tests; (3) the formal prohibition of discrimination within the registration process; (4) the increased availability of bilingual registration materials; (5) the large increase in the number of states permitting registration by mail; (6) the sharp decline in the length of state residency requirements, from a year or more in most states in 1960 to the current, almost uniform level of a month or less; (7) the movement of closing dates— that is, the last date one can register to vote in a given election—closer to the date the election is held; and (8) the implementation of minimum national standards for absentee registration.

Clearly these are significant changes in the voter registration system that must have affected the average costs of voting for citizens in the United States. However, from the standpoint of explaining declining voter turnout, these changes present a serious problem: *all of them go in the wrong direction*. Each of these changes acted to liberalize the system—to make it *easier* to register, not harder—and therefore *reduced* the costs of voting. This means that, had nothing else changed after 1960 save the voter registration system, turnout would actually have gone *up*, not down as shown by the data.

This is part of the reason the post-1960 decline in U.S. voter turnout is frequently termed "the puzzle of participation."[17] Although turnout has trended steadily downward election after election, certain well-

17. Brody 1978, pp. 287–324.

known societal changes, such as the easing of registration requirements, should logically have produced the opposite result: an *increase*
in turnout.[18] Solving the puzzle of participation, therefore, entails not
only accounting for the observed decline in turnout, but also explaining
how countervailing forces *promoting* voter turnout failed to have an
observable effect.

The analysis of voter registration presented here certainly suggests
this puzzle will not be solved on the level of costs. The voter registration
system appears to have been a source of reduced costs to the U.S. voter,
and no other changes in the legal structure of voting seem plausible as
a significant source of increased costs (if anything, other changes, such
as easier absentee balloting, probably *reduced* the costs). It follows that
the changes in U.S. society responsible for declining turnout must be
changes that affected the *benefits* of voting, not the costs. I now turn
to a consideration of these changes.

Two obvious candidates present themselves, one of which can be
immediately ruled out, whereas the other deserves serious consideration. The one that can be ruled out is changes in the basic structure of
electoral competition. Since 1960 this basic structure has remained
intact: neither the type of electoral districts, nor the proportionality of
seat allocation in Congress, nor the number of legislative bodies, nor
the number of parties in those legislative bodies has changed much, if
at all, in the last three decades. Therefore although the structure of
electoral competition is a general factor in *low* U.S. voter turnout, it
cannot possibly be a factor in *declining* U.S. voter turnout.

Changes in the Individual-Level Characteristics of U.S. Voters

Changes in the individual-level characteristics of U.S. voters, on the
other hand, present quite a different picture. As shown in chapter 1, a
series of individual demographic and attitudinal characteristics of U.S.
citizens actually *promote* voter turnout (for example, education levels,
levels of civic duty, following politics in the media, and so on), in
contrast to most other aspects of the U.S. system. But the last three
decades have witnessed dramatic change in the demographic[19] and

18. Another example is the dramatic increase in educational attainment, a point
discussed in detail later in the chapter.
19. I use the term "demographic" in the loose sense of meaning objective (not
attitudinal or behavioral) individual characteristics. Thus demographic characteristics by
this definition include characteristics such as occupation and income that by virtue of
their changeable status (one can change jobs or lose or gain income, whereas one's race
cannot be changed) are sometimes not considered to be true demographic categories.

attitudinal profile of Americans.[20] If these changes have included the various turnout-relevant characteristics of Americans and if these changes have been in the "right" direction, then one of the few turnout-promoting aspects of the U.S. system may have eroded, causing turnout to fall.

I next investigate this possibility by looking at characteristics that experienced changes in distribution over the period in question (1960–88)[21] and have at least surface plausibility as predictors of turnout.

POLITICAL CYNICISM.   The first cluster of characteristics to look at are those tapping political cynicism. The data in table 2-1 make it clear that there has been an astonishing increase in political cynicism over the last several decades. In 1964 a little more than one-fifth of the electorate (22 percent) felt the government could be trusted only some (or none) of the time. By 1980 this figure had skyrocketed to almost three quarters of the electorate (74 percent). Although by 1988 this figure had declined somewhat to a little under three-fifths (59 percent) of the electorate, the percentage of the population feeling mistrustful of the government was still nearly three times as high at the end of this period as at the beginning. This change is quite substantial by any standard.

A similar pattern obtains for views on whether the government is dominated by "big interests." In 1964 under one-third of the electorate (31 percent) endorsed this assessment, whereas by 1980 over three-quarters (77 percent) felt big-interest domination did characterize the government. Again there is some drop-off in this view during the 1980s, but in 1988 two-thirds (67 percent) of the electorate still believed that

20. For a useful general compendium of information on both demographic and attitudinal change, see Miller and Traugott 1989. For more detail on demographic change (Miller and Traugott's demographic data are limited by their reliance on the relatively small-sample National Election Studies), see the various publications put out by the Bureau of the Census that summarize Current Population Survey data (series P-20 through P-25 and P-60). The census monograph series sponsored by the Russell Sage Foundation also contains a wealth of relevant information (see, for example, Levy 1987).

For useful summaries of some of the key data on attitudinal change, see Lipset and Schneider 1983, Gant and Luttbeg 1991, and Conway 1991.

21. If levels of a given characteristic were stable over this time period, it makes it quite unlikely that that characteristic is part of the turnout decline story—lacking distributional change, the *effect* of that characteristic would have had to change substantially across time (see Teixeira 1987). Interestingly, however, relatively few relevant characteristics did exhibit flat trend lines across this entire period. The ones that came closest were citizen duty and personal trust, which exhibited flat trend lines in the 1960s and 1970s. In the 1980s, however, the NES did not retain most of these items, so it cannot be said with any confidence that levels of these characteristics were truly stable over the entire 1960–88 period. (In fact reasonably good evidence, both from one item retained in the NES and from other surveys, exists that citizen duty, in particular, *did* decline in the 1980s. See the final section of this chapter for further discussion.)

TABLE 2-1. *Political Cynicism, by Indicator, 1964–88*[a]

Percent

Question and answer[b]	1964	1968	1972	1976	1980	1984	1988	Change 1964–88[c]
Can government be trusted?								
Never[d] or only some of time	22.3	37.3	45.8	65.3	74.3	55.1	58.8	36.5
Most of time	63.2	55.3	48.8	31.3	23.6	41.2	36.9	−26.3
All the time	14.5	7.5	5.4	3.4	2.1	3.7	4.2	−10.3
Is government run by big interests?								
Run by big interests	30.9	43.6	58.6	73.7	76.9	58.6	67.3	36.4
Run for benefit of all	69.1	56.4	41.4	26.3	23.1	41.4	32.7	−36.4
Does government waste tax money?								
A lot	48.1	60.6	67.0	76.3	80.0	66.2	64.0	15.9
Some	45.2	35.2	30.6	20.6	17.9	30.1	33.5	−11.7
Not very much	6.7	4.2	2.4	3.1	2.0	3.7	2.5	−4.2
Is government competent?								
Doesn't know what it's doing	27.8	39.2	42.2	52.7	65.0	n.a.	n.a.	37.2
Run by smart people	72.2	60.8	57.8	47.3	35.0	n.a.	n.a.	−37.2
Is government crooked?								
Many are	30.0	26.3	37.7	44.3	48.5	33.4	41.8	11.8
Not many are	51.0	54.0	47.5	42.1	42.7	51.6	46.6	−4.4
Hardly any are	19.0	19.6	14.8	13.6	8.8	15.0	11.6	−7.4

SOURCE: Author's tabulations from National Election Study data.
n.a. Not available
a. Data for all questions are only available from 1964. For one of the questions data stop in 1980. To facilitate comparisons across time, "don't know" answers have been removed from tabulations.
b. Full question wordings are in appendix C.
c. 1960–80 only for "Is government competent?"
d. Volunteered answer.

big interest domination of government was a fact of life—over twice the proportion at the beginning of the period.

The patterns for other aspects of political cynicism—that the government wastes tax money, doesn't know what it is doing, and is crooked—are basically the same, if somewhat less pronounced. Cynical assessments of the government rose between 1964 and 1980, subsided somewhat during the 1980s,[22] but wound up substantially higher in 1988 than in 1964.[23]

22. The data for government competence, however, stop in 1980. Therefore it is not known whether this aspect of political cynicism experienced the same partial recovery in the 1980s observable for the other attributes in the table.
23. The latest data indicate that cynicism about politics is higher in 1992 than it was in 1988 (Schneider 1992). This continues a trend toward increased cynicism that dates

On the face of it these changes seem tailor-made for explaining declining voter turnout. Cynicism has obviously increased dramatically over time, and because more cynical citizens are presumably less motivated to vote, the result should be precisely the observed sharp decrease in turnout. The intuitive plausibility of this story has lent it both journalistic and popular currency ("You can't get people to vote, they're too cynical"; "Why should people vote—the government's full of crooks"; and so on).

There is one serious problem with this story, however. Analysis has shown that feelings of political cynicism have *no significant,*[24] *independent*[25] *effect* on an individual's likelihood of voting. It follows that, because cynicism has little to do with turnout, an increase in cynicism will have little effect on turnout levels. Thus the dramatic rise in cynicism, despite its intuitive plausibility, cannot be part of the turnout decline story.

SOCIOECONOMIC STATUS. Another cluster of characteristics that experienced substantial change over the 1960–88 period was that tapping different aspects of socioeconomic status (SES): education, occupation, and income. Each of these characteristics is believed to affect turnout.[26] Education, for example, increases cognitive skills, which presumably makes it easier to learn about a complex and abstract subject like politics. It also increases the ability to handle bureaucratic obstacles such as those entailed by registration. For both reasons more education should make individuals more likely to vote.

Occupation affects voter turnout in a different way. Nonmanual occupations are believed to provide more mental stimulation, access to information, and opportunity for insight into complex social mechanisms. Therefore individuals in those occupations should be more likely

---

back to the mid-1980s (the decrease in cynicism that took place in the 1980s was mostly confined to Reagan's first term).

24. Based on models estimated by the author on NES data covering the 1964–88 period. See also Citrin 1974, Shaffer 1981, and Abramson and Aldrich 1982 for discussions about the lack of relationship between political cynicism or trust and turnout.

25. By "independent" I mean that that characteristic's effect on voter turnout is not because of its relationship with some other characteristic that affects turnout. If lack of independence does obtain, the characteristic may appear to have a significant relationship to turnout on the *bivariate* level, but when inserted in a properly specified *multivariate* model, that significant effect will disappear (see appendix B for a discussion of model specification and the role of multivariate analysis).

26. See Wolfinger and Rosenstone 1980, and Conway 1991 for more detailed discussion of how different aspects of SES affect turnout.

to vote than those in manual occupations and especially housewives, who are out of the labor force entirely.

Finally a higher income is said to allow a citizen to "lift his head" from the preoccupations of daily life and take the time and emotional energy necessary for a nonessential such as voting. In addition a higher income may increase an individual's felt stake in the system and therefore in the outcome of the election, making it more likely the individual will vote.

All these effects may be summed up by saying that higher SES makes it more likely that individuals will find elections meaningful and will be motivated to vote,[27] whereas lower SES makes it less likely. Hence a trend toward lower SES could conceivably be part of the explanation for declining voter turnout.

The problem of course is that the exact opposite has taken place. There has been a massive upgrading of socioeconomic status since 1960 (table 2-2). The most dramatic change has been the tremendous increase in educational attainment. Although almost half of the electorate (49 percent) had less than a high school education in 1960, by 1988 less than one-quarter (22 percent) of the electorate had this low a level of education. And on the other end of the scale, the percentages of both those with some college (thirteen to fifteen years of education) and college graduates about doubled (from 12 to 23 percent and from 10 to 20 percent, respectively).

These changes in educational attainment are the most salient changes in the SES distribution, both because the education distribution has changed the most and because education is, by far, the strongest promoter of voter participation among the SES characteristics.[28] However, the occupation and income distributions also changed fairly substantially (table 2-2).

The most significant change in occupation distribution by far was the large decrease in the proportion of housewives. Housewives were just about one-quarter of the electorate (26 percent) in 1960, but only a little more than one-tenth (12 percent) in 1988. Other upgrading changes included a decline (4 points) in the blue-collar category and increases in all white-collar categories, both low (clerical-sales up

27. To the extent education acts to facilitate negotiation of the registration process, it may play a direct, cost-cutting role.

28. See appendix B, especially the model summarized in table B-1. Wolfinger and Rosenstone 1980 and Teixeira 1987 also contain detailed discussions of education, occupation, and income and their relative importance to voter participation.

TABLE 2-2. *Socioeconomic Status, by Indicator, 1960–88*[a]

Percent

Characteristic	1960	1964	1968	1972	1976	1980	1984	1988	Change 1960–88
Education (years)									
0–8	30.0	24.8	23.1	19.9	16.7	12.0	10.8	9.9	− 20.1
9–11	19.0	19.9	17.7	17.8	14.9	15.0	12.1	12.1	− 6.9
12	29.0	31.4	31.8	33.0	35.1	36.2	35.7	35.7	6.7
13–15	12.0	12.7	14.2	16.1	18.5	20.6	24.7	22.5	10.5
16 or more	10.0	11.1	13.1	13.1	14.7	16.2	16.7	19.8	9.8
Occupation									
Housewives	26.4	31.2	29.0	26.9	21.6	16.5	13.2	11.9	− 14.5
Out of the labor force, except housewives	15.9	11.9	14.3	18.1	24.3	24.6	26.8	25.2	9.3
Blue collar	20.0	19.3	19.8	18.9	16.5	17.9	14.1	16.2	− 3.8
Service	7.3	7.3	5.7	5.2	7.0	6.9	8.8	7.9	0.6
Farm	4.6	3.4	2.5	1.6	1.4	1.1	2.2	1.5	− 3.1
Clerical-sales	12.0	11.1	11.7	12.5	12.5	13.3	16.9	16.5	4.5
Professional-technical and managerial-administrative	14.0	15.9	17.0	16.7	16.7	19.6	18.0	20.8	6.8
Family income (1988 dollars)									
Less than 7,500	16.0	19.1	11.6	12.1	12.7	10.8	13.4	13.9	− 2.1
7,500–19,999	38.9	28.4	28.0	27.6	28.0	26.7	28.6	27.5	− 11.4
20,000–39,999	34.6	35.9	42.4	39.2	36.7	35.4	32.8	33.3	− 1.3
40,000 or more	10.5	16.6	18.0	21.1	22.5	27.1	25.1	25.4	14.9

SOURCE: Author's tabulations from National Election Study data.
a. Details on coding of categories are in appendix C.

about 5 points) and high (professional-technical and managerial-administrative up about 7 points).

Turning to family income levels, the income distribution shifted basically upscale during the overall time period. In 1960, 55 percent of the electorate had family incomes of less than $20,000 (1988 dollars). By 1988 the percentage with family incomes this low had fallen to 41 percent (this figure was actually down to 38 percent in 1980, but crept back upward during the 1980s). Conversely at the upper end of the income scale, percentages increased. Only 11 percent had family incomes of more than $40,000 in 1960, compared to one-quarter with incomes this high in 1988.

Across the board then and particularly in terms of educational attainment, socioeconomic status was substantially *upgraded* between 1960 and 1988. This means that the changing distribution of socioeconomic status cannot possibly be responsible for the decline in U.S. voter turnout, because the direction of change has been entirely wrong. In fact the changing SES distribution should have promoted *higher* voter turnout, not lower.

Model estimations in fact strongly support this assessment.[29] All other things equal, turnout in 1988 would have been 3.9 percentage points higher than in 1960 simply on the basis of the changing distribution of income, occupation, and education (especially the latter; over two-thirds of this effect is from educational upgrading alone). But of course all other things have *not* been equal, hence the observed decline in turnout, rather than the 4-point increase one would predict on the basis of socioeconomic upgrading.

But what are the other factors that have not been equal, that have actually been acting to *depress* turnout? So far two sets of seemingly relevant distributional changes have not provided much clarity on this issue. The substantial increase in political cynicism turns out not to affect turnout levels, and the sustantial upgrading of socioeconomic status has actually been a countervailing force, providing an upward "push" on turnout.

Thus the "puzzle of participation" alluded to in the section on changes in voter registration has only been deepened by the changes examined so far in this section. Specifically turnout-depressing factors must now be found that not only account for the observed decline in turnout, but also for the neutralization of the upward push on turnout provided by socioeconomic upgrading.[30] Put another way "more" turnout decline must now be accounted for than when this investigation was begun. I shall refer to this augmented decline in turnout as the "SES-adjusted" decline in turnout.

SOCIAL CONNECTEDNESS.   Another widely commented on set of changes in U.S. society during this period has to do with the social "connectedness" of individuals. The idea is that interpersonal, community, and general social ties provide a substantial proportion of an individual's motivation to vote, because these ties can provide external encouragement to vote, as well as an enhanced sense of an election's meaningful-

29. This model estimate and others presented in this chapter are, unless otherwise noted, based on model B.1 in appendix B. This model is based on self-reported, not validated vote because only self-reported vote covers the entire 1960–88 time period. In addition, other problems with the validated vote (see appendix A) make it undesirable to use in this context.

30. Not to mention the upward push on turnout of unknown magnitude provided by post-1960 liberalization of the registration system.

ness.[31] Therefore if social connectedness has trended downward, this may help account for some or all of the SES-adjusted turnout decline discussed above.

Some characteristics believed at least partially to reflect social connectedness are marital status, church attendance, and age. Those who are married and live with their spouses have the interpersonal tie with their partner; those who attend church relatively often have the interpersonal and community ties generated by such attendance;[32] and those who are older tend to be more "settled down,"[33] with deeper roots in communities and society and more stable, long-established ties with other individuals.[34] Individuals with these attributes should therefore have a higher level of social connnectedness and be more likely to vote.

The data in table 2-3 show that social connectedness, as measured by these characteristics, has indeed trended downward over the 1960–88 period.[35] Marital status shows the most dramatic change, with

31. On the role of social connectedness in turnout, see Knack 1991a; Popkin 1991a, chap. 10; Pomper and Sernekos 1989; and Strate and others 1989.

32. It is also possible that those who attend church frequently develop political skills that facilitate voting. See Verba and others 1991, especially pp. 30–44, for some evidence relating church attendance to skills that facilitate participation (though their evidence is about political participation in general, not the specific act of voting).

33. It is also possible that aging promotes acquisition of bureacratic skills that facilitate registration and voting, as argued by Wolfinger and Rosenstone 1980, especially chap. 3 (though note that their evidence about the diminishing marginal effect of age at higher educational levels neither proves nor disproves this contention, but simply reflects the shape of the probit curve [see Nagler 1991 and appendix B]). This analysis seems most applicable to young people who have just entered the electorate and have little experience with the political system. However, I am skeptical that skill acquisition (at least bureaucratic skill acquisition) can satisfactorily explain why age continues to promote turnout up to the age of seventy-five, because the skills involved are not that complex and should be relatively easy to acquire.

34. Of course some age-related variation in turnout is explained by age-related variation in political attributes that affect turnout (for example, political involvement, sense of government responsiveness, partisanship), as well as age-related variation in more concrete aspects of community attachment, such as home ownership and length of time in current home (which also affect turnout) (see Strate and others 1989). The fact remains, however, that age continues to have a strong effect on turnout, *even with all these other characteristics controlled for*. My interpretation is that this controlled effect of age (that is, the effect of age that is *not* explained by its relation to other characteristics) at least partially reflects the relationship of age to social connectedness.

35. It is important to note that table 2-3 does not exhaust the roster of characteristics pertinent to social connectedness. Other clearly relevant characteristics include residential mobility, home ownership, and union membership. All of these characteristics, however, do not seem particularly useful for looking at declining turnout.

For example, residential mobility, although a very strong predictor of turnout, has not been uniformly measured by the NES over the time period in question. As a result, apparent increases in residential mobility between 1960 and 1988 may be artifacts of the differential NES coding procedures. Moreover where NES coding can be made most uniform (under or over four years in same home), the distribution shows little change.

TABLE 2-3. *Social Connectedness, by Indicator, 1960–88*
Percent

Characteristic	1960	1964	1968	1972	1976	1980	1984	1988	Change 1960–88
Marital status									
Single[a]	21.0	24.1	29.2	33.1	37.2	39.6	43.2	45.2	24.2
Married, spouse present	79.0	75.9	70.8	66.9	62.8	60.4	56.8	54.8	−24.2
Church attendance[b]									
Never	12.4	9.9	12.8	19.0	20.0	23.3	22.4	21.1	8.7
Seldom	30.5	30.2	34.4	32.0	28.4	28.7	28.7	28.5	−2.0
Often	16.4	16.8	15.2	23.0	26.5	23.1	24.9	25.2	8.8
Regularly	40.7	43.1	37.6	26.0	25.0	24.9	24.0	25.2	−15.5
Age									
18–28[c]	11.6	16.3	16.4	25.2	25.6	24.3	22.3	19.5	7.9
29–36	18.1	15.9	14.0	14.2	16.0	17.7	20.1	20.9	2.8
37–44	19.5	18.2	17.9	13.6	11.7	12.9	14.4	17.2	−2.3
45–64	35.2	34.5	34.8	31.0	28.5	27.7	25.3	24.6	−10.6
65–74	11.1	10.1	11.7	10.2	11.7	11.4	10.6	10.5	−0.6
75 or older	4.4	5.1	5.3	5.8	6.6	6.1	7.3	7.4	3.0

SOURCE: Author's tabulations from National Election Study data.
a. Includes divorced, separated, and widowed.
b. Question wording for church attendance changed between 1960 and 1988. For discussion of this problem and attendant coding decisions, see appendix C.
c. Category does not include 18- to 20-year-olds until 1972.

slightly more than one-fifth of the electorate (21 percent) being single in 1960, compared to almost half (45 percent) in 1988. Church attendance also dropped substantially with the proportion never attending church rising from 12 to 21 percent and the proportion attending regularly falling from just over two-fifths (41 percent) to about one-quarter (25 percent).[36] Finally the electorate became

---

Finally census data suggest that residential mobility (measured as under or over one year, and including children) was no higher in 1985 than in 1960. See U.S. Bureau of the Census 1985.

Home ownership, also a fairly strong predictor of turnout, was simply not measured by the NES in 1960, so home ownership levels in the base year of the period are not known. More important, home ownership declined only slightly during the years covered (1964–88).

Union membership (actually measured as having a union member in the family) has declined somewhat over the 1960–88 time period (down 8 points), but I do not find a significant effect of union membership on turnout, once other demographic and political variables are controlled for. However, even if union membership was treated as significant, the relationship would be weak and the contribution to turnout decline marginal.

36. Coding ambiguity in the church attendance measure can be partially eliminated by combining the "regularly" and "often" categories (see appendix C). In this case frequent church attendance still falls, though less sharply, from 57 to 50 percent.

younger,[37] with the proportion under 29 increasing about 8 percentage points (from 12 to 20 percent; much of this is because of the enfranchisement of eighteen- to twenty-year olds by the Twenty-Sixth Amendment in 1971), whereas, at the other end of the age spectrum, the proportion in the forty-five- to sixty-four-year-old group fell 10 points (from 35 to 25 percent).

The decrease in social connectedness indicated by these data seems substantial and a plausible source of downward pressure on turnout in the 1960–88 period. Model estimations[38] suggest that this downward pressure did indeed exist—that, all else equal, turnout would have fallen during this time period as a result of a decrease in social connectedness. However, the *magnitude* of this turnout-depressing effect—though fairly close—is actually somewhat smaller than the magnitude of the turnout-elevating effect of socioeconomic upgrading. Because of this the *decrease* in levels of social connectedness combined with the *increase* in levels of socioeconomic status would still have produced, all else equal, a modest *increase* in turnout of about 0.7 percent over the 1960–88 period.

Clearly declining turnout in this time period has still not been explained adequately, though some progress has been made in accounting for SES-adjusted turnout decline (that is, at least the countervailing force provided by socioeconomic upgrading has been largely canceled out and thereby accounted for by the decrease in social connnectedness just identified). Therefore, distributional trends on other characteristics must be examined as possible explanations for turnout decline.

One possible source of downward pressure on turnout is suggested by the discussion of decreasing social connectedness. If general social connectedness is relevant to turnout, it makes sense that *political* connectedness would also be relevant, because voting is inescapably a political act. The idea here is that the various ways individuals tend to be connected to politics in the United States—through their identification with or knowledge about parties, through their psychological and media-based involvement in public affairs, and through their sense of a responsive link between individuals and government[39]—determine

37. The trend toward a younger electorate applies to the overall 1960–88 period. During the 1980s, however, the electorate actually got *older* (see table 2-3) and will continue to do so in the future as the baby boom generation moves through the life cycle.

38. Detailed in appendix B.

39. This sense of government responsiveness is different from the feelings of cynicism toward the government discussed earlier. Both negative (cynical) and positive (not cynical) feelings constitute a sort of attachment or link to the government. The sense that

to a significant extent how meaningful these individuals find elections and therefore how likely they are to vote. If political connectedness has trended downward, this may help account for some, or all, of the SES-adjusted turnout decline that remains unexplained.

Given the many analyses of America's declining political parties[40] and the widespread perception of popular disenchantment with the parties, the connections between Americans and political parties seem a particulary plausible place to look for a relevant decline in political connectedness. Table 2-4 displays the changing distributions of some key characteristics tapping Americans' feelings about, and knowledge of, their political parties. Those who identify relatively strongly with a political party, those who are concerned about which party wins an election, those who see important differences between the parties, and those who have relatively high levels of knowledge about the parties and their candidates should all be relatively likely to find an election meaningful and therefore relatively likely to vote.

These data do not suggest a massive disconnection of Americans from their political parties, but rather a modest overall downward trend. Party identification, for example, shows the independent category[41] stable over the time period, with the weak partisan or leaner category going up 5 points (from 52 to 57 percent) and the strong partisan or leaner category going down 5 points (from 36 to 31 percent). This is a downward trend in partisanship, but not a large one (the drop between 1960 and 1980 was larger, but, as the data show, levels of partisanship recovered somewhat in the 1980s).

The trend in concern over which party will win the election also shows a downward trend, but again a fairly modest one. About 65 percent of the electorate said they cared a great deal which party won the election in 1960, compared to 61 percent in 1988, a drop of only 4 points. (Again the drop was larger between 1960 and 1980, but concern over the election outcome picked up in the 1980s).

The other two indicators, which are more on the level of perception and understanding of the parties, present a mixed picture. The proportion of the electorate seeing important differences in what the parties

---

the government just does not listen or care, on the other hand, suggests a lack of attachment, positive or negative, to the government.

40. A particularly useful account is provided by Wattenberg 1990.

41. By independents I mean only *pure* independents. Those who say they are independents, but admit they lean toward one or another of the parties, are best treated as weak partisans. See Keith and others 1986 for further discussion.

TABLE 2-4. *Party-Related Characteristics, 1960–88*[a]

Percent

Characteristic	1960	1964	1968	1972	1976	1980	1984	1988	Change 1960–88
Party identification									
Independent, apolitical	12.3	8.7	11.9	14.6	15.3	15.1	12.7	12.2	−0.1
Weak partisan, leaner	51.7	53.4	58.5	60.4	61.1	58.7	58.0	56.6	4.9
Strong partisan	36.0	37.9	29.6	25.1	23.5	26.2	29.3	31.2	−4.8
Care which party wins election?									
Don't care very much	34.8	34.5	34.9	39.6	43.6	44.1	35.2	39.0	4.2
Care a good deal	65.2	65.5	65.1	60.4	56.4	55.9	64.8	61.0	−4.2
Are there important differences between parties?									
No	49.7	45.0	48.3	53.9	52.8	42.0	37.5	40.4	−9.3
Yes	50.3	55.0	52.3	46.1	47.2	58.0	62.5	59.6	9.3
Knowledge of parties and candidates									
Very low	4.8	2.9	3.4	6.4	6.1	4.6	7.4	11.3	6.5
Low	20.3	20.0	17.5	25.0	25.1	27.0	23.4	23.5	3.2
Medium	32.2	32.2	27.0	31.3	29.6	29.4	26.4	22.8	−9.4
High	26.1	26.4	26.0	21.6	19.0	21.4	17.9	17.9	−8.2
Very high	16.6	18.5	26.0	15.7	20.3	17.6	24.9	24.5	7.9

SOURCE: Author's tabulations from National Election Study data.

a. Question wording and basic coding decisions are described in appendix C.

stand for has, contrary to some expectations, actually gone up. Just about half of the electorate felt there were important differences be- tween the parties in 1960, whereas by 1988 this figure had risen to about three-fifths of the electorate—a gain of 9 percentage points.

Knowledge of parties and candidates,[42] on the other hand, shows what appears to be a general downward trend, but hardly an over- whelming one. The two lowest knowledge categories go up 10 points (from 25 to 35 percent), whereas the next two highest categories go down 17 points (from 58 to 41 percent). But partially counterbalancing these trends, the very highest knowledge category went up 8 points, from 17 percent to 25 percent. The counterbalancing shift at the upper

42. "Knowledge" is measured by a simple count of the number of statements of likes and dislikes a person could make about the parties and candidates. A summation of likes and dislikes in this manner worked far better (that is, it was more robust and statistically significant) than alternative specifications of a variable based on likes and dislikes (for example, net effect—likes minus dislikes—for respondent's preferred party). See appen- dix C for question wording and coding of the knowledge variable and appendix B for relationship of different levels of knowledge to turnout.

end of the scale means that the magnitude of the overall downward shift cannot be large.

The disconnection of Americans from their political parties thus appears to be a source of downward pressure on turnout but probably a modest one. Model estimations[43] confirm this assessment. Had nothing else changed between 1960 and 1988 save these connections—affective and perceptual—between Americans and their political parties, turnout would have dropped only 0.4 percent. (The drop is almost entirely because of declining partisanship and concern over the election outcome; a slight turnout-*elevating* effect from the increased perception of important differences between the parties was almost exactly counterbalanced by a slight turnout-depressing effect from decreasing concrete knowledge about those parties.)

Again the SES-adjusted decline in voter participation over the 1960–88 period has still not been explained. Once the effect of socioeconomic upgrading is taken into account, the combined effects of the decline in social connectedness *and* the erosion of Americans' ties to political parties would have produced, all else equal, virtual stability in voter turnout levels (more specifically, a very slight increase in turnout of about 0.3 percentage point). The answer must therefore lie beyond connections to the political parties in other common ways in which Americans maintain connections to the political system: through their psychological and media-based involvement in politics and through their sense of government responsiveness.

POLITICAL INVOLVEMENT AND SENSE OF GOVERNMENT RESPONSIVENESS.   Data are shown here on the changing distribution of some key characteristics tapping involvement, as well as the most common measure of sense of government responsiveness (table 2-5).[44] Those who follow an election campaign in the newspapers or on television,[45] those who have a high

43. Model estimations are detailed in appendix B.
44. The literature is profoundly confusing about "efficacy"—internal and external, political and personal—with different names sometimes given to the same efficacy measure and vice versa. For the record the measure I am using is usually called "external political efficacy" (though it is sometimes called just "external efficacy" or just "political efficacy") and is derived from two common NES questions on whether ordinary people have a say in government and whether public officials care what ordinary people think (see appendix C, table C-3, for exact question wording and scale construction).
45. The contention that campaign newspaper reading and TV watching should be viewed as measures of campaign involvement has been disputed. For example, some argue that reading the paper about a campaign is really a form of political *behavior*—moreover, behavior that simply expresses intent to vote, rather than any psychological attribute

level of general interest in a campaign, and those who follow overall public affairs closely should all feel more involved in an election—and therefore more likely to find it meaningful and to vote—than those who lack these attributes. Similarly those who believe the government is responsive to the wishes of ordinary people are more likely to find an opportunity to cast a ballot meaningful and thereby be more likely to vote than those who are skeptical of government responsiveness. It follows that if these particular connections of Americans to politics have eroded over time, this may account for some or all of the turnout decline as yet unexplained.

The data in table 2-5 do suggest a substantial downward trend in these attributes over the 1960–88 period. In terms of political involvement, the most dramatic change is in the extent Americans follow campaigns in the newspapers. The proportion of Americans reading many articles about the campaign dropped from over half (55 percent) in 1960 to under one-fifth (18 percent) in 1988, whereas the proportion reading none at all increased from exactly one-fifth (20 percent) to over one-half (51 percent).[46] This is a tremendous decrease in a very

---

(Abramson, Aldrich, and Rohde 1990, pp. 117–18).

However, analysis of NES data on whether respondents expected to vote in an upcoming election does not support the latter assertion: campaign newspaper reading cannot be reduced to an individual's expectation to vote, and trends in campaign newspaper reading do not track trends in individual voting expectation. The former assertion—that campaign newspaper reading is a form of political behavior—is reasonable as far as it goes, but does not logically contradict the notion that campaign newspaper reading is an indicator of campaign involvement.

In fact, there is good evidence (Bennett 1990b) that campaign newspaper reading (and other campaign media usage) is a critical part of what people mean when they indicate interest in the campaign or involvement in politics. That is people feel that if they are reasonably engaged with the election process, they will take the relatively simple and nontaxing step of reading an article or two in the newspaper. This in turn may lead to voting in the election—though not necessarily—making campaign newspaper reading a sort of *intermediate* form of political participation.

A more interesting question perhaps is whether campaign newspaper reading is simply a *manifestation* of involvement in the campaign or whether it actually *engenders* involvement in the campaign (through the very process of newspaper reading or the demanding nature of the print media or both). In all likelihood it is both, though it is difficult, if not impossible, to know for sure.

46. The magnitude of this drop was probably somewhat inflated by altered question placement in 1988 (the campaign newspaper reading question was asked preelection, rather than postelection, as has been traditionally the case). Examination of 1988 campaign newspaper reading data by interview completion period, however, suggests that the extent of this inflation was only modest. For example, those respondents who were interviewed in the last week before the election had campaign newspaper reading levels only a little higher (4 points higher on "many articles"; 5 points lower on "no articles") than those interviewed in the middle of September. This leads me to believe that the exceptionally low levels of campaign newspaper reading reported in the 1988 NES data are largely a reflection of very low campaign involvement in 1988, rather than an artifact

TABLE 2-5. *Political Involvement and Sense of Government Responsiveness, by Indicator, 1960–88*[a]

Percent

Characteristic	1960	1964	1968	1972	1976	1980	1984	1988	Change 1960–88
Campaign newspaper reading[b]									
No articles	20.0	21.4	24.6	42.4	26.0	29.2	23.1	51.4	31.4
Some articles	25.1	24.9	26.7	21.6	35.3	45.4	52.4	30.7	5.6
Many articles	54.9	53.7	48.7	35.9	38.7	25.4	24.4	17.8	−37.1
Campaign TV watching[b]									
No programs	13.3	10.9	10.8	11.7	10.5.	14.1	13.9	16.7	3.4
Some programs	40.0	47.8	47.7	58.1	55.1	62.5	60.8	42.8	2.8
Many programs	46.7	41.3	41.6	30.2	34.4	23.4	25.3	40.5	−6.2
Campaign interest									
Not much interested	25.1	25.1	20.8	27.4	21.3	26.0	24.8	25.0	−0.1
Somewhat interested	37.3	36.6	40.4	41.1	42.6	44.2	46.8	47.2	9.9
Very much interested	37.6	38.2	38.9	31.5	36.1	29.8	28.4	27.8	−9.8
Following government and public affairs									
Little of the time[c]	37.5	28.1	36.3	27.3	30.1	38.7	37.1	40.7	3.2
Some of the time	41.7	41.6	30.7	36.2	31.6	34.9	36.4	36.9	−4.8
Most of the time	20.8	30.3	33.0	36.6	38.3	26.4	26.4	22.4	1.6
Sense of government responsiveness (political efficacy)[b]									
Low	15.7	21.3	30.6	31.9	35.6	31.8	24.8	42.8	27.1
Medium	22.6	26.3	24.7	28.3	28.9	33.8	25.2	27.3	4.7
High	61.7	52.4	44.7	39.8	35.4	34.3	49.9	29.9	−31.8

SOURCE: Author's tabulations from National Election Study data.

a. Basic question wording and coding decisions are described in appendix C.

b. Question wording for these questions changed between 1960 and 1988. Question placement was substantially altered in 1988 for campaign newspaper reading and TV watching. For discussion of these problems and attendant coding decisions, see appendix C.

c. Combines "hardly at all" and "every now and then" (1964 on).

important aspect of campaign involvement and, as it turns out, a powerful predictor of turnout.[47]

Other aspects of political involvement also show decreases, though not as dramatic as with campaign newspaper reading. The proportion of the electorate watching many programs about the campaign on TV

of question placement. Further support for this interpretation is provided by data from surveys taken in Wichita, Kansas in 1990 and 1991 (Research Center 1990a, table VIII a–e; 1990b, questions 20A–27B; and 1991b, tables 16, 17) showing campaign newspaper reading going up by only modest amounts—that is, similar to the amounts quoted above

dropped from 47 to 41 percent, the proportion that was very much interested in the campaign fell from 38 to 28 percent and the proportion that followed public affairs some or most of the time fell from 63 to 59 percent. These are hardly overwhelmingly decreases, but, combined with the drastic fall in campaign newspaper reading, they suggest a very substantial withdrawal of the American electorate from the electoral process.

The sense of government responsiveness also shows a very substantial fall over this period. In 1960 over three-fifths of the electorate (62 percent) had a strong sense of government responsiveness (high "political efficacy"). By 1988 this had slipped to less than half of that figure (30 percent). On the other end of the scale, just 16 percent of the electorate in 1960 had a weak sense of government responsiveness (low "political efficacy"), whereas by 1988 this figure had more than doubled to over two-fifths (43 percent) of the electorate.[48] Again this suggests

---

for 1988—during periods running from considerably *before* a given election (more than one month) to periods actually *after* that election (one week).

47. See appendix B for an empirical discussion of the strength of campaign newspaper reading as a predictor of turnout in a multivariate context. Exactly *why* campaign newspaper reading has a strong relationship to turnout is a more difficult issue to settle. It is possible that campaign newspaper reading is simply a "truer" measure of campaign involvement than a number of other indicators, because following the campaign in the papers requires some effort and therefore some genuine sense of involvement to foster the necessary motivation. Conversely, *lacking* such a sense of involvement, one of the first things people may *neglect* to do is follow the campaign in the papers.

Another possibility is that the very nature of campaign newspaper reading—the quality of the information, the active way it is absorbed (especially relative to other media)—substantially *enhances* people's feelings of involvement in the campaign. This would also lead to campaign newspaper reading being a strong predictor of turnout.

There is no clear way to choose between these two interpretations. My own feeling (supported by some focus group results—see Research Center, 1991a, pp. 1–34) is that both explanations play a role, with an initial sense of involvement helping motivate people to start following the campaign in the paper, and the process of following the campaign, once started, actually *increasing* people's sense of involvement.

In this context, it is also important to stress that campaign newspaper reading is *not* a proxy for *overall* newspaper reading. In fact, overall levels of newspaper reading have no independent effect on an individual's likelihood of voting. Nor can declining campaign newspaper reading be viewed as a simple product of generally declining newspaper readership. Declining daily newspaper readership tracks declining campaign newspaper reading very poorly. In addition, the proportion of the population that reads a newspaper at least once a week has remained stable (about 90 percent), so most people who are so motivated still have an opportunity to follow the campaign in the papers. Again, this suggests that the involvement factor is key.

48. The response categories to the efficacy questions were changed in 1988, from agree or disagree to a 5-point scale including a neutral, middle response. It is possible that people who might normally have given efficacious responses to these questions were drawn to the middle category, thereby exaggerating the proportion of low-efficacy citizens in this particular year and, hence, the overall drop in efficacy since 1960. Use of

quite a significant break in the perceived link between government and ordinary citizens.

The erosion of political and campaign involvement and a sense of government responsiveness thus appears to have been a source of downward pressure on turnout levels during the 1960–88 period, perhaps a very strong one. Model estimations are consistent with this assessment. The decreases in political and campaign involvement and in a sense of government responsiveness have easily the strongest effect on turnout levels of any of the other groups of characteristics considered here. In fact when changes in levels of involvement and sense of responsiveness are included in model estimations, it is possible to account for a very respectable three-quarters (73 percent) of the turnout decline observed in the National Election Study (NES) data (table 2-6)[49] (7.1 of 9.7 percentage points).[50]

RELATIVE CONTRIBUTIONS OF CHARACTERISTICS.   Table 2.6 also assesses the relative contributions of different factors to predicted turnout decline based on the probit model presented in appendix B. The first cluster of factors—education, occupation, and income ("socioeconomic status")—are all negatively signed, indicating that these factors made negative contributions to turnout decline (that is, actually served to *increase*, rather than decrease, turnout levels). Education is far and away the crucial factor here, its influence being about three times as great as occupation and income put together. Combined, the three SES characteristics *increased* the predicted probit by .171, a figure almost

---

alternative scoring methods for the 1988 data, however, fails to bring levels of low efficacy below 37 percent, indicating that most of the observed drop in efficacy is real, not an artifact of question wording (see Abramson, Aldrich, and Rohde 1990, pp. 118–19, for a confirmatory analysis).

49. The model performs about equally well in accounting for changes in turnout levels in the South and non-South. However, the model does not do particularly well in accounting for changing turnout levels among *black* southerners. (It severely underpredicts the large [25-point] increase in turnout in the NES data.) This suggests that black southerners were subject to highly specific cost and benefit changes not captured in the model that drove up their turnout levels. This is consistent with what we know about the tremendous reduction in registration barriers in the South in the 1960s, a phenomenon with impact primarily on southern blacks.

50. To decompose turnout decline into components attributable to different factors, it was necessary to assess turnout decline by comparing the probability of the predicted average (that is, of the average *probit*) across years, rather than the average of the predicted probabilities. Fortunately predictions of aggregate decline tend not to be sensitive to choice of method (here results are virtually identical in either case), so use of the predicted average method presents no serious problems.

TABLE 2-6. *Explaining the Differential in Turnout, 1960–88*

Characteristic	Predicted decline[a]	Percent of predicted decline[a]	Percent of SES-adjusted decline[a]
Socioeconomic status			
Education	−.118[b]	−46.0[b]	...
Occupation, income	−.053[b]	−20.7[b]	...
All socioeconomic status	−.171[b]	−66.7[b]	...
Social connectedness			
Age	.034	13.3	8.0
Marital status	.034	13.3	7.9
Church attendance	.077	29.9	17.9
All social connectedness	.145	56.5	33.9
Other demographic characteristics			
Race, region	.029	11.2	6.7
Party-related characteristics			
Partisanship, concern over outcome	.016	6.4	3.8
Difference between parties	−.013[b]	−5.1[b]	−3.1[b]
Knowledge of parties and candidates	.013	4.9	2.9
All party-related characteristics	.016	6.2	3.7
Political involvement and efficacy			
Campaign involvement through media	.105	40.7	24.4
Campaign and political interest	.027	10.5	6.3
Political efficacy	.107	41.7	25.0
All political involvement and efficacy	.238	92.8	55.7
Total probit drop	.257	100.0	100.0
Percentage-point decline in turnout predicted by probit model		7.1	
Percentage-point decline in turnout reported in ANES survey		9.7	
Percent of turnout differential explained by model		73.2	

SOURCE: Author's computations based on model in appendix B.
a. Figures in columns may not sum exactly because of rounding.
b. Minus sign indicates factor acted to *increase* turnout.

two-thirds the magnitude of the entire probit decline predicted by the model.

The second group of characteristics—age, marital status, and church attendance ("social connectedness")—all make positive contributions to turnout decline, with church attendance making the largest single contribution. Together, these social connectedness characteristics decrease the predicted probit by .145, about half of the overall decline predicted by the model. This predicted decline, combined with that attributable to race and region[51] ("other demographic"), just about counterbalances the upward push on turnout attributable to upgrading of socioeconomic status. Hence were the accounting procedure to stop at this point—with only social and demographic characteristics taken into consideration—very little change in turnout levels would be predicted over the 1960–88 period.

This is where changes in political connectedness come in, represented by the last two clusters of characteristics in table 2-6 ("party-related characteristics" and "political involvement and efficacy"). As the table shows, these factors together can account for almost all (99 percent) of the decline predicted by the model. Almost all of this effect, in turn, can be attributed to political involvement and efficacy factors (93 percent of predicted decline), rather than party-related characteristics, such as partisanship, and so on (only 6 percent of predicted decline). Finally of the involvement and efficacy factors, campaign involvement through the media[52] and political efficacy are of prime and roughly equal importance (each accounts for about two-fifths of predicted decline).

These results are rearranged in the third column. This rearrangement uses the concept of SES-adjusted turnout decline developed earlier. To reflect the fact that SES upgrading served to promote turnout and thus made the amount of turnout decline to be explained larger than that observed in the data, the predicted probit *increase* from these characteristics (.171) is added to the overall probit drop (.257) to produce the amount of probit decline actually explained by the other, non-SES variables in the model (.428). The probit drop from individual characteristics or sets of characteristics is then divided by .428 to find the proportion of adjusted decline accounted for by these variables. These proportions are shown in column three.

51. Race (black/nonblack) and region (South/non-South) were included as controls in the model (sex had such a weak effect on turnout, once other characteristics were controlled for, that I simply eliminated it from the final model). The effect on turnout levels alluded to here stems from distributional shifts in race and region (that is, more blacks and more southerners in the voting pool). Generally most hypothesized effects of race and region on turnout levels stem not from distributional changes, but from hypothesized *effect* changes. (For example, it is argued that being a southern black, by itself, no longer depresses turnout as much as it did in 1960.) Possible effects of such changes on turnout levels are discussed in the next section. The general issue of changing turnout differentials by region and, particularly, by race, is discussed in detail in the first part of chapter 3.

52. Declining campaign newspaper reading is by far the most important influence here.

These figures allow the findings from the decomposition to be presented more cleanly, with the positive contributions to turnout decline adding up to 100 percent (rather than well over, as in column two). By this accounting the contributions to turnout decline break down into more than one-half (56 percent) from decreases in political involvement and efficacy, about one-third (34 percent) from decreases in social connectedness, and the rest (10 percent) from the changing distribution of race, region, and various party-related characteristics.

The model findings suggest that the American electorate has been affected by three large-scale trends in the last thirty years, which together help explain a good part of the observed drop in turnout levels. The first big trend, socioeconomic (particularly educational) upgrading actually pushed turnout up. The other two big trends pushed turnout down: a substantial decline in social connectedness, as manifested in a younger, less married, and less church-going electorate; and a generalized withdrawal from the political world, as manifested by declining psychological involvement in politics and a declining belief in government responsiveness. (Interestingly, withdrawal or disconnection from the parties as particular political entities appears to be only a minor part of this story.) The latter two developments depressed the average benefits of voting sufficiently among the electorate to produce reduced turnout levels, despite the mitigating effects of the first development.

This is a relatively simple and compelling story that makes good intuitive sense. Several cautions, however, need to be kept in mind when interpreting these findings.

First, the analysis presented above is based on a statistical model that, like all models, is only an approximation of a very complicated reality.[53] It is possible, therefore, that there were (and are) other important factors affecting turnout levels that are not captured in this model.[54]

Second, even within the framework of the model, not all of the decline in turnout is accounted for. Specifically, as shown in table 2-6, the model cannot account for about one-quarter of the decline in turnout observed in the NES data. This means that although the model illumi-

---

53. As the statistician, Box, put it: "All models are wrong, but some are useful."
54. In fact if it is assumed that turnout levels at any given time are a complex result of a variety of influences—some positive, some negative—there is no mathematical limit to the potential number of other factors there could be. The potential influence of a wide range of factors is particularly plausible, given the nature of voting as low-cost, low-benefit action (see Aldrich [forthcoming] for a fully developed argument along these lines).

nates a good part of the story behind declining turnout, it probably does not provide a complete explanation.

Third, looking outside the framework of the model, there appears to be an additional amount of turnout decline to be accounted for that was not captured by the NES data. This is because the aggregate ("real world") data show a decline in turnout of 12.6 percentage points (see table 1-3), about 3 points more than the NES data show. Although there are problems with directly comparing NES and aggregate data, there still seems to be some additional amount of turnout decline that the model presented here did not address and, therefore, does not account for. This underscores the point that the model, although providing a useful window into the processes affecting turnout decline, does not, in all likelihood, provide a complete explanation for that decline.

Finally the analysis presented above is really about identifying the factors that, in a *proximate* sense, have led to declining turnout levels. But this type of analysis does not reveal where these proximate factors came from or the extent to which they may be functioning as indicators of underlying social phenomena. For example, if declining psychological involvement in politics and sense of government responsiveness have led to declining turnout, what caused citizens to become less involved and believe less in responsive government? Unfortunately, poor data make it difficult, if not impossible, to develop a very detailed understanding of these underlying causes, but I do think this issue is worth keeping in mind when interpreting the research findings presented here (and as a subject for further research).

Other Possible Sources of Turnout Decline

This discussion suggests the desirability of looking for other sources of turnout decline that were not included in the model estimations. One possibility is changes in the *effect* of race (black) and region (South) on turnout, as opposed to changes in distribution of these characteristics (already included in the estimations summarized in table 2-6). As discussed earlier most hypothesized impacts of race or region on turnout levels stem not from distributional changes, but from hypothesized effect changes (for example, it is argued that being a southern black, by itself, no longer has the same effect on turnout as it did in 1960).

I did find some evidence of a change in the effect of being a southern black on turnout after 1965—that is, for presidential elections, 1968 and onward, being a southern black depressed a citizen's likelihood of turnout substantially less than in 1960 and 1964. In addition I found some weak evidence of an effect change over the same time period for being a white southerner.[55] In either case, however, the estimated impact of the effect changes went in the wrong direction for explaining turnout decline. Specifically the estimated impact of these effect changes on turnout would have been, all else equal, to *increase* turnout 1 to 2 percentage points[56] over the 1960–88 period.[57]

Obviously then, changes in the effect of region or race do not go very far in accounting for the "missing" turnout decline. A possibly more fruitful source may be the decline in social connectedness discussed earlier in this chapter. At that point, I mentioned that the aspects of social connectedness included in the model did not exhaust the roster of social connectedness characteristics conceivably relevant to turnout decline (though a brief look at the data on these other characteristics did not suggest a high level of relevance). To test whether these other characteristics could be playing a role in turnout decline, I inserted them in models that included all the variables in table 2-6 and covered as many years as the characteristics tested would permit.[58] The results were not encouraging. Home ownership, for example, is a significant predictor of turnout, but changes so little over the 1964–88 time period that its impact on turnout levels is negligible.

Nor does union membership have much of an impact.[59] Although union membership declined more than home ownership, the relationship between union membership and turnout is so weak that the impact of this decline on turnout levels was also negligible. In fact I estimated the *combined* negative impact of declining home ownership and de-

55. No evidence whatsoever exists of an effect change for sex on turnout over this time period, contrary to a thesis that is occasionally advanced by political observers.

56. The estimate is closer to 2 points if the very weak white southern interaction term is included in the estimations, and closer to 1 point if this interaction term is excluded.

57. It seems likely that to some extent these estimates are capturing the effects of registration law changes from the 1960s, because these changes are believed to have had the most impact on southern blacks. Thus this finding, although not explaining turnout decline directly, does provide some evidence on the turnout-promoting effect of registration law changes, which, along with the turnout-promoting effect of socioeconomic upgrading, forms a critical part of the "puzzle of participation" alluded to earlier in the chapter.

58. Data on some of these characteristics were not collected in all presidential years, 1960–88. See appendix C for more information on data availability by year for different characteristics.

59. Actually the variable in the NES data is whether the respondent is in a union *family*, rather than a union member himself or herself. I do not believe this presents any particular problems for analysis.

clining union membership on turnout levels at only about 0.3 percent. This suggests that the impact of the decline in social connectedness, at least in any way that can be measured,[60] may already be captured fairly well by the model summarized in table 2-6.

Another possible source of additional downward pressure on turnout might be from the level of party mobilization. This could be a factor even if, as discussed earlier, the erosion of individual-level affective and perceptual connections between citizens and parties has played only a very minor role in declining turnout (see table 2-6). For example, it is theoretically possible that the role of parties themselves in actively organizing citizens—party mobilization—has fallen drastically, while individual citizens' sense of partisanship has declined only modestly (see table 2-4). Certainly much anecdotal evidence exists that generally speaking "parties aren't what they used to be," and, in many communities, are not the strong institutions they once were.

The problem with this line of argument is that it is relatively difficult to come up with hard evidence that supports it. For example, levels of direct contact by parties, as measured by an NES item that asks respondents whether anyone from one of the parties came around and talked to them about the election, changed relatively little over the 1960–88 time period and, to the extent they did, the change was in the "wrong" direction (that is, *up* slightly, not down).[61] Although one could raise questions about this item as an indicator of party mobilization,[62] it is nonetheless food for thought that respondents' self-reports of direct party contact have not decreased over time.

60. It is still possible of course that other aspects of social connectedness not well captured in the NES data—or any other time series data set—could be responsible for some or all of the "missing" turnout decline. This would be the argument, I would presume, of Knack and others who argue for the primary salience of declining social connectedness to falling voter turnout. (Knack 1991a, 1992a has even been involved in the piloting of some items for the NES that he believes could capture some of these missing aspects of social connectedness. The problem of course is that even if these items "pan out" in terms of their relationship to turnout, data will be lacking on their distributional change over time and, therefore, the extent to which they are truly salient to declining turnout levels.)

61. Party contact was actually 1.8 percentage points higher in 1988 than in 1960. Indeed 1960 was the low point for the entire period, so party contact was at least somewhat higher in all the intermediate presidential elections as well.

62. It is possible that citizens do not adequately distinguish between people from interest groups and people from the parties contacting them. If this is true, citizens might be reporting unchanged levels of party contact simply because decreased frequency of party contact has coincided with increased frequency of interest group contact, and citizens tend to conflate the two types of contact.

Another difficulty with the declining party mobilization argument is that, on a pure organizational level, parties are stronger than ever. That is, regardless of other ways in which American political parties may have declined, the structural strength of American parties as organizations has, if anything, actually increased.[63] Again, although organizational strength is probably not a particularly good indicator of mobilization, the trend on this indicator underscores the difficulties of finding hard evidence supporting the party demobilization argument.

Does this lack of hard evidence mean that a decline in party mobilization should be completely ruled out as a possible contributor to turnout decline? I do not think so. First, changes over time have not been (and perhaps never will be) adequately measured for too many important aspects of party mobilization. These include the quality of contacts between party and citizen (that is, how well, if at all, do citizens know local party workers?); the nature of party organization in local communities (that is, how many links do local parties have with social groups, community institutions, and organizational networks, and how strong are those links?); and the quality and type of party outreach activities (that is, how much has television simply supplanted many of the ways parties used to reach out to ordinary citizens?). I believe enough anecdotal evidence exists that parties have demobilized—become weaker and more diffuse—in these ways so that a possible role for party demobilization in turnout decline should still be considered.

It is also possible that demobilization, if not a direct contributor to turnout decline, has played a role indirectly as an underlying cause of the disconnection from politics described in the previous section. Unfortunately the aspects of party mobilization enumerated above are the most plausible candidates for causing such disconnection, but because of the lack of hard data on these aspects, their possible role cannot be empirically evaluated. Still I think the theoretical plausibility of such a relationship (that is, between demobilization and political disconnection) suggests this possibility should be kept in mind.

Thus if available data do not allow party demobilization to be ruled out as a possible source of turnout decline, neither do they allow it to be ruled in.[64] Much the same might be said of the possible role of

63. See, for example, Gibson and others 1985; Huckshorn and others 1986; and Herrnson 1988.
64. But see Rosenstone and Hansen (forthcoming) for an argument that demobiliza-

declining competitiveness of elections. Although it is certainly clear that elections for the House of Representatives have become substantially less competitive, it is less clear that elections for president, governor, and senator[65]—the elections that draw the heaviest turnouts—have declined seriously in competitiveness. And in at least one section of the country (the South) competitiveness has clearly increased, as the old one-party (that is, the Democratic party) system has been replaced with a two-party system. Available data, then, do not permit a clear judgment on whether changing electoral competitiveness has been a source of downward pressure on turnout levels.

I turn now to two possible sources for which available data *do* directly suggest that contributions to turnout decline have been made. The first is changes in election calendars.[66] As discussed in chapter 1, frequent elections are believed to attenuate the meaningfulness of any individual election, especially where balloting for important offices is spread across a number of elections instead of being concentrated in one general election. Changes in election calendars since 1960 have in fact directly increased election frequency (for instance, the rise in presidential primaries from fifteen states in 1960 to thirty-two states in 1988) and shifted important offices away from the presidential general election ballot (such as the movement of governors' races to off-year elections by sixteen states, thereby dropping the number of states that hold gubernatorial elections during presidential years from twenty-eight in 1960 to twelve in 1988). Because both of these changes are in the "right" direction to depress turnout levels, the plausibility that changing election calendars are a factor in turnout decline is further suggested.

Model estimations[67] confirm that changing election calendars probably played a role—albeit a modest one—in turnout decline. I found that the combined impact of the rise in spring primaries and the decline

tion—though very broadly defined and not restricted to the direct role of parties—has been a central part of the turnout decline process.

65. Though it is true that the proportion of senatorial incumbents reelected with 60 percent or more of the vote has increased over time (Ornstein, Mann, and Malbin 1992, table 2-11).

66. This possibility was originally raised by Boyd 1981, 1986, 1989. See his articles for detailed discussion of the issue.

67. Based on the model in appendix B with variables added for gubernatorial elections and number of spring primaries. The coding for spring primaries follows the procedure used in Boyd 1989 (see appendix C for details). I also initially included a variable for number of fall primaries, but did not find a significant effect for that variable (but see Boyd 1981, 1986, 1989 for an alternative estimation).

in concurrent gubernatorial elections in presidential years should have been, all else equal, to depress turnout about 1.7 percentage points (most of this because of the decline in gubernatorial elections).[68] Thus changing election calendars are apparently another factor reducing the meaningfulness of presidential elections for citizens and thereby contributing to declining turnout.

The second source for which available data directly suggest a role in falling turnout is the decline in citizen duty, an aspect of political connectedness not previously included in model estimations. Citizen duty taps the extent to which citizens feel an obligation to participate in the political system (by voting), regardless of other factors that may militate against such participation. Citizen duty items have been asked only irregularly on the NES, and most of them were eliminated from the survey after 1980. Perhaps this was partially because the trend line on these data was so flat during the 1960s and 1970s—that is, whatever else was happening in American society, people's sense of citizen duty did not appear to be changing.

However, the NES did retain one citizen duty item on the survey through the 1980s, and it turns out that this item does show quite a lot of change over the decade. The specific item asked people whether they thought they should not bother to vote in an election if they did not care much about it. The proportion that thought they should bother to vote, even under these circumstances, has gone down from 59 percent in 1980 to 42 percent in 1988—a very substantial 17-point drop in eight years.[69]

Confirmatory evidence for this drop in citizen duty comes from *Washington Post*/ABC surveys in 1983 and 1991. On these surveys respondents were asked a somewhat different citizen duty item—

---

68. It is interesting to note that this turnout-depressing effect from changing election calendars roughly counterbalances the turnout-*increasing* effect from the changing influence of race and region on turnout. Assuming that this latter effect is also primarily structural in origin (that is, mostly stems from relaxation of registration laws in the 1960s, particularly in the South), this would mean that the two structural changes identified as influences on turnout levels (changes in election calendars and registration laws) tend to cancel one another out and make little net contribution to explaining turnout decline.

69. Abramson, Silver, and Anderson 1987 argue that this drop is probably artifactual because this item is now asked alone, while before it was asked after two other citizen duty items (which promoted a "dutiful" response to the third item). I am not persuaded that evidence from one relatively old (1952) NES is sufficient to disregard the 17-point drop in the proportion disagreeing with this item. Besides, even taking their evidence on a question-ordering effect at face value, the effect they show is not close enough to account for a decline of this magnitude.

whether they thought their own votes really mattered. Because a similar item was also asked on the 1980 NES, it is possible to assess the extent to which this aspect of citizen duty changed during the 1980s by using the 1980 NES as a benchmark.[70]

The results were astonishing. Although the earlier NES data show tremendously high proportions expressing the belief that their votes mattered, the *Washington Post*/ABC data show that this belief has eroded drastically in recent years. From 91 percent saying their vote mattered in 1980, the proportion expressing such a belief fell to 86 percent in 1983 and to 73 percent in the most recent poll in 1991. (Interpolating the latter two figures, this would put the level of this aspect of citizen duty at about 78 percent at the time of the 1988 election.) Once again this is a very substantial drop of about 18 points over an eleven-year time period.

Using the same technique described earlier in this section in connection with union membership and home ownership, I estimated models that included these citizen duty items to see if these declining levels of citizen duty could be playing a role in turnout decline. Turnout impact estimates[71] based on these models strongly suggest this was the case. Specifically the estimated impact of these decreases in citizen duty on turnout should have been, all else equal, to decrease turnout levels about 2 to 4 percentage points (almost all in the 1980s).[72]

Thus the model does not include at least two possible sources of turnout decline for which some reasonably hard evidence can be adduced. It is interesting that one of these sources—and the one with apparently the most impact—taps yet another connection of Americans to their political system, suggesting, once again, that a multifaceted decline in political connectedness has played a central role in bringing down U.S. turnout levels.

---

70. Note, however, that *Washington Post*/ABC did alter the item somewhat, changing it from "So many other people vote in the national elections that it doesn't matter much to me whether I vote or not" to "My own vote doesn't really matter in an election." I do not believe, however, that this change seriously damages comparability, because the basic thrust of the item was very similar and would appear to tap the same underlying citizen commitment (or lack thereof) to the political process.

71. See appendix B for a description of how the impact of specific variables on turnout levels is estimated.

72. The estimate is closer to 2 points, if the 1983 *Washington Post*/ABC citizen figure is used, closer to 4 points if the 1983 and 1991 *Washington Post*/ABC figures are interpolated to produce a 1988 figure.

Conclusion

The following conclusions have been reached from this investigation of the decline in U.S. voter turnout since 1960.

First the decline in voter turnout since 1960 has been substantial and serious and is in no way merely an artifact of available data. Nor is the decline in turnout simply a matter of fewer people negotiating the onerous U.S. registration system, because even those registered are showing less of a propensity to vote.

Second this decline in voter turnout does not appear to a be a matter of increased voting *costs*, because the registration system, the chief source of costs to U.S. voters, has actually become less stringent since 1960. It follows that the root cause of declining turnout has been a reduction in the perceived *benefits* of voting.

Third the turnout-reducing drop in the perceived benefits of voting may be traced in large part to trends in the individual-level character- istics of citizens. Specifically three big trends have affected the Ameri- can electorate in the last thirty years that together explain a good amount of the observed drop in turnout levels. The first big trend, socioeconomic (particularly educational) upgrading actually pushed turnout up. The other two big trends pushed turnout down: a substan- tial decline in social connectedness, as manifested in a younger, less married, and less church-going electorate, and a generalized withdrawal or diconnection from the political world, manifested most dramatically by declining psychological involvement in politics and a declining belief in government responsiveness. These latter two trends depressed the average benefits of voting sufficiently among the electorate to produce substantially reduced turnout levels, despite the mitigating effects of the first trend.

Finally of the two turnout-depressing trends just mentioned—one social, one political—the ongoing process of political disconnection appears to have played by far the largest role. This role is underscored by indications that citizen duty may be yet another aspect of political connectedness that is eroding and pushing down turnout levels.

3

A Class Bias in American Politics?

It has been shown that much of the decline in U.S. voter turnout can be traced to ongoing processes of social and political disconnection that are reducing the perceived benefits of participating for many citizens. This gives us some idea of the motivational barriers impelling more and more citizens to stay home on election day.

But this analysis tells little about the *impact* of increased nonvoting. Specifically, it does not tell *who* is not voting and *what difference* such nonvoting may make to American politics. This chapter explores these very important questions in detail.

Who Is Not Voting?

The basic contour of declining voter participation has been described, but what of specific subgroups in the electorate—groups segmented by race, age, economic class, and other factors? Has the decline in turnout been uniform across these subgroups or has it been sharper for some than for others?

For two general reasons uniform turnout decline should *not* be expected across subgroups in the population. The first is that the factors impelling turnout downward may not have trended uniformly across all social groups. For example, the generalized withdrawal from politics may have been sharper among certain groups than others. If this is true, turnout decline would tend to be greater for the group experiencing the sharpest withdrawal from politics.

The second reason deals with the theoretical relationship between the *probability* of voting and the influence of different factors on that

58

probability. Briefly put the theory says the influence of a given factor will be greatest on those individuals with about an even (50–50) chance of voting and substantially less on those already very likely to vote.[1] Hence two subgroups, one with a 50 percent likelihood of voting and the other with an 85 percent likelihood, could experience identical downward shifts in levels of a given characteristic (say, efficacy) but experience very different shifts in their average turnout level (the group at 50 percent would experience a much greater decline in turnout).

Given all this, varied turnout decline across population subgroups seems quite natural and a moderate lack of uniformity no necessary cause for concern. However, a number of popular theories about the decline in turnout say it has been so concentrated among certain subgroups—the poor, minorities, the young—that differential turnout decline is indeed a cause for concern. According to these theories, the demographic skew in turnout rates has become substantially more severe over time, thereby seriously distorting the American political process. In what follows, I test these theories against available data to see whether and to what extent these skews have actually changed over time.

The Class Gap in Voting Rates

Perhaps the most popular theory concerning demographic skews and nonvoting posits a widening class gap in turnout. This theory, elaborated by such influential commentators as Edsall, Burnham, and Piven and Cloward,[2] says that as turnout has been falling over time and the decline has been concentrated among the poor and lower class, thereby dramatically sharpening the already existing class gap in participation. The widening of this class gap in turn is believed to be responsible for a variety of political ills—the most serious being a turn away from the poor (now allegedly unrepresented) in the policy discourse of the country.

The data shown here address the first part of the argument. Has the class gap in participation substantially widened over time?[3] These data, drawn from the massive census survey conducted in November of every election year, as well as the National Election Studies, show

1. Also substantially less on those very *un*likely to vote. See Teixeira 1987, pp. 41–43, and appendix B for more discussion on the basic turnout model.
2. Edsall 1984, pp. 180–83, Burnham 1987, esp. pp. 123–30, and Piven and Cloward 1980.
3. The second part of the argument—the presumed effect of a class gap on political outcomes—is discussed in detail later in this chapter.

self-reported[4] turnout rate trends for all three components of socioeconomic status—income, education, and occupation (tables 3-1 and 3-2).

The reasons for using two different data sources are as follows. The census survey (more specifically known as the Voter Supplement file to the November Current Population Survey) is, all else equal, the best data source on the changing demographics of voter turnout because of the very large sample size (from 92,000 to 114,000 respondents of voting age per survey, which is about 50 times the size of a typical National Election Study). These very large sample sizes make it possible to compare voting rates across relatively small demographic categories with a good degree of confidence.

However, an important problem with these data exists—available machine-readable data are limited to the 1972–88 period because the data tapes have been lost for the 1968 and 1964 presidential elections (1964 was the first year the survey was taken). Thus full analyses of the census data could only be done for the five presidential elections between 1972 and 1988. However, where possible I have tried to match my own tabulations with tabulations contained in the published census reports for 1964 and 1968 so as to present as extensive a time series as possible.[5]

Because of this time coverage problem, I present additional data on voting rate demographics from the National Election Studies (NES).[6]

4. It should be emphasized that these data do not represent the "true" turnout rates of these demographic groups—no such statistics are kept by election authorities—but rather the *self-reports* of survey respondents as to whether they voted in a given election or not. As such, these data, in an absolute sense, will always *overstate* the turnout rate of a given group because of the phenomenon of vote *overreporting* (see appendix A). The data, however, are still quite useful for looking at *patterns* of turnout—that is, for comparing the turnout rates of demographic groups and examining how these rates have changed over time. But a stand-alone figure from one of these surveys of the form, "X percent of Y group voted in the Z election," is generally not that useful because that figure will generally be a substantial overestimate of the true situation in that election.

5. Also note that a consistent time series from the Census Voter Supplement can only be constructed using the voting age population as a base rather than the eligible electorate. The Voter Supplement is administered to a sample of the entire VAP (including noncitizens) and has traditionally based its published reports on that population—including the reports from 1964 and 1968, the only source of data from those years. In addition, because the census substantially changed its procedures for identifying noncitizens in 1978, a time series for the eligible electorate alone is suspect even for the 1972–88 period, for which data tapes *are* available. For all these reasons census data are presented here on the basis of the VAP as a whole as in standard census reports. (However, all analyses for 1972–88 were also run with an approximation of the eligible electorate, to check for possible biases introduced by including noncitizens.)

6. Self-reported turnout data are used here though the NES does currently include a validated turnout measure as well (in which the NES attempts to check a respondent's

The NES data, despite the relatively small sample sizes involved, can be fully analyzed back to 1960, whereas the census data go back to only 1964 at best and sometimes only 1972. Thus the NES data provide a useful supplement. However, when voting rate trends seem to differ between the two data sources, and cannot be explained by differing population bases,[7] I generally give the census data more interpretive weight.

The data on turnout rates by income are examined first (table 3-1). It is here that the widening class gap would be expected to be most obvious, both because income level is generally the most politically salient aspect of class and because the poor are the group typically believed to be the most disadvantaged by evolving turnout patterns.

The first thing these data make clear is that the decline in turnout in the last several decades has not been confined to low-income groups. In fact the decline in turnout has been generalized across all income groups, including the very highest. For example, the census data show that, between 1972 and 1988, turnout dropped about 4 percentage points among the highest income group (those with family incomes of more than $60,000 in 1988 dollars),[8] compared to 6 points among the population as a whole.

Similarly the NES data say that turnout declined about 8 points among the highest income group[9] between 1960 and 1988, compared to 9 points among the population as a whole. Clearly then not just low-

---

self-report of voting against local records). Unfortunately the validated turnout data do not start until 1964 and then skip twelve years to 1976. Thus the data are difficult to use in a time series context, particularly as a supplement and check to the census.

In addition close scrutiny of the validated data reveal they are susceptible to fairly serious biases that would at least partially offset the advantage of eliminating the self-reporting bias. Most serious is that the methodology and almost certainly the accuracy of NES voter validation has changed quite substantially from 1964 to 1988 (Traugott 1989) so that observed changes over time in validated voting rates are likely to reflect both changes in the real world *and* changes in NES procedures (see appendix A for more discussion of problems with NES validation procedures). This further limits the usefulness of the validated data in a time series comparison context. (However, all analyses run on the self-reported data were also run on the validated data—for the years available—to check for possible biases introduced by self-reporting.)

7. The NES data are based on the eligible electorate, whereas the census data are based on the voting-age population as a whole.

8. The methodology by which respondents in different years were assigned to a uniform set of income categories is explained in appendix C.

9. Because of data limitations it was necessary to code the top income group as $50,000 or more, rather than $60,000 or more as could be done with the census data. This biases the measured turnout level of the top category slightly downward, relative to the census, and possibly the amount of turnout decline slightly upward.

TABLE 3-1. *Self-Reported Turnout Rates, by Family Income, 1960–88*
Percent

Characteristic	1960	1964	1968	1972	1976	1980	1984	1988	Change[a]
Family income				Census data					
(1988 dollars)									
Less than 7,500	n.a.	n.a.	n.a.	47.2	43.3	42.9	43.2	39.8	−7.4
7,500–14,999	n.a.	n.a.	n.a.	53.5	50.5	50.0	50.8	47.4	−6.1
15,000–19,999	n.a.	n.a.	n.a.	54.8	53.6	54.4	55.7	54.1	−0.7
20,000–29,999	n.a.	n.a.	n.a.	64.1	60.0	59.5	60.6	60.5	−3.6
30,000–39,999	n.a.	n.a.	n.a.	70.2	67.0	67.2	66.5	66.2	−4.0
40,000–59,999	n.a.	n.a.	n.a.	78.5	74.5	72.6	72.0	72.3	−6.2
60,000 or more	n.a.	n.a.	n.a.	79.1	76.5	73.9	75.5	75.4	−3.7
Family income by sextile									
Lowest sextile	n.a.	n.a.	n.a.	49.2	45.1	44.7	44.3	40.7	−8.5
Second sextile	n.a.	n.a.	n.a.	54.0	51.6	51.6	52.6	50.1	−3.9
Third sextile	n.a.	n.a.	n.a.	58.8	56.1	56.8	57.5	54.5	−4.3
Fourth sextile	n.a.	n.a.	n.a.	67.0	62.2	62.5	63.0	60.9	−6.1
Fifth sextile	n.a.	n.a.	n.a.	71.6	69.0	69.5	69.4	66.4	−5.2
Highest sextile	n.a.	n.a.	n.a.	78.8	75.8	73.7	74.8	74.1	−4.7
Total	n.a.	69.3	67.8	63.0	59.2	59.2	59.9	57.4	−5.6
Family income				NES data					
(1988 dollars)									
Less than 7,500	65.4	63.8	59.0	55.8	52.3	53.3	51.7	45.2	−20.2
7,500–14,999	69.4	69.6	64.6	63.6	63.9	63.5	69.6	57.2	−12.2
15,000–19,999	83.6	79.6	69.7	66.0	71.1	73.1	71.2	69.4	−14.2
20,000–29,999	85.0	81.1	79.4	72.2	71.7	70.1	72.5	69.3	−15.7
30,000–39,999	80.6	82.5	85.6	81.2	74.1	74.6	79.9	76.6	−4.0
40,000–49,999	88.5	91.0	87.6	87.3	83.3	82.0	84.5	83.5	−5.0
50,000 or more	94.3	87.0	91.0	89.3	89.3	83.0	88.9	86.5	−7.8
Family income by sextile									
Lowest sextile	64.5	62.1	61.2	58.6	56.7	57.3	53.8	46.9	−17.6
Second sextile	72.5	71.2	64.6	63.6	64.8	66.8	70.0	58.7	−13.8
Third sextile	80.0	81.1	77.4	67.8	70.3	72.4	70.3	68.2	−11.8
Fourth sextile	83.0	78.5	79.1	74.5	71.0	70.7	78.0	72.6	−10.4
Fifth sextile	86.3	83.9	85.7	83.5	78.8	80.6	82.1	80.9	−5.4
Highest sextile	88.1	88.7	89.5	88.6	87.1	83.0	88.4	86.3	−1.8
Total	79.0	77.7	75.8	72.8	71.6	71.4	73.6	69.7	−9.3

SOURCE: Author's tabulations of Bureau of the Census and National Election Study data.
n.a. Not available.
a. For census data, change is 1972–88. For NES data, change is 1960–88.

income voters are turning away from the ballot box; high-income voters are also becoming progressively less likely to participate in the voting process.

But if the decline in turnout has been general, it is still possible that the class gap in turnout may have widened substantially, as a result of sharper turnout decline among low-income groups. Here the census and NES stories diverge. The census data show only a modest increase[10] in the turnout gap between the bottom and the top of the income distribution—less than 4 percentage points (from 31.9 to 35.6 points) over the 1972–88 period.[11]

The NES data, on the other hand, show the gap widening fairly substantially—from 29 to 41 points—over the full 1960–88 period. However, comparison with the census data suggests this figure is inflated. Most of the increase in the NES class gap in turnout (8 points) occurs in the 1972–88 period, precisely the period when the census data show only a 4-point increase in the gap. Assuming the census estimate is correct[12] for 1972–88, and assuming that the 1960–72 NES data are

10. A common way of exaggerating such moderate changes should be mentioned here. It consists of taking the amount of turnout decline for a given group and expressing it as a *percentage* of the group's original turnout rate—that is, as a percentage of a percentage. The problem with this method is that it is very sensitive to the size of the group's original turnout rate, which forms the denominator for this particular computation. The lower the original turnout rate, in fact, the greater the change estimate, all else equal, this method will produce. (The same is true of any other method using the original turnout rate as a denominator.)

Thus the method is ideally suited for inflating the amount of change taking place among low-turnout groups. Take, for example, identical 10-percentage-point declines in turnout among two groups: group A, voting at 40 percent; and group B, voting at 80 percent. According to this method, group A's turnout rate changed twice as much as group B's (25 percent to 12.5 percent). But this result simply reflects the fact that group A had a much lower level of turnout to begin with.

Moreover depending on the focus of inquiry, this method actually produces different substantive results with the same data—for example, if one chooses to look at *nonvoting* rates instead of voting rates. The *nonvoting* rates for groups A and B are, respectively, 60 percent and 20 percent. If turnout declined (nonvoting increased) the same 10 percentage points for each group, group A's nonvoting rate only increases 16.7 percent, but group B's nonvoting rate increases 50 percent. Thus the big change shifts from group A to group B, though the data has remained the same. This is not the mark of a very robust method.

11. By setting the maximum family income category lower than shown in table 3-1, I was able to develop rough estimates of increases in the class gap in turnout since 1968 and 1964 using the published census reports (though note that these reports excluded individuals in one-person households from family income–based tabulations, further vexing comparisons with later years). These estimates show increases in the class gap consistent with those given above for 1972–88 (slightly larger for 1968–88 and slightly smaller for 1964–88). Although these estimates should be treated cautiously because of the altered income categorization, they buttress the case for a moderate, rather than large or dramatic, increase in the turnout class gap.

12. The low census estimate cannot be attributed to using the voting-age population

equally inflated, yields a more modest estimate of a 6-point increase in the class gap between 1960 and 1988.

But what if income groups are defined in a different way?—by *relative* position in the income structure. Some argue this is the crucial distinction, because the size of groups based on real income may shift over time, but the bottom 20 percent remains at the bottom (and presumably similarly disadvantaged relative to the top 20 percent). Such relational data may also be found in table 3-1 (here based on *sextiles*—dividing the income distribution into six equal-sized groups).[13]

Based on these relational groups, the census data continue to show a fairly modest increase in the class gap. Turnout in the top sextile declined by about 5 percentage points between 1972–88, compared to 8 percentage points in the bottom sextile. This increased[14] the class gap between top and bottom from about 30 to 33 percentage points, hardly a huge change and one consistent with theoretical expectations of modest differences in turnout decline across subgroups.[15]

The NES data again tell a different story, showing a substantial 16-point increase in the class gap, from 23.6 to 39.4 points over the 1960–88 period. And here again comparison with the census data suggests this figure is inflated. Most of the increase in the NES sextile-based class gap (9 points) occurs in the 1972–88 period, the same period when the census data show only a 4-point increase in the gap. Using the assumptions described earlier—that the census estimate is correct for 1972–88 and that the 1960–72 NES data are equally inflated—this

---

as a base. Simulating the NES universe within the census data yields an even *lower* estimate of the increase in the class gap (2 percentage points).

Indeed this should generally be true when moving from a voting-age to citizen-eligible population base. This is because the proportion of aliens has gone up steadily since 1970, and because aliens tend to be low SES, the increase in aliens will be concentrated in these low-SES categories. Thus when using the voting-age population as a base, the growing concentration of aliens will increasingly and disproportionately depress the voting rates of low-SES categories over time. This in turn should slightly *increase* the change in the class gap over that measured among citizen-eligibles. Thus using the voting-age population as a base, as I do here, should generally *over*estimate, not underestimate, the change in the class gap.

13. The methodology for assigning respondents to sextiles, given the categorical nature of the income data in both the census and NES, is explained in appendix C.

14. Most of the increase really stems from the 1988 election in particular rather than a steady change over time. In fact the class gap in the 1984 election was very close (within 1 point) to that in the 1972 election.

15. These findings are also consistent with the detailed analysis of census data conducted by Leighley and Nagler 1991. Their analysis, conducted somewhat differently than my own, shows a similarly stable class gap in turnout (defined relationally) between 1972 and 1988.

suggests a moderate increase in the class gap of about 6 points between 1960 and 1988.[16]

Of course none of this means there is no income-based class gap in turnout. Far from it—this class gap is obviously quite large. The point is that the magnitude of this gap has not changed dramatically over time and, if it is a problem, it is much the same problem as existed three decades ago when the current era of turnout decline began.

Although the data do not support the idea of a substantially enlarged class gap based on income, it is possible other measures of socioeconomic status—education or income—may show a different pattern. Looking first at the census data, it is apparent that turnout rates for citizens at all levels of educational attainment have been declining significantly over time (table 3-2). Even the top educational group— those with a college degree or more—has experienced a 10-point drop in turnout since 1964, not much less than the overall turnout drop recorded by the census (12 points).

In addition the decline in turnout is clearly much larger among the lowest group in this distribution. Those with only eight years or less of education experienced a turnout drop of about 22 points, over twice the drop for college graduates.[17] Because of this, the education gap in turnout increased from about 29 points in 1964 to 41 points in 1988.[18]

16. Once again alternative estimations using a census universe that approximates the NES universe show even *lower* estimates of the 1972–88 increase in the relational class gap (2 percentage points). In addition the validated NES data diverge here from the self-reported data and show only a modest (7-percentage-point) increase in the relational class gap over the 1964–88 time period.

17. It is interesting that the drops in turnout among other education groups (nine to eleven years, high school graduate, some college) are also quite large—from 18 to 24 points. In light of this, it may seem strange that overall turnout declined only 12 points (especially because the only group for which turnout declined *less* than the overall average [college graduates] went down a healthy 10 points, not that much less than the overall figure). The reason for this puzzling result is the educational upgrading discussed earlier. Because educational upgrading shifts substantial proportions of the population into higher-turnout education categories, it is possible for turnout to drop much more sharply *within* individual education groups than among the population as a whole (on which the turnout-*promoting* effects of shifts across education categories make themselves felt).

18. The very poorly educated (zero to eight years of education) are a somewhat different group of people today than they were at the beginning of the 1960s. Then it was not so uncommon for individuals to finish their education before high school. Today of course it is relatively unusual, because of the tremendous distributional shifts out of very low education categories in the last thirty years (see table 2-2). As a result, the group "left behind" in the zero to eight-years category is, in all likelihood, a group with demographic, social, and attitudinal characteristics that are particularly uncongenial to voter participation (for an interesting discussion of this left-behind, low-education group, see Bennett 1991). In light of this, it seems surprising that the increase in the education gap is not even larger than it is.

TABLE 3-2. *Self-Reported Turnout Rates, by Education and Occupation, 1960–88*

Percent

Characteristic	1960	1964	1968	1972	1976	1980	1984	1988	Change[a]
				Census data					
Education									
0–8 years	n.a.	59.0	54.5	47.4	44.1	42.6	42.9	36.7	−22.3
9–11 years	n.a.	65.4	61.3	52.0	47.2	45.6	44.4	41.3	−24.1
High school graduate	n.a.	76.1	72.5	65.4	59.4	58.9	58.7	54.7	−21.4
Some college	n.a.	82.1	78.4	74.9	68.1	67.2	67.5	64.5	−17.6
College graduate or more	n.a.	87.5	84.1	83.6	79.8	79.9	79.1	77.6	−9.9
Occupation									
Professional-technical	n.a.	n.a.	n.a.	82.3	78.3	78.0	76.0	75.7	−6.6
Managerial-administrative	n.a.	n.a.	n.a.	76.0	71.9	71.8	74.1	71.9	−4.1
Clerical-sales	n.a.	n.a.	n.a.	72.8	67.8	66.7	66.2	62.4	−10.4
Operatives-craft	n.a.	n.a.	n.a.	55.0	50.7	50.0	50.2	44.9	−10.1
Laborers	n.a.	n.a.	n.a.	48.6	43.7	43.5	41.9	38.2	−10.4
Service	n.a.	n.a.	n.a.	57.9	51.5	51.3	51.6	46.2	−11.7
Farm	n.a.	n.a.	n.a.	63.6	62.5	61.5	52.4	49.8	−13.8
Housewives	n.a.	n.a.	n.a.	60.2	58.0	58.7	60.3	57.1	−3.1
Unemployed	n.a.	n.a.	n.a.	50.2	43.9	40.9	43.9	38.3	−11.9
Student	n.a.	n.a.	n.a.	60.4	50.9	45.2	46.1	42.2	−18.2
Unable to work	n.a.	n.a.	n.a.	31.9	36.3	37.6	36.0	37.7	5.8
Retired/other	n.a.	n.a.	n.a.	62.4	58.8	60.6	63.2	63.8	1.4
Total	n.a.	69.3	67.8	63.0	59.2	59.2	59.9	57.4	−11.9
				NES data					
Education									
0–8 years	67.3	67.8	60.4	58.0	60.9	58.6	58.0	50.0	−17.3
9–11 years	71.5	71.3	68.6	60.8	58.2	54.8	56.1	49.8	−21.7
High school graduate	87.3	81.9	83.8	75.3	69.7	69.7	69.7	62.3	−25.0
Some college	88.0	88.6	79.1	83.9	83.3	75.8	81.5	78.4	−4.6
College graduate or more	93.0	87.7	89.4	89.9	87.7	90.7	90.6	92.4	−0.6
Occupation									
Professional-technical	88.7	86.5	88.4	87.9	88.5	88.6	86.3	89.9	1.2
Managerial-administrative	88.6	86.1	85.1	84.1	81.6	85.7	87.7	80.3	8.3
Clerical-sales	89.5	86.3	84.6	78.9	77.8	76.9	80.6	73.5	−16.0
Operatives-craft	79.5	77.5	72.2	71.3	67.0	59.4	64.4	52.3	−27.2
Laborers	80.0	50.0	73.3	57.7	58.4	60.7	60.6	55.6	−24.4
Service	75.0	68.9	63.6	63.9	65.0	69.6	60.1	56.4	−18.6
Farm	79.3	75.5	75.7	72.2	67.6	82.4	67.4	72.4	−6.9
Housewives	69.5	75.1	73.9	66.9	65.7	66.2	69.8	69.5	0
Total	79.0	77.7	75.8	72.8	71.6	71.4	73.6	69.7	−9.3

SOURCE: Author's tabulations of census and NES data; and U.S. Bureau of the Census 1965, 1969.

n.a. Not available.

a. For census data, change is 1964–88 for education and total; 1972–88 for occupation. For NES data, change is 1960–88.

The NES data, however, show a larger increase in the education gap, with turnout dropping about 17 points among those with zero to eight years of education and remaining essentially stable among those with a college education.[19] Hence the education gap widened from about 26 points in 1960 to 42 points in 1988. Moreover if one compares the period when the census and NES data match up directly (1964–88), the NES data show an even larger, 23-point increase in the education gap, nearly twice that shown by the census data. (The NES 1964–88 estimate is larger than the NES 1960–88 estimate because the NES shows a gap-*narrowing* trend between 1960 and 1964.)

These figures suggest the NES-based estimate of the 1960–88 increase in the education gap is substantially inflated. It can be deflated by assuming that the census data are correct and that the NES data for 1960–88 are as inflated as the direct census-NES matchup for 1964–88 suggests. The result is a more modest estimate of an 8-point increase in the education class gap. Note that this is even lower than the census-based estimate covering 1964–88 only, reflecting the fact that the census data do not cover the 1960–64 period, when the gap apparently narrowed. This suggests that the correct figure for the increase in the education gap between 1960 and 1988 is probably somewhere between this 8-point NES-based estimate and the 12-percentage-point change shown by the census estimate, but no higher.

The occupation data present the most confused picture of all. Partially this reflects the fact that occupations are not really *ordinal* in nature—that is, occupational categories cannot be meaningfully ranked in a logical order from low to high (in contrast to the income and education categories). This makes it harder to determine if the turnout gap is growing by occupation, because it is not clear which occupational categories should enter into such a determination.

For convenience, however, I adopt the convention that blue-collar categories[20] are "low" and professional categories[21] are "high" (though

19. I am very skeptical that the turnout of college graduates did not change over time, as the NES data claim. Here I think one must go with the superior sample size and reliability of the census data and assume that the turnout of college graduates has in fact declined since the 1960s. Possible reasons the NES data may be off, besides basic sampling error, include (1) the possibly worsening bias toward inclusion of politically interested respondents in the NES, many of whom may be highly educated; (2) the possibility that the highly educated are those most susceptible to "interview" effects—that is, the stimulus to voting provided by the preelection-postelection panel structure of the NES (Traugott and Katosh 1979, pp. 368–76); and (3) the possibility that the tendency of the highly educated to overreport voting in the NES may be worsening over time (Silver, Anderson, and Abramson 1986).

20. Represented here by the operatives-craft and laborers categories.

21. Represented here by the professional-technical category.

why clerical-sales workers, given what we know of their current pay levels and social status, should not be considered just as low—if not lower—than most blue-collar workers, is very unclear). Using this convention to look at the census data, two things are immediately clear.

The first is that turnout decline was general across all occupational groups. Even the highest occupational group, professional-technical, experienced a decline in turnout of about 7 points from 1972 to 1988— actually greater than the drop among the population as a whole.

The second is that lower occupational groups did in general experience somewhat larger decreases in turnout. Turnout dropped 10 points among both blue-collar categories, operatives-craft and laborers. (Interestingly the drop in turnout was just as large among the supposedly white-collar clerical-sales category and largest of all among the service category.) Because of this, the occupation gap in turnout (using operatives-craft as low and professional-technical as high) increased somewhat from 27 points in 1972 to 31 points in 1988.[22]

The NES data show a substantially larger increase in the occupation gap over time. Between 1960 and 1988, the NES has turnout in the professional-technical group remaining stable (actually going *up* slightly) with turnout among the operatives-craft group declining an astonishing 27 points. By these measures the occupation gap in turnout skyrocketed 28 points over the period, going from a mere 9.2 points in 1960 to 37.6 points in 1988.

However, a variety of reasons exist for believing that the NES data substantially overstate the size of this gap. They include (1) the stability

22. Larger increases in the occupation gap can be derived from the census data if one is willing to use the data going back to 1964 that are only available in published reports and use highly aggregated occupational categories. Using the best approximations I could make of the "low" and "high" occupational categories described earlier, I found an 11-point increase in the occupation class gap going back to 1968 and an 8-point increase in this gap going back to 1964, figures somewhat higher than those reported above. (Edsall 1984 and Burnham 1987, who rely heavily on these early census data, report similar findings.)

I am very skeptical of these figures, however, because of the difficulty of constructing truly comparable occupational categories over time, a difficulty enhanced by the unavailability of the 1964 and 1968 data tapes. Unfortunately occupational coding systems have changed drastically over time (three different coding systems have been used since 1964), so it is very unclear that manual workers, as defined in 1964, or professional-technical workers, as defined in 1968, have well-defined counterparts in 1988 and that therefore one is comparing apples with apples. Lending credence to the possible existence of coding effects is the pattern of change in the occupation gap: most of the change takes place from 1968 to 1972, when the 1960 census occupational coding system was replaced with the quite different 1970 census system (see also Leighley and Nagler 1991 on this point).

of the professional-technical turnout rate in the NES, a stability that seems highly suspect on the same grounds that the stability of the NES college graduate turnout rate seemed suspect; (2) the instability of the NES occupational coding system (*five* different occupational coding systems have been used since 1960) with possible title upgrading out of lower occupational groups; (3) the occupation gap in the NES data (only 17 points in 1972 compared to 27 points in the census data for the same year), suggesting a considerable NES underestimate of the gap in that year; and (4) the fact that most of the increase in the NES occupation gap in turnout (21 points) occurs in the 1972–88 period, the same period when the census data show only a 4-point increase[23] (assuming the census data are correct and deflating the 1960–72 NES occupation gap increase as done previously implies a quite modest increase of 5 points over the 1960–88 period).

Thus the NES data showing a dramatically widening occupation gap in turnout should be treated very cautiously. At best they raise the possibility that the increase in the occupation gap may have been larger than that implied by the census data, especially if the entire 1960–88 period is considered. Beyond this the most reasonable conclusion to draw, because it is consistent with both data sources, is that the occupational gap in turnout probably widened modestly over time, with turnout among manual and blue-collar workers declining faster than among professional and white-collar workers.

After reviewing turnout rate trends for all three components of socio-economic status—income, education, and occupation—the weight of the evidence does not suggest a dramatically widening class gap in voter participation. Rather the evidence suggests a generalized decline in turnout across socioeconomic groups with only a modest widening of the gap between the top and bottom of the social structure. The modest nature of the decline is especially clear for turnout by income level, the characteristic most people have in mind when they think of class as a social grouping.

In fact the modest widening of the income class gap seems quite consistent with the theoretical expectation that, given a societywide

23. As before, the low census estimate is not attributable to using the voting-age population as a base. In fact, approximating the NES universe (that is, removing non-citizens) with the census data actually *lowers* the estimate of the increase in the occupation turnout gap (3 percentage points). Here, also, the validated NES data diverge from the self-reported NES data, showing much less of an increase in the occupation turnout gap, particularly from 1976 onward.

TABLE 3-3. *Self-Reported Turnout Rates, by Race, 1960–88*
Percent

Race	1960	1964	1968	1972	1976	1980	1984	1988	Change[a]
					Census data				
Race									
White	n.a.	70.7	69.1	64.5	60.9	60.9	61.4	59.1	−11.6
Black	n.a.	58.5	57.6	52.1	48.7	50.5	55.8	51.5	−7.0
Other	n.a.	46.0	41.8	38.7	26.8	30.9	30.1	31.0	−15.0
Race, Hispanics separated									
White	n.a.	n.a.	n.a.	65.7	62.4	62.8	63.3	61.8	−3.9
Black	n.a.	n.a.	n.a.	52.2	48.9	50.8	56.1	52.1	−0.1
Other	n.a.	n.a.	n.a.	38.8	26.6	30.9	30.2	31.2	−7.6
Hispanic	n.a.	n.a.	n.a.	37.5	31.8	29.9	32.7	28.8	−8.7
Hispanic citizens only	n.a.	n.a.	n.a.	n.a.	42.6	44.3	50.0	48.0	5.4
Race, non-South									
White	n.a.	74.7	71.8	67.5	62.6	62.4	63.0	60.4	−14.3
Black	n.a.	72.0	64.8	56.7	52.2	52.8	58.9	55.6	−16.4
Race, South									
White	n.a.	59.5	61.9	57.0	57.1	57.4	58.1	56.4	−3.1
Black	n.a.	44.0	51.6	47.8	45.7	48.2	53.2	48.0	4.0
Race, Hispanics separated, non-South									
White	n.a.	n.a.	n.a.	n.a.	64.1	64.3	65.0	63.3	−0.8
Black	n.a.	n.a.	n.a.	n.a.	52.5	53.5	59.5	56.8	4.3
Race, Hispanics separated, South									
White	n.a.	n.a.	n.a.	n.a.	58.6	59.2	59.8	58.5	−0.1
Black	n.a.	n.a.	n.a.	n.a.	45.7	48.3	53.3	48.2	2.5
Total	n.a.	69.3	67.8	63.0	59.2	59.2	59.9	57.4	−11.9
					NES data				
Race									
White	81.9	79.6	77.1	73.8	72.6	72.3	75.2	71.9	−10.0
Black	52.9	64.9	67.7	64.7	65.1	66.7	65.6	59.7	6.8
Race, Hispanics separated									
White	n.a.	n.a.	n.a.	n.a.	n.a.	73.1	76.0	72.4	−0.7
Black	n.a.	n.a.	n.a.	n.a.	n.a.	67.7	65.4	60.2	−7.5
Hispanic	n.a.	n.a.	n.a.	n.a.	n.a.	52.1	62.1	65.7	13.6
Total	79.0	77.7	75.8	72.8	71.6	71.4	73.6	69.7	−9.3

SOURCE: Author's tabulations of census and NES data; and U.S. Bureau of the Census 1965, 1969.
n.a. Not available.
a. Earliest year to 1988.

turnout-depressing change (like declining efficacy), the effect of the change will be somewhat less on groups with a very high probability of voting (for example, the highest income groups) and somewhat more on groups with a lower probability of voting (for example, the lowest income groups). This sounds quite different, and is quite different, from the popular conception that the poor are simply dropping out of politics, leaving the electoral field to the affluent.

The Racial Gap in Voting Rates

Another popular theory concerning demographic skews and nonvoting posits a large and growing racial gap in voting rates, particularly between whites and blacks. The idea is that turnout decline has been particularly serious among minorities and that the large racial gap in turnout contributes to distorted political priorities by ensuring that the minority political agenda can be safely ignored. This idea was a staple of Jesse Jackson's various presidential campaigns and still finds a sympathetic home among many minority and liberal commentators.

The data in table 3-3 allow one to assess the size of the racial gap in turnout and the extent to which it has been changing. Looking first at the census data, two interesting things stand out. The first is that the turnout gap between blacks and whites, when compared to the large turnout differentials by income, education, and occupation (tables 3-1 and 3-2), was relatively low throughout the 1964–88 period. The largest gap was in 1972 (12.4 percentage points) and the smallest gap in 1984 (5.6 points). These white-black turnout gaps grow only slightly when Hispanics, most of whom are classified as white by the census, are separated out: a high of 13.5 points (1976) and a low of 7.2 points (1984). Note also that the turnout gap between white non-Hispanics and *citizen* Hispanics is not much larger than the white-black differential and has narrowed in recent years (from 20 points in 1976 to 14 points in 1988). These figures compare to turnout gaps that regularly reach 30 points and more on various SES indicators.[24]

---

24. These results make sense, given that race, once other variables are controlled, is a very weak predictor of voter turnout (see model B-1 in appendix B). It turns out in fact that a great deal of the turnout differential between whites and blacks simply reflects the lower average SES of blacks (that is, poorer, less educated, and so on). Indeed if one controls just for *demographic* characteristics, it turns out that blacks are actually *more* likely to vote, all else equal (see model B-2 in appendix B). It is only when one controls for demographic *and* attitudinal variables, as in model B-1, that the likelihood of voting for whites and blacks becomes roughly equalized. Thus, blacks go from being *less* likely

The second thing is that the gap in white-black turnout has been *declining*. According to the census data, white turnout declined about 12 percentage points from 1964 to 1988, while black turnout declined only 7 points. As a result the gap in white-black turnout actually narrowed by 5 points over the period.[25] (Hispanics can only be separated out from 1972 on,[26] but these data also show a narrowing of the white-black turnout gap by about 4 points.)

The data on racial turnout rates by South[27] versus non-South clarify the dynamics of this narrowing turnout gap. In the South, black turnout actually *increased* by 4 percentage points between 1964 and 1988, a trend no doubt traceable to the Voting Rights Act of 1965 and other reforms. Southern white turnout, on the other hand, dropped about 3 points in the same period.[28] As a result the southern white-black turn-

---

to vote on the descriptive level to appearing *more* likely to vote when controlling for demographics to appearing about equally likely to vote when controlling for demographics and attitudinals.

One way of thinking of this is that in terms of turnout blacks are *disadvantaged* demographically but *advantaged* attitudinally. Once these respective sources of disadvantage and advantage are controlled, race has little effect on anyone's likelihood of voting.

25. Leighley and Nagler 1991, p. 13, report both higher white-black turnout differentials and a slight widening of this differential, at least between 1980 and 1988. However, these estimates are based on "correcting" the census data using NES-validated vote-misreporting estimates for whites and blacks. There are good reasons to be skeptical of this correction procedure.

The basic problem is that the allegedly higher misreporting rate for blacks appears to reflect to a large extent the tendency of blacks to live in areas with poor voting record quality and access, factors that promote more observed "misreporting." Once record quality and access are controlled in fact, half of the misreporting differential between blacks and whites disappears (see Presser, Traugott, and Traugott 1990, p. 16). For these reasons, the Leighley and Nagler adjusted estimates must be considered suspect.

26. Actually this separation can only be performed cleanly for 1976 on (the Hispanic variable is not included in the 1972 data file). However, I was able to use the 1976 distribution of Hispanics by race to "back out" the Hispanics from the 1972 national results and estimate white non-Hispanic, and so on, voting rates. This estimation procedure becomes progressively more difficult below the national level, so I show subnational "Hispanics separated" results for 1976 on only.

27. The South is defined here as the standard southern regional grouping of states used by the Census Bureau. Alternative estimations using the traditional "Old Confederacy" definition of the South show no important differences from the trends shown in table 3-3. See the appendix C section on NES demographic-social structural variables, for the states defined as the South under each definition.

28. Note that this drop compares quite favorably to the overall turnout drop of 12 points shown by the census data and the 14-point drop observed for whites outside the South. This suggests that southern whites, as well as blacks, were subject to some turnout-promoting factors in this period. Presumably, these factors for southern whites were rooted in the rise of real party competition in the South, which should have increased the benefits of voting. However, the turnout-promoting effect of these party competition changes was only enough to slow the decline in turnout among southern whites, rather

out gap narrowed substantially from 16 points in 1964 to 8 points in 1988.

The data for the rest of the country (the non-South) tell a different story. According to these data the white-black turnout gap was less than 3 points outside the South in 1964 (compared to 16 points in the South). In the subsequent twenty-four years, both black and white turnout fell sharply outside the South, white turnout by 14 points and black turnout by about 16 points. Because of these changes the white-black nonsouthern turnout gap increased slightly (to 5 points) rather than decreasing, as in the South. Thus the results observed at the national level are actually the resultant of two counterposed trends in different regions of the country, with the southern gap-narrowing trend large enough to outweigh the slight gap-widening trend in the rest of the country.

The NES data generally confirm the national-level story.[29] Between 1964 and 1988 the NES data show the turnout gap between whites and blacks narrowing by about 3 percentage points (from 15 points in 1964 to 12 points in 1988). In addition the data from 1960 suggest the extent of change in the racial turnout gap may have been substantially larger if the full 1960–88 period is considered.[30]

This review of turnout rates by race shows conclusively that, although turnout differentials by race continue to exist, these differentials are not terribly large and moreover have been declining, not increasing, over time. In addition racial turnout differentials by region have converged so that the black-white turnout gap in the South, the historic problem area for black voter participation, is now only slightly larger than in the rest of the country. Thus contrary to the gloomy assessments of some commentators, this is one area of voter participation in which things have actually gotten better, not worse.

---

than producing an actual turnout *increase* as among southern blacks. This reflects the fact that southern blacks benefited greatly from the elimination of registration barriers, a factor that had much less effect on whites.

29. The NES data, suspect even at the national level with relatively small groups like blacks, cannot be used with confidence for such groups at the subnational level. The sample sizes are simply too small. (But see Cassel 1979 for a useful and appropriately cautious attempt to use the NES data to examine differential racial turnout trends in the South.)

30. The NES 1960 data should be viewed skeptically, however, due to (1) the general NES problem of small sample sizes and relatively poor reliability; (2) the lack of confirmatory data from the census survey; and (3) the fact that literacy tests, perhaps the principal means of disfranchising southern blacks, were not abolished until 1965, making the timing of the sudden jump in black turnout from 1960 to 1964 somewhat suspicious.

TABLE 3-4. *Self-Reported Turnout Rates, by Age, 1960–88*
Percent

Age group	1960	1964	1968	1972	1976	1980	1984	1988	Change[a]
					Census data				
18–20	...	...	...	48.3	38.0	35.7	36.7	33.2	−15.1
21–24	n.a.	51.3	51.1	50.8	45.6	43.1	43.5	38.3	−13.0
25–34	n.a.	64.7	62.5	59.7	55.4	54.6	54.6	48.0	−16.7
35–44	n.a.	72.8	70.8	66.3	63.3	64.4	63.5	61.3	−11.5
45–54	n.a.	76.1	75.1	70.9	67.9	67.5	67.6	66.6	−9.5
55–64	n.a.	75.6	74.7	70.7	69.7	71.3	72.1	69.3	−6.3
65–74	n.a.	71.4	71.5	68.1	66.4	69.3	71.8	73.1	1.7
75 or older	n.a.	56.7	56.3	55.6	54.8	57.6	61.3	62.2	5.5
Total	n.a.	69.3	67.8	63.0	59.2	59.2	59.9	57.4	11.9
					NES data				
18–20	...	...	...	52.6	43.3	55.7	45.7	32.2	−20.4
21–24	55.4	58.1	56.0	65.9	62.0	48.9	53.4	49.1	−6.3
25–34	74.4	71.3	71.9	70.9	65.8	65.4	70.0	61.2	−13.2
35–44	78.7	83.4	78.5	79.0	79.3	77.3	78.9	74.2	−4.5
45–54	86.7	81.9	85.4	80.1	81.5	79.3	80.9	78.4	−8.3
55–64	80.5	82.2	79.4	77.0	78.4	79.1	82.8	77.4	−3.1
65–74	85.5	77.9	75.8	73.2	76.0	82.8	83.9	81.6	−3.9
75 or older	62.8	76.9	64.9	60.2	63.8	68.3	68.2	70.0	7.2
Total	79.0	77.7	75.8	72.8	71.6	71.4	73.6	69.7	−9.3

SOURCE: Author's tabulations of census and National Election Study data; and U.S. Bureau of the Census 1969.
n.a. Not available.
a. Earliest year to 1988.

The Age Gap in Voting Rates

Another theory about demographics and nonvoting puts the onus for declining turnout on the young. By this account younger members of the electorate have dropped out of politics in recent decades, whereas older members have continued to vote at high rates. The result has been the political disfranchisement of the younger segments of the electorate. The data shown here on turnout rates by broad age groups allow the validity of this claim to be assessed (table 3-4).

The census data show that an age gap in political participation is not a recent invention.[31] In 1964, the first year for which census data are available, turnout among the youngest age group (21–24) was about 20 percentage points lower than among the oldest high-turnout age

31. The relatively broad age categories in table 3-4 correspond to the age categories used in the published census reports for 1964 and 1968. I had to use these age categories to ensure continuity across years because the data tapes for 1964 and 1968 are not available.

group $(65-74)^{32}$ and about 25 points lower than among those aged 45–54. Thus, the younger segment of the electorate voted much less often than the older segment, even at the beginning of the turnout decline era.

The census data also show that turnout decline has been general across most age groups.[33] Between 1964 and 1988, turnout declined 6 points for those 55–64, 10 points for those 45–54, 12 points for those 35–44, 17 points for those 25–34, and 13 points for those 21–24 (turnout also dropped 15 points just from 1972 to 1988 among the newly enfranchised 18- to 20-year-old group). It appears, therefore, that nonvoting is becoming increasingly common among Americans of all ages, not just the young.

The broad patterns and trends in the NES data are consistent with those in the census data. The NES data show, as do the census data, a large age gap in turnout in the early 1960s and a generalized decline in turnout across most age categories during the last three decades. Thus neither census nor NES data seem to indicate that the decline in turnout is a phenomenon confined to young voters.

Still, it cannot be denied that turnout decline has been most rapid among the younger segments of the electorate. This has increased the age gap in participation (using the 21–24 and 65–74 age groups as reference points) from about 20 points in 1964 to 35 points in 1988, a fairly substantial change.[34] Such patterns, plus some recent increases in voter turnout among the elderly, have led some observers to propose a variant on the apathetic youth theory of turnout decline.

A Cohort Phenomenon?

Their theory is that declining voter turnout is primarily because of increased nonvoting among youth *and* those who were young relatively recently. Both the currently young and recently young represent new *cohorts* of voters who have entered the electorate and are replacing

32. Until the age of roughly 75, aging, all else equal, tends to promote voter turnout (see Wolfinger and Rosenstone 1980, pp. 37–38; and appendix B). After this age, however, the effect tends to be negative, reflected in the lower turnout levels recorded for the 75-and-over group. Despite the relationship between age and turnout just described, the turnout rate in 1964 was slightly lower for the 65–74 age group than for both the 45–54 and 55–64 age group. However, by 1988 the ordering had been reversed, so that the 65–74 age group was indeed the highest turnout age group.

33. Interestingly the very oldest age groups, 65–74 and 75 and older, experienced *increases* in turnout (2 points and 6 points, respectively).

34. The increase in the age gap is less (only about 7 points) if 55- to 64-year-olds are substituted for 65- to 74-year-olds.

generations of older voters who are passing from the scene. This view, argued most forcefully by Miller,[35] asserts that rates of nonvoting have tended to be unusually high among these entering cohorts of voters ("post–New Deal," 1968–88), and has basically outweighed the continuing commitment of earlier generations ("New Deal," 1932–64, and "pre–New Deal," before 1932) to electoral politics.

Reasons certainly exist for believing that cohort effects are at least part of the turnout decline story. For example, every successive 18- to 20-year-old group that has entered the electorate since the enfranchisement of this group in 1972 has voted at a lower rate than the group preceding it (see the census data in table 3-4). However, it is one thing to say that cohort effects may contribute to turnout decline, quite another to ascribe the entire turnout decline phenomenon to such effects.

In fact careful scrutiny of the relevant data does not support the cohort interpretation of declining voter turnout (tables 3-5 and 3-6). These data give a direct look at specific cohorts (defined by the year they entered the electorate) and how their turnout rates have changed over time. This, in turn, makes it possible to untangle—at least somewhat—the easily conflated effects on turnout of *age, period,* and *cohort.*[36]

In the current context these effects may be distinguished as follows: (1) an age or life-cycle effect refers to the (generally) positive effect of aging on an individual's likelihood of voting; (2) a period effect refers to how the social and political character of a period affects an individual's general likelihood of voting (in this case, presumably a negative effect); and (3) a cohort effect refers to how being part of a cohort that has shared the same formative experiences affects an individual's likelihood of voting (in this case, presumably a negative effect on the recent cohorts and a positive effect on earlier cohorts). The problem of course is that all three effects typically operate at once, sometimes in the same direction—for example, cohort and age effects should both be positive for earlier cohorts in the electorate—so that it is easy to confuse one effect with another.

This is precisely where the cohort explanation of declining turnout runs into problems. Looking at turnout rates by cohort based on the

35. Miller 1992.
36. See Glenn 1977 for a good discussion of cohort analysis and the critical need to distinguish these three types of effects.

TABLE 3-5. *Self-Reported Turnout Rates, by Cohort, Census Data,*
1972–88
Percent

Cohort	1960	1964	1968	1972	1976	1980	1984	1988	Change[a]
21 or older in 1912	n.a.	n.a.	n.a.	46.2	39.2	32.0	32.9	...	...
21–24 in 1916	n.a.	n.a.	n.a.	60.6	51.1	48.2	43.9	...	...
21–24 in 1920	n.a.	n.a.	n.a.	64.6	60.9	57.5	48.3	43.2	−21.4
21–24 in 1924	n.a.	n.a.	n.a.	66.3	63.6	60.3	58.4	50.6	−15.7
21–24 in 1928	n.a.	n.a.	n.a.	70.2	64.3	66.0	66.1	60.6	−9.6
21–24 in 1932	n.a.	n.a.	n.a.	70.3	68.1	68.3	69.4	66.7	−3.6
21–24 in 1936	n.a.	n.a.	n.a.	71.2	68.6	71.2	71.6	70.0	−1.2
21–24 in 1940	n.a.	n.a.	n.a.	70.8	70.3	72.7	72.9	73.4	2.6
21–24 in 1944	n.a.	n.a.	n.a.	71.6	70.0	71.0	71.5	73.6	2.0
21–24 in 1948	n.a.	n.a.	n.a.	70.2	68.3	69.6	72.5	70.1	−0.1
21–24 in 1952	n.a.	n.a.	n.a.	68.5	66.8	67.5	71.2	69.0	0.5
21–24 in 1956	n.a.	n.a.	n.a.	65.9	64.3	66.4	68.3	68.9	3.0
21–24 in 1960	n.a.	n.a.	n.a.	62.6	64.0	65.8	65.6	67.7	5.1
21–24 in 1964	n.a.	n.a.	n.a.	60.5	60.5	64.3	65.2	64.6	4.1
21–24 in 1968	n.a.	n.a.	n.a.	57.7	57.3	61.4	63.3	63.2	5.5
21–24 in 1972	n.a.	n.a.	n.a.	50.8	51.5	56.3	60.6	61.3	10.5
18–20 in 1972	...	...	...	48.3	46.9	51.6	57.8	57.4	9.1
18–21 in 1976	...	...	...	...	38.9	45.1	51.8	51.3	12.4
18–21 in 1980	...	...	...	...	...	36.4	45.3	44.2	7.8
18–21 in 1984	...	...	...	...	...	...	37.5	40.0	2.5
18–21 in 1988	...	...	...	...	...	...	...	33.7	...
Total	n.a.	69.3	67.8	63.0	59.2	59.2	59.9	57.4	−5.6

SOURCE: Author's tabulations of census data.
n.a. Not available.
a. Earliest year to 1988 except for total, which is 1972–88.

census data (table 3-5) reveals relatively low turnout rates among the
post–New Deal cohorts and relatively high rates among the New Deal
cohorts, rates that have increased or remained stable over time. It is
tempting to interpret these stable and, especially, increasing turnout
rates among the New Deal cohorts as prima facie evidence that turnout
decline must be attributable to the newer cohorts in the electorate.

The problem is that turnout rates among some (that is, relatively
young) New Deal cohorts *should* have been rising, *because of the very*
nature of a cohort as a group of people who uniformly get older over
time. In other words, because individuals in these cohorts were getting
older over time, and older people are more likely to vote, turnout
increases of some magnitude among these cohorts were natural and
only to be expected. (Note that the sharply rising turnout rates among

TABLE 3-6. *Self-Reported Turnout Rates, by Cohort, NES Data, 1960–88*
Percent

Cohort	1960	1964	1968	1972	1976	1980	1984	1988	Change[a]
21 or older in 1912	73.7	76.2	57.7	52.4	43.5	75.0	...	...	...
21–24 in 1916	88.9	81.0	70.0	61.4	47.6	50.0	...	...	...
21–24 in 1920	84.5	76.2	76.9	67.1	78.2	60.0	73.3	75.0	−9.5
21–24 in 1924	84.8	75.6	80.3	75.0	68.8	67.9	62.5	75.0	−9.8
21–24 in 1928	77.0	84.6	77.8	73.9	80.0	77.5	65.5	58.6	−18.4
21–24 in 1932	86.1	87.6	75.9	73.5	76.1	82.9	76.5	72.2	−13.9
21–24 in 1936	87.9	81.3	85.6	77.7	77.6	85.5	82.4	83.3	−4.6
21–24 in 1940	79.8	80.2	81.3	76.2	84.5	81.3	86.4	81.9	2.1
21–24 in 1944	76.6	84.9	89.5	78.4	76.8	82.6	80.7	78.9	2.3
21–24 in 1948	85.9	84.3	77.6	85.1	76.7	78.3	86.3	79.8	−6.1
21–24 in 1952	70.3	74.6	79.6	80.9	84.5	77.0	83.5	72.3	2.0
21–24 in 1956	69.4	78.6	79.4	80.9	80.2	75.8	78.5	81.3	11.9
21–24 in 1960	55.4	64.0	72.5	69.5	80.0	78.8	80.9	79.1	23.7
21–24 in 1964	...	58.1	67.5	70.5	71.8	79.4	77.2	77.5	19.4
21–24 in 1968	...	...	56.0	71.6	67.5	71.8	79.2	77.5	21.5
21–24 in 1972	...	...	...	65.9	63.6	69.1	79.6	76.9	11.0
18–20 in 1972	...	...	...	52.6	63.8	60.3	72.0	70.3	17.7
18–21 in 1976	...	...	...	...	47.8	47.7	64.0	65.3	17.5
18–21 in 1980	...	...	...	...	...	56.6	58.1	54.6	−2.0
18–21 in 1984	...	...	...	...	...	...	45.5	48.4	2.4
18–21 in 1988	...	...	...	...	...	...	...	39.0	...
Total	79.0	77.7	75.8	72.8	71.6	71.4	73.6	69.7	−9.3

SOURCE: Author's tabulations of National Election Study data.
a. Earliest year to 1988.

the very youngest [post-1968] cohorts in table 3-5 are another vivid example of this dynamic.) Thus the proper question is not *whether* the turnout rates of New Deal cohorts have gone up, but *how much*. If turnout rate increases have been less than expected (that is, the fairly large increases normally expected simply as a result of aging), then New Deal cohorts have indeed been affected by general turnout decline trends. The effect of these trends has simply been masked by positive aging effects, which have acted as a countervailing force to the various influences depressing turnout (these influences are really the "period effects" described earlier).

This is exactly what appears to have happened. Using the relative turnout rates by age in 1972 as an indicator of expected turnout increase over the life course,[37] turnout rate increases between 1972 and 1988 among later New Deal cohorts, 1952–64, have all been less than expected given the number of years they aged. For example, turnout among the 1952 cohort should have increased about 3 percentage points as these individuals aged from 41–44 in 1972 to 57–60 in 1988. Instead turnout remained stable.

Similarly the 1956 cohort should have experienced a 5-point increase in turnout between 1972 and 1988, instead of the 3-point increase that actually obtained. Finally turnout among the 1960 and 1964 cohorts should have increased 9 and 10 points, respectively, as these cohorts aged from 29–36 in 1972 to 45–52 in 1988. Instead turnout rose only 5 points for the 1960 cohort and 4 points for the 1964 cohort, 4 points and 6 points less, respectively, than one would have expected from the unimpeded action of aging effects. (These latter differences are quite close to the overall 5.6-percentage-point drop in turnout among the population as a whole.) It therefore appears that general turnout decline forces affected the 1952–64 cohorts and slowed the increases in turnout that would normally have occurred as a result of the aging process.

Interestingly, however, the earlier New Deal cohorts, 1932–48, appear to have been genuinely unaffected by turnout decline influences between 1972 and 1988. For example, the 1940–48 cohorts experienced either stable turnout or a slight increase between 1972 and 1988, when turnout-depressing period influences should have made their turnout rates drop. (These cohorts, in contrast to the 1952–64 cohorts, had no expectation of positive age effects to prop up turnout because they were already 45–56 in 1972.) This implies that for whatever reason negative period effects were not operative for these cohorts in the 1972–88 period.

The NES data suggest, however, that the early New Deal cohorts did not completely escape turnout decline influences in the 1960–88 period (table 3-6). Although one must be cautious in interpreting these data,[38] they do imply that these cohorts were substantially affected by

37. This is the earliest year for which age categories can be sufficiently disaggregated to allow estimation of age differences in turnout by four or multiples of four (that is, the amount of time a cohort ages between presidential elections).

38. The cell sizes for particular cohorts within individual NES surveys tend to be relatively small, so estimates about any particular cohort will be far less reliable than those of the census. The best strategy is to look for results that generalize across a group of cohorts and form a pattern.

turnout decline trends in the earlier part of the period between 1960 and 1972.[39] For this period, these cohorts all show either less increase in turnout than one would expect from aging effects or actual turnout decline when one would have expected stability or a slight increase. Thus even the early New Deal cohorts appear to have been affected by turnout decline influences[40] if the entire 1960–88 period is taken into consideration.

To sum up, a review of turnout rates by age and cohort shows the following trends. First turnout decline has been general across most age groups, rather than just among the young. However, turnout has declined faster among the young, so an already existing age gap in participation has widened.

In addition it appears that more recent cohorts entering the electorate may have contributed disproportionately to turnout decline. But earlier cohorts also appear to have been affected by and made contributions to turnout decline, so here again responsibility for turnout decline cannot be allocated to just one part of the electorate.

Indeed all the material reviewed in this section indicates that turnout decline has not been the responsibility of any one demographic category, no matter how these categories are defined (by income, education, occupation, race, age, and so on). It has been, as it were, a collective enterprise with almost all demographic categories contributing.

That said, it is also true that turnout decline has been somewhat more rapid among those groups least likely to vote in the first place[41] (that is, the poor, the poorly educated, those in "lower" occupational categories, the young, and so on). Because of this lack of uniformity in turnout decline, turnout rate gaps by income, education, occupation, ·and age have all increased over time. However, these gap-widening trends have generally been moderate and do not appear to have created a dramatic new problem with the representativeness of the electorate. In fact the clearest effect of these trends has been simply to aggravate already existing demographic skews in voting. Thus if a problem exists

39. The NES data for 1972–88 are also consistent with the story told by the census data for the later New Deal cohorts—that is, the NES data also show smaller turnout increases over the period for these cohorts than would be expected from the unimpeded action of aging effects.

40. The questions of exactly *which* turnout-depressing influences were strongest on which cohorts and why are interesting ones. For a beginning discussion, see Teixeira 1987, pp. 94–99.

41. One exception here is blacks, whose turnout has declined more slowly than that of whites and has even *increased* in the southern region of country.

with the representativeness of the electorate, it is much the same problem that existed three decades ago when the current era of turnout decline began.

Comparing the Demographic Profile of Voters and Nonvoters

Several factors lead one to expect a substantial shift over time in the characteristics of nonvoting Americans, away from the very lowest socioeconomic categories and toward a more middle-class social composition. First, turnout decline has been generalized across most demographic categories, swelling the ranks of nonvoters with the affluent as well as the poor, the college graduate as well as the high school dropout. And second, the electorate as a whole, from which nonvoters are drawn, has become more affluent, educated, and white collar through a process of socioeconomic upgrading. In fact data on the demographic composition of the nonvoting pool, the voting pool, and the entire electorate do show such shifts over time. Turning first to the census data, substantial upgrading in the character of the nonvoting pool, especially in terms of educational levels, is evident (table 3-7).

For example, although about three in ten nonvoters in 1972 had eight years or less of education and over half were high school dropouts, by 1988 only 16 percent had eight years or less of education and less than one-third were high school dropouts. Conversely in 1972 just 5 percent of nonvoters were college graduates and under 15 percent had attended college at all, whereas by 1988 10 percent of nonvoters were college graduates and over one-quarter had attended college. Clearly the old stereotype of the nonvoter as high school dropout is becoming less and less applicable.

Occupational upgrading of the nonvoting pool is also evident, though less dramatic. Easily the largest change is the declining proportion of housewives among nonvoters, a figure that fell from about 28 percent in 1972 to 15 percent in 1988. Other significant changes include a rise in the proportion of nonvoters with high-end white-collar jobs[42] (from about 8 percent in 1972 to 12 percent in 1988) and a rise in the proportion with clerical-sales jobs (from about 10 to 16 percent). The data also show a slight decline in the proportion of nonvoters in the quintessentially blue-collar operative-craft category (from 22 to 20 percent), a finding of some interest given the newly emerging stereotype of the nonvoter as a disaffected blue-collar worker.

42. Professional-technical or managerial-administrative.

Interestingly the upgrading described above is not evident at the level of income. For example, the proportion of nonvoters in the two highest income categories ($40,000 or more in family income) remained stable between 1972 and 1988 at about 11 percent. Similarly the proportion of nonvoters in the two *lowest* categories (less than $15,000) was virtually unchanged (38 percent in 1972; 39 percent in 1988). What change there was took place in the middle three categories of the income distribution, which included roughly the same proportion of nonvoters in 1988 as in 1972, but which shifted toward the lowest of these three categories. To a large extent this lack of income upgrading for nonvoters probably reflects the populationwide stagnation of family income levels after 1973[43] (in contrast to the continuation of educational and occupational upgrading after this date).

The data in table 3-7 provide two additional items of interest: first, the nonvoting pool has become substantially younger, chiefly from growth in the 25- to 44-year-old range (an age group that was virtually coterminous with the baby boom generation in 1988); and second, the nonvoting pool has remained almost exactly the same percentage black (about 13 percent) over time. The latter point underscores the extent to which nonvoting is not a particularly racial issue, despite attempts by certain political forces, such as those linked to Jesse Jackson, to portray it in such terms.

However, even if the nonvoting pool has been upgraded in some important ways between 1972 and 1988, it is still worth asking whether this pool, relative to the population at large, has become substantially more biased over time. Certainly some of the widening gaps in participation identified previously (that is, by income, education, occupation, and so on) raise some concerns along these lines.

The data in table 3-7 can also be used to address this question through construction of a bias measure comparing representation of a demographic category within the nonvoting pool to representation of that category within the overall population (here I simply divide the share of that category among nonvoters by the corresponding share among the entire population). These computations suggest two observations concerning bias and the nonvoting pool.

43. Mishel and Frankel 1991 and Congressional Budget Office 1988 provide extensive documentation on the stagnation in family income growth. However, it is also possible that some of the distributional change observed, particularly within the middle categories, is attributable to coding problems in constructing comparable income categories across time rather than to shifts in the real-world income distribution.

TABLE 3-7. *Self-Reported Voters and Nonvoters, by Indicator,*
Census Data, 1972, 1988
Percent

	1972			1988		
Characteristic	Nonvoters	Voters	All	Nonvoters	Voters	All
Education						
0–8 years	29.2	15.5	20.6	16.0	6.9	10.8
9–11 years	21.2	13.5	16.4	16.3	8.5	11.8
High school graduate	34.8	38.7	37.3	41.8	37.5	39.3
Some college	9.6	16.8	14.1	16.0	21.6	19.2
College graduate or more	5.2	15.5	11.6	9.9	25.5	18.9
Occupation						
Professional-technical	4.2	11.4	8.8	6.1	14.1	10.7
Managerial-administrative	4.0	7.5	6.2	5.6	10.6	8.5
Clerical-sales	10.3	16.3	14.1	15.5	19.0	17.5
Operatives-craft	21.6	15.6	17.8	19.6	11.8	15.1
Laborers	3.7	2.1	2.7	3.7	1.7	2.5
Service	8.9	7.2	7.8	11.7	7.5	9.3
Farm	2.0	2.1	2.1	2.1	1.5	1.8
Housewives	27.7	24.7	25.8	14.9	14.7	14.8
Family income (1988 dollars)						
Less than 7,500	15.4	8.0	10.7	16.9	8.2	11.9
7,500–14,999	22.9	15.3	18.1	22.2	14.6	17.8
15,000–19,999	14.5	10.2	11.8	20.5	17.6	18.9
20,000–29,999	20.9	21.7	21.4	16.4	18.4	17.5
30,000–39,999	15.3	21.0	18.9	13.1	18.7	16.4
40,000–59,999	6.3	13.5	10.8	5.7	10.8	8.6
60,000 or more	4.7	10.3	8.2	5.2	11.7	9.0
Age						
18–20	11.3	6.2	8.1	9.5	3.5	6.0
21–24	13.3	8.0	10.0	12.0	5.6	8.3
25–34	21.5	13.5	16.4	29.3	20.0	24.0
35–44	14.9	17.2	16.3	18.0	21.1	19.8
45–54	13.5	19.3	17.2	10.7	15.8	13.6
55–64	11.0	15.6	13.9	8.7	14.6	12.1
65–74	8.0	10.0	9.3	6.2	12.6	9.9
75 or older	6.6	4.8	5.5	5.6	6.8	6.3
Race						
White	85.4	91.1	89.0	82.4	88.4	85.8
Black	12.8	8.2	9.9	12.6	9.9	11.1
Other	1.8	0.7	1.1	5.1	1.7	3.1

SOURCE: Author's tabulations of Bureau of the Census data.

The first observation is that "lower" demographic categories (for example, less than $7,500 in family income, or eight years or less of education) tend to have bias measures above 1, indicating they are *overrepresented* in the nonvoting pool,[44] whereas "higher" categories

44. The farther above 1, the more overrepresented the category is.

(for example, more than $60,000 in family income or college graduate) tend to have bias measures below 1, indicating that they are *underrepresented*.[45] The second observation is that bias as measured by these computations has not changed much since 1972.

For example, the bias measure for those with eight years or less of education changed only from 1.42 in 1972 to 1.48 in 1988 (indicating a slight decrease in representativeness through increased overrepresentation of those with eight years of education or less among nonvoters), whereas the bias measure for college graduates changed only from 0.45 to 0.52 (indicating a slight *increase* in representativeness through decreased underrepresentation of college graduates).[46] Similar small changes in bias obtained for other demographic categories. Thus the bias of the nonvoting pool remained fairly stable between 1972 and 1988, experiencing most commonly[47] only slight increases in the overrepresentation of lower demographic categories, and slight decreases in the underrepresentation of higher demographic categories.[48]

The NES data (table 3-8), which cover the full 1960–88 period, generally confirm the story told by the census data. In some ways in fact they make the results sharper. For example, the NES data show even heavier educational upgrading among nonvoters with the proportion of high school dropouts in the nonvoting pool dropping from almost three-quarters (72 percent) in 1960 to a little over one-third (35 percent) in 1988. These data[49] also show a larger shift out of the housewife category, which shrank from 38 percent of nonvoters in 1960

45. The farther below 1, the more underrepresented the category is.

46. These low estimates of change in bias levels are not attributable to using the voting-age population as a base. In fact when noncitizens are removed from the census sample (all of whom are included in the nonvoting pool, because they are not eligible to vote), estimates of change in bias levels are generally *reduced*. This presumably reflects the fact that noncitizens tend to have low SES levels and that their relative share of the VAP has grown somewhat over time.

47. The pattern of change within categories, however, was not uniformly as it was within the education category. For example, the lowest income groups became *less* not more overrepresented, as did blacks. Conversely, the oldest age groups become *more* not less underrepresented.

48. Bias trends in the voting pool tell a less ambiguous story, showing most commonly slight increases in the overrepresentation of low demographic categories *and* slight increases in the underrepresentation of high demographic categories. The fact that bias result can look different simply because analysis shifts from nonvoters to voters illustrates that this method is subject to some of the same problems (sensitivity to focus of inquiry and size of denominator) that bedevil the percentage-of-a-percentage method.

49. The NES data differ, however, in showing an increase in the proportion of nonvoters in the basic blue-collar (operative-craft) category over time. In my opinion this result reflects to a large extent the tendency of the NES to overestimate change in the turnout rates of basic blue-collar workers.

TABLE 3-8. *Distribution of Self-Reported Voters and Nonvoters, by Indicator, NES Data, 1960, 1988*
Percent

Characteristic	1960			1988		
	Nonvoters	Voters	All	Nonvoters	Voters	All
Education						
0–8 years	47.1	25.8	30.3	16.1	7.0	9.8
9–11 years	25.3	16.9	18.6	18.8	8.1	11.3
High school graduate	17.4	32.1	29.0	43.6	31.3	35.0
Some college	6.8	13.2	11.8	16.3	25.7	22.8
College graduate or more	3.4	12.0	10.2	5.3	28.0	21.1
Occupation						
Professional-technical	3.9	8.2	7.3	4.5	17.2	13.4
Managerial-administrative	3.9	8.0	7.2	5.4	9.6	8.3
Clerical-sales	6.0	13.6	12.0	14.3	17.2	16.4
Operatives-craft	18.5	19.0	18.9	22.7	10.9	14.4
Laborers	1.3	1.4	1.4	2.2	1.2	1.5
Service	8.3	6.6	7.0	10.8	6.1	7.5
Farm	4.7	4.8	4.8	1.5	1.7	1.6
Housewives	37.8	22.9	26.0	11.9	11.8	11.3
Family income (1988 dollars)						
Less than 7,500	26.5	13.2	15.9	22.5	8.2	12.6
7,500–14,999	26.2	15.6	17.8	25.9	15.3	18.6
15,000–19,999	15.6	20.9	19.8	8.8	8.8	8.8
20,000–29,999	18.5	27.6	25.7	18.9	18.9	18.9
30,000–39,999	9.0	9.8	9.7	11.4	16.5	14.9
40,000–59,999	2.4	4.8	4.3	5.4	12.1	10.0
50,000 or more	1.9	8.0	6.7	7.2	20.3	16.2
Age						
18–24	6.5	2.1	3.1	10.4	4.4	6.2
25–34	26.0	20.1	21.4	29.2	20.1	22.9
35–44	25.5	25.1	25.2	20.7	25.8	24.3
45–54	12.2	21.2	19.4	8.8	13.8	12.3
55–64	14.6	16.0	15.7	9.7	14.4	13.0
65–74	7.6	11.8	10.9	6.5	12.6	10.7
75 or older	7.6	3.4	4.3	7.3	7.4	7.3
Race						
White	78.1	94.0	90.7	78.0	87.2	84.4
Black	18.8	5.6	8.4	16.2	10.5	12.2
Other	3.1	0.4	1.0	5.8	2.4	3.4

SOURCE: Author's tabulations of National Election Study data.

to only 12 percent in 1988. Finally the NES data show marked income upgrading of the nonvoting pool with fewer low-income nonvoters (down 5 points in the lowest two income categories, from 52.7 to 48.4 percent) and more high-income nonvoters (up 8 points in the two highest income categories, from 4.3 to 12.6 percent).

In terms of bias the NES data also show relatively modest changes over the 1960–88 period. For example, bias on the lowest income category changed from 1.67 to 1.79, while bias on the highest income category changed from 0.28 to 0.44. Although there were some changes of larger magnitude,[50] the data do not seem to indicate a radical shift in the representativeness of the nonvoting pool over the 1960–1988 period.

This comparison of the demographic profile of voters and nonvoters has revealed the following. First, the character of the nonvoting pool, has been upgraded substantially over time so that the stereotype of the nonvoter as a poor, high school dropout no longer obtains. Second despite this upgrading, the demographic structure of the nonvoting pool does not mirror the demographic structure of the electorate as a whole, but rather tends to overrepresent lower demographic categories and underrepresent higher demographic categories. But finally, this bias in the nonvoting pool has changed only moderately over time, indicating no drastic increase in the extent to which the demographic profile of nonvoters is skewed relative to the electorate as a whole.

Does Nonvoting Make a Difference?

The second big question addressed in this chapter is what difference does nonvoting make to political and policy outcomes? It is certainly a common perception that nonvoting *does* make a difference, and a fairly large one, to political outcomes. This is, for example, the view of the observers cited at the beginning of the previous section (Edsall, Burnham, and Piven and Cloward), as well as virtually a religious principle of Jesse Jackson's Rainbow Coalition and various other left-leaning organizations. And, of course, this view is a staple of political reporters and others whenever they comment on voter turnout, or the lack of it in any given election.

The reasoning behind this viewpoint is not hard to uncover. The nonvoting pool is in fact substantially skewed toward lower SES categories (poorer, less educated, more likely to be in blue-collar or service

50. Again, change within the operatives-craft category is distinctive, with these workers going from slightly underrepresented to very overrepresented in the nonvoting pool. (As pointed out in the previous note, however, there are very good reasons to be skeptical of the magnitude of this change.) Other relatively large changes include those for high school graduates (from quite underrepresented to somewhat overrepresented) and blacks (much less overrepresented).

occupations) regardless of whether and how much this skew has changed over time (tables 3-7 and 3-8). It follows that if more nonvoters voted it would help Democrats or more liberal candidates, because low-SES individuals tend to be relatively liberal and pro-Democrat. Conversely their absence from the voting pool hurts these same candidates by depriving them of some portion of their natural support base.

This argument seems clear enough as far as it goes. However, the argument does not specify *how much* nonvoter mobilization would help Democratic candidates, only that mobilizing nonvoters would be *some kind* of help (that is, it specifies the *direction* not the *magnitude*, of change for the Democratic candidate). As it turns out, this distinction is crucial because changing the outcome of an election by expanding the voting pool is far more difficult than is generally believed.[51]

A variety of reasons makes this so, including (1) the nonvoting pool, which while not a faithful representation of the entire population, is hardly a monolith of the disadvantaged; (2) partisan skews by demographic group, which, especially compared to other countries, are not overwhelming (skews in political attitudes even less so); (3) the fact that nonvoters are particularly likely to disregard partisan and other preferences and surge in the direction of a candidate who appears to be winning; and (4) the simple mathematics standpoint that it is a great deal easier to change an election outcome by switching the preferences of existing voters than by adding new voters.[52]

The Problem of Nonvoter Mobilization

The last point deserves some expansion.[53] The basic problem of nonvoter mobilization is that given a plurality for, say, the Republicans

51. As believed by the general public, that is. Political scientists have generally been cognizant of the difficulty of changing electoral outcomes through nonvoter mobilization. See, for example, Wolfinger and Rosenstone 1980; Petrocik 1981, 1987; Shaffer 1982; Bennett and Resnick 1990; Calvert and Gilchrist 1991; Cavanaugh 1991; and Gant and Lyons 1992.

52. The basic idea is that every existing voter who switched, for example, from the Democrats to the Republicans, provides the Democrats with *two* net votes (that is, the Democrats have one *more* vote and the Republicans have one *less* vote). In contrast every additional mobilized nonvoter provides the Democrats with only a *fractional* net vote equal to the support differential between the two parties among nonvoters. For example, if the Democrats are supported by 60 percent of nonvoters and the Republicans by 40 percent of nonvoters—a fairly high pro-Democratic differential—every additional mobilized nonvoter provides the Democrats with, on average, only 60 percent minus 40 percent of a vote, or just 0.2 net votes. Thus even under a relatively favorable scenario, it still takes ten nonvoters to generate as many net votes as one vote switcher.

53. I am indebted to Cavanaugh 1991 for a great deal of the discussion that follows. Also, consult his article for a basic formalization of the mathematics behind the nonvoter mobilization problem.

among existing voters, that plurality has to be entirely made up by the Democrats among the newly mobilized nonvoters. But even under optimistic scenarios the number of newly mobilized nonvoters will be relatively small compared to the number of existing voters (for example, a 10-percentage-point increase in presidential turnout is still only one-fifth the size of the 1988 presidential electorate [50 percent]). Because of this, the intensity of support for the Democrats among the smaller numbers of mobilized nonvoters must be much higher than the level of support for the Republicans among the much larger numbers of existing voters. Otherwise, the strategy will not work.

But assumptions of such support levels among nonvoters are typically unrealistic. To use the example above (50 percent existing turnout, 10 percent increase), and assuming an existing 54 to 46 percent Republican advantage (which approximates the 1988 presidential election), the level of Democratic support among newly mobilized nonvoters would have to be 70 percent to 30 percent—*five times* the percentage-point plurality of the Republicans among existing voters. To say this is unlikely to happen is to understate the case considerably.

The only way to avoid such an unrealistic assumption is to posit an even larger turnout increase—say 20 percent. But this is also unrealistic. And even here the level of Democratic support would still have to be 60 to 40 percent among the mobilized nonvoters for the strategy to work—hardly an easy goal to attain in and of itself.

Thus the basic dynamics of electoral arithmetic are such that a nonvoter mobilization strategy typically involves unrealistic assumptions about support levels among nonvoters or levels of increase in turnout or both. Conversely the fact that such unrealistic assumptions are necessary to reverse an electoral outcome suggests that most existing outcomes are fairly robust and unlikely to change through simply expanding the voting pool. These points are further illustrated by consideration of some generic types of mobilization scenarios.

Selective Mobilization of Candidate Supporters

The most trivial case to be considered here is the case of selective mobilization of a given candidate's supporters (that is, more of that candidate's supporters turn out while *none* of the other candidate's do). This scenario is, I believe, what many people—and politicians—have in mind when they claim that turnout decided the outcome of a given election. The scenario is based on the fact that the most valuable type of turnout for any given candidate is turnout among that candidate's supporters. By definition their voting rate for the candidate is 100 percent, higher than that candidate's support will be among any demographic group or geographical community. Thus understandably candidates tend to see turnout rates among their supporters as a key explanation for electoral success, because every mobilized voter is "pure gold." Conversely, because any given margin of defeat logically could have been made up by simply mobilizing an additional number of supporters equal to the margin of defeat (assuming no counter-mobilization), turnout rates among supporters are also a convenient and semiplausible explanation for defeat.

A critical problem with these explanations is that turnout rates among supporters of different candidates are very difficult to ascertain because the true level of support for different candidates *among the electorate as a whole* on election day is generally unknown. This is not to say that obtaining such information is completely impossible. By applying proper estimation techniques to preelection polling data, it is technically possible to develop a reasonable estimate of differential candidate support among the electorate as a whole. But these estimates take some effort to develop and are hardly the stuff of public knowledge. Thus if it is generally not known how many supporters of a given candidate there are in the electorate as a whole, how can it be known whether the turnout rate of that candidate's supporters on election day was low, high, or about what would be expected?

The short answer is it cannot be known with any certainty. But this does not stop politicians and commentators from blaming "poor turn-out" of a candidate's supporters for a variety of electoral outcomes. Indeed the de facto "unknowability" of such turnout rates adds to their attraction as electoral explanations. Under such circumstances it is quite difficult to check, for example, whether turnout among supporters of different candidates was already about equal on election day, making a low-mobilization explanation for defeat less reasonable. Thus such an explanation can always be trotted out, with little fear of immediate empirical refutation.

But the very difficulty of assessing such claims empirically should promote skepticism about explanations for electoral outcomes that hinge on the mobilization rate of a given candidate's supporters. Moreover the implicit and implausible assumption that additional mobilization would have been *selective*—that is, produced no counter-mobilization of the other candidate's supporters—must also be treated skeptically. All this suggests that low mobilization among supporters is more the stuff of post hoc candidate justification than a significant determinant of electoral reality.

Selective Mobilization of Key Demographic Groups

A less trivial and somewhat more plausible scenario is based on the concept of mobilizing nonvoters from key demographic groups that demonstrate strong political leanings. (In what follows, I concentrate on mobilization of Democratic-leaning demographic groups, because this is how the scenario is typically presented.) The basic idea is that certain demographic groups with known Democratic sympathies (blacks, Hispanics, the poor) are also generally known to have relatively low turnout rates. It follows that, if these turnout rates could be raised—perhaps just equalized with other demographic groups—it should help the Democrats and lead to changes in electoral outcomes.

One advantage to this scenario is that, because the distribution of these demographic groups among the electorate is generally and publicly known (in contrast to the distribution of candidate supporters), one can easily estimate turnout rates for these demographic groups. Just how low these rates actually are and how much they would have to increase to match or surpass turnout rates among other groups can thus be easily determined. Finally, these estimated turnout rate increases can be combined with information on the Democratic proclivities of these groups (for example, from exit polls) to produce fairly concrete estimates of the impact of these turnout increases on Democratic fortunes.

For those who advocate such scenarios, however, this advantage can turn into a disadvantage because their assertions about the probable effects of increased mobilization usually turn out to be incorrect when tested, an inconvenient and politically embarrassing eventuality. An example is the 1988 election, in which the Democrats endured yet another presidential defeat at the hands of the Republicans—a defeat that was, as usual, accompanied by relatively low turnout rates among blacks, Hispanics, and the poor (tables 3-1 and 3-3). Elements within the Democratic party (chiefly Jesse Jackson and his Rainbow Coalition) immediately claimed that the defeat could be attributed to these low turnout rates among the Democrats' core constituencies.[54]

The numbers, however, show otherwise. In fact the numbers show that even very large—indeed, absurdly large—increases in turnout

54. For sustained arguments along these lines, see Williams 1989 and Southern Regional Council 1989.

among blacks, Hispanics, and the poor would still have left Michael Dukakis far behind George Bush. For example, if black turnout had matched turnout among the general population, an increase of 6 percentage points, the Democrats would have netted about 865,000 additional votes.[55] If black turnout had matched that of whites,[56] an increase of 10 points, the net Democratic gain would have been about 1,442,000 votes. And, if black turnout had somehow been *10 points higher* than turnout among whites (that is, 20 points higher than it was in reality), the Democratic gain would have amounted to about 2,884,000 voters.

But Dukakis lost the election by *more than 7 million votes*, which means that even if blacks had turned out in much larger numbers than they did, or even much larger numbers than they are ever likely to, he still would have been defeated. This suggests that the 1988 election was decided more by overall levels of support among the population than by relative turnout rates among different groups.

This view is borne out by the analogous figures for Hispanics. If Hispanic turnout had matched turnout among the general population, the net gain for the Democrats would have been about 292,000 votes. If Hispanic turnout had matched that of whites, the Democrats would have netted about 453,000 votes. Finally, under the unlikely scenario that Hispanic turnout exceeded white turnout by 10 points, the Democrats would have gained about 776,000 voters.

Thus even heavy increases in turnout among Hispanics would not have reversed the outcome of the 1988 election. In fact if both Hispanics *and* blacks had voted at rates 10 points higher than whites—a preposterous scenario—the overall net gain for the Democrats, 3,660,000 votes, would still have fallen far short of the number Dukakis needed for victory.[57]

---

55. I base these estimates on the turnout differentials shown in table 3-3, second panel, census data, plus Democratic voting rates by group from the 1988 CBS/*New York Times* exit poll. I also assume throughout this analysis that new voters from a given group would have voted Democratic at about the same rate as group members who did vote: 85 percent for blacks, 69 percent for Hispanics, and 62 percent for the poor.

These estimates differ somewhat from those in my earlier articles (Teixeira 1989a, 1989b), primarily because the exit poll–based turnout differential estimates I used earlier were smaller for blacks and the poor and, especially, much larger for Hispanics. The latter difference reflects the fact that previously I had to use an estimated turnout differential based on the Hispanic VAP, whereas here I am able to use a turnout differential based on Hispanic citizens only—a much smaller differential, as shown in table 3-3.

56. White non-Hispanics.

57. For similar calculations on the effects of increased turnout in the 1988 election,

It could still be argued that the Democratic turnout problem was not so much a matter of race as of economic class. The turnout rate of the poor in 1988 was 36 points less than that of the rich (table 3-1). What if the poor had turned out at higher levels?

If turnout among those with less than $12,500 in family income[58] had matched that of the population as a whole, the Democrats would have netted about 1,703,000 voters. If poor turnout had matched rich turnout (where "rich" is defined as more than $50,000 in family income), the net gain would have been about 3,468,000 votes. Finally if some sort of unprecented poor people's mobilization had taken place and the poor had managed to turn out at a level 10 points higher than the rich, the Democrats would have gained about 4,449,000 votes—not enough, by itself, to reverse the 1988 electoral verdict.

But what about the combined voting power of blacks, Hispanics, and poor people of all colors—the so-called Rainbow Coalition? Given that a substantial fraction of blacks and Hispanics are poor, any attempt to calculate these figures for this combined group must eliminate double-counting. The simplest way to do this is to add up the projected vote increments for Hispanics, blacks, and the white poor (not the poor as a whole). Assuming the highest turnout scenarios (for blacks and Hispanics, 10 points higher than whites; for the white poor, 10 points higher than the white rich), the computations still show only 4,677,000 additional net votes for the Democrats.

These results seem clear enough. However, it could still be argued that the electoral college, by concentrating the results of increased turnout in a few key states, could magnify the impact of the mobilization scenarios discussed above. Jesse Jackson, for example, claimed that relatively modest increases in black registration and turnout in eleven key states would have won the 1988 election for Dukakis.

Again such a scenario is relatively easy to test. In fact I was able to test not only the state-level effects of increased black turnout, but also the state-level effects of increased turnout among Hispanics and the white poor.

---

see Abramson, Aldrich, and Rohde 1990, pp. 108–109. Abramson, Aldrich, and Rohde 1987 also contains analogous calculations for the 1984 election.

58. Here I use less than $12,500 and greater than $50,000 as "poor" and "rich" categories, respectively, because these categories correspond to the income breakdowns in the 1988 CBS/*New York Times* exit poll. However, I retain the turnout rate differentials in table 3-1—which should *overestimate* the gap between these two categories—to make the strongest possible case for this scenario.

With a "modest" 5-point increase in black turnout, not a single state would have switched from Dukakis to Bush. With a 10-point increase in black turnout in every state that Bush won, only two states would have switched: Maryland and Illinois, for a total of 34 electoral votes. Finally, with a 20-point increase in black turnout, far beyond the realm of a "modest" increase, only Pennsylvania is added to the two other states, producing a still-lopsided Dukakis loss of 367–171 in the electoral college.[59]

Of course devotees of this sort of mobilization theory could go beyond the claim made by Jackson and maintain that, if Hispanics and the white poor also had been mobilized at the levels just envisioned for blacks and these turnout increases were mediated by the electoral college, the results would be quite different. But increasing Hispanic and white poor turnout by 20 points in every state Bush won adds only California to the Democratic column, primarily because of the state's large Hispanic population and the relative closeness of the election there.

In sum if turnout among blacks, Hispanics, and the white poor had *all* been 20 points higher in every state Bush won—a mobilization advocate's dream come true—Dukakis still would have lost the 1988 election 320–218 in the electoral college. Because these 20-point increases would have been difficult, if not impossible, to achieve (especially without a Republican countermobilization of *other* demographic groups) and would not have actually changed the outcome anyway, it suggests just how difficult it is to change election outcomes through selective mobilization. Conversely the difficulty of changing outcomes through selective mobilization suggests most existing electoral outcomes are fairly robust and not, in any meaningful sense,[60] determined by relative turnout rates.

59. For slightly different calculations (primarily based on exit poll data) that tell basically the same story, see Galston and Kamarck 1989.
60. To say meaningfully that an electoral outcome has been "determined" by low turnout, it should be the case that bringing the low-turnout group up to some standard—the population average or the rate of the high-turnout group—actually would have changed the outcome of the election. Otherwise, the statement has little meaning.
Conversely to say that an electoral outcome was determined by high turnout, it should be the case that bringing the high-turnout group *down* to some standard—the population average, the historical turnout rate for that group, the rate of some low-turnout group— would have changed the election's outcome. There is, to put it mildly, a lot of loose talk about elections being determined by high turnout in situations where these elementary criteria do not even begin to obtain.
A good example of this is the 1991 defeat of David Duke by Edwin Edwards in the

None of this is to say, however, that mobilizing key demographic groups could not *technically* have won the 1988 election for the Democrats. For example, if *every black* in the United States had voted in 1988 (and not a single additional white had voted), Dukakis would probably have won. Or, if turnout among the poor had been just 20 points higher, and *every one of these additional poor people had voted Democratic*, this, too, would have been enough to swing the election. But these scenarios are the stuff of political science fiction.

However, as silly as they seem, these scenarios do illustrate an important point. When people say "turnout is the problem" or "if turnout had just been higher," they are usually basing their election assessments on just such fantasies. That is, they envision either preposterously high turnout increases for a group or preposterously high voting rates for their candidate among new voters or both. The lack of realism of such assumptions further underscores the shaky credibility of selective demographic mobilization as an electoral influence.

General Mobilization of Nonvoters

The most plausible form of mobilization scenario is simply expanding the voting pool through general mobilization of nonvoters. Under this scenario, no one gets to "pick" the nonvoters who get added to the voting pool. They are drawn more or less at random from the nonvoting pool without regard to political proclivities or demographic affiliation.

But because nonvoters are on average concentrated in demographic groups that on average are relatively supportive of the Democrats, even random additions of nonvoters should help the Democrats—or so the theory goes. The problem, however, is that there is very little evidence this theory is actually true.

The weakness of the theory can be seen most clearly by looking at the extreme case of general nonvoter mobilization, 100 percent voter participation.[61] In other words, what if they gave an election and every-

---

contest for Louisiana governor. It was frequently asserted that the key to Edwards's victory was dramatically high turnout among the state's black population. In reality, turnout had little to do with it, the key lying instead in the support levels among whites and blacks for Edwards. Given these support levels (blacks broke 96–4 for Edwards and whites 45–55) and given the distribution of blacks and whites in the population (blacks are about 31 percent of the VAP and whites about 67 percent), Edwards could easily make up his deficit among white voters from black voters, *even at very low black turnout levels*. In fact, my estimates suggest that Edwards would have won the election even if black turnout had been an abysmal 16 percent. So much for the election being determined by black turnout.

61. In chapter 4, I discuss the political effects of less extreme scenarios of general nonvoter mobilization in connection with the issue of registration reform.

body came? Would it make a difference? The answer, it turns out, is not much.

This basic result is consistent across a number of studies, election years, and data bases. For example, the 1988 CBS/*New York Times* post-election poll shows that if nonvoters had voted, the election result would have been the same—except that Bush would have won by a wider margin. Similarly, Bennett and Resnick[62] found that, according to NES data, complete mobilization of nonvoters in 1980 and 1984 would have produced the same outcome, slightly decreasing Reagan's victory margin in the first instance and slightly *increasing* it in the second instance. Finally Petrocik[63] presents NES-based evidence[64] covering every presidential election from 1952 to 1984 and found that complete mobilization would not have changed the outcomes of any of these elections, with the possible exception of 1980.[65] In fact Petrocik found that the typical effect of complete mobilization would have simply been to increase the victory margin of the winner.

The relatively minor impact of full nonvoter mobilization on presidential election outcomes is further illustrated by the data in table 3-9. These data compare the reported presidential vote of voters to the expressed presidential preference of nonvoters and then combine reported vote and expressed preference to show how the entire electorate would have voted under 100 percent turnout. The data clearly show that in no instance would the winner among voters[66] have been changed if all nonvoters had voted.[67] This suggests that although nonvoter candidate preferences can be somewhat different from those of voters, they are not likely to be different enough to change most election outcomes even under conditions of complete general mobilization.

62. Bennett and Resnick 1990, p. 795.
63. Petrocik 1987.
64. Petrocik 1987, pp. 239–59, also uses a 1974 national survey conducted by the National Opinion Research Center. In addition Petrocik does not simply combine the expressed preferences of voters and nonvoters, but attempts to simulate how nonvoters, as "peripheral" members of the electorate, might be expected to cast their ballots as they surge into the voting pool.
65. Though note that this result does not accord with the basic tabulation of voter and nonvoter presidential preferences from the NES (see table 3-9).
66. I should stress that this means the winner among *NES* voters. As alert readers will note, Nixon won the 1960 election, according to voters surveyed by the NES. But more important for the purposes of the argument made here, this anomalous result holds up even when the NES nonvoters are added to NES voters.
67. The pattern of results reported here is basically the same if validated voters and nonvoters are used instead of self-reported voters and nonvoters (except that validated vote data are not available for 1960 or 1968).

TABLE 3-9. *Self-Reported Voters and Nonvoters, by Presidential Vote or Preference, 1960–88*[a]

Percent

Vote or preference	Nonvoters	Voters	All
1960			
Democratic vote or preference	50.8	48.9	49.3
Republican vote or preference	49.2	50.6	50.3
Other vote or preference	0	0.5	0.4
1964			
Democratic vote or preference	79.7	67.4	70.0
Republican vote or preference	20.3	32.4	29.9
Other vote or preference	0	0.2	0.1
1968			
Democratic vote or preference	44.6	40.9	41.7
Republican vote or preference	40.4	47.6	46.0
Other vote or preference	15.0	11.5	12.2
1980			
Democratic vote or preference	46.8	39.4	41.1
Republican vote or preference	45.1	50.8	49.5
Other vote or preference	8.2	9.8	9.4
1984			
Democratic vote or preference	38.6	41.4	40.8
Republican vote or preference	61.2	57.7	58.4
Other vote or preference	0.3	0.9	0.8
1988			
Democratic vote or preference	44.4	46.6	46.0
Republican vote or preference	54.3	52.3	52.8
Other vote or preference	1.3	1.2	1.2

SOURCE: Author's tabulations of National Election Study data.

a. The NES did not ascertain the presidential preference of nonvoters in 1972 and 1976.

It is also worth noting that the presidential preferences of nonvoters, relative to those of voters, appear to have changed. Although in every election through 1980 nonvoters were somewhat more Democratic-leaning than voters, this situation reversed itself in the last two elections. That is, in both 1984 and 1988, levels of Republican support among nonvoters were actually *higher* than among voters, meaning that the Republican victory margins would probably have gone *up* if all nonvoters had decided to show up at the polls. Hence not only is it incorrect to assume that general nonvoter mobilization would substantially help the Democrats win elections, but it may even be incorrect to assume that the Democrats would be helped at all.

The conclusion from this analysis of nonvoter mobilization scenarios seems inescapable. Most electoral outcomes are not determined in any meaningful sense by turnout and are not likely to change even with highly implausible levels of nonvoter mobilization. Or, to put it more bluntly, nonvoting—in a short-term, election-outcome-specific sense— does not as a rule make much of a difference.

Does this mean that nonvoting *never* makes a difference to election outcomes—that elections are never determined by the level of turnout? No, it just means that very specific—and relatively unusual—conditions have to be met for turnout to play such a determining role. These conditions were well summarized by Cavanaugh as follows: first, the election must be close to begin with, because of partisan balance or other political trends, or both; second, a very large turnout increase can be expected relative to the normally expected turnout level for the election; and third, a group of nonvoters with distinctly lopsided candidate preferences is available for mobilization.[68]

These conditions are not likely to obtain very often.[69] But when they do, it becomes much more reasonable to speak of turnout—at least potentially—determining the outcome of an election. For example, the outcome of the 1983 Chicago mayoral election, in which normally low black turnout levels increased tremendously, was probably determined by turnout levels. This example suggests that turnout *can* determine the outcome of at least some elections. But it also illustrates just how unusual conditions have to be for this to happen: Chicago blacks had a historically low turnout rate, but increased their participation by 30 percentage points and voted 99 percent for Harold Washington. The overwhelming majority of U.S. elections do not and will not take place in electoral settings where anything resembling these conditions exists.

Comparing the Policy Preferences of Voters and Nonvoters

It could still be argued that, although nonvoting may not make a difference to election outcomes, the policy preferences of voters and nonvoters make a difference to the *meaning* of those outcomes. The idea is that nonvoters' policy preferences are so different from those of voters that, were nonvoters to vote, elected officials would respond to

68. Cavanaugh 1991.
69. This is especially true at the state or national level. It is considerably more probable that these conditions will obtain in local elections for the simple mathematical reason that base turnout levels are typically very low in these elections. This makes it comparatively easy to generate a turnout increase with a relative weight that is large compared to the base turnout.

a far different set of policy preferences than they currently do. Thus although the same individuals might get elected, the outcome in terms of policy might be quite different.

Some support for this argument is provided by data that show significant demographic differences between the voting pool and the overall electorate (tables 3-7 and 3-8). Most important, for this scenario the data show that the overall electorate contains proportionally more low-SES individuals and proportionally fewer high-SES individuals than the pool of actual voters. Because lower-SES individuals are generally believed to have more "left" or liberal policy preferences than higher-SES individuals, it seems to follow that more participation of nonvoters would encourage elected officials to pursue a more liberal policy mix.

As always with these scenarios, however, the real question is not whether nonvoter participation would make a difference, but rather *how much* of a difference that participation would make. If the difference is small, it makes little sense to speak of nonvoting as seriously skewing the policy outputs of government, at least in an immediate sense. If the difference is large, such a viewpoint becomes more defensible.

The data in table 3-10[70] allow the extent of this difference to be evaluated. Turning first to the issue of the partisan complexion of the electorate, the data show that a fully mobilized electorate (right-hand column) would be no more Democratic than the current electorate (center column) is. In fact, there would be a very slight *decline* of half a percentage point in voters with Democratic leanings (from 47.9 to 47.4 percent of the electorate).

It is true, however, that a fully mobilized electorate would be somewhat less Republican—those with Republican leanings would decline 4.3 percentage points from the current electorate.[71] But it is the independent category, not the Democrats, that would gain from this Republican loss. Indeed the fully mobilized electorate would simply be less

70. I use the validated, rather than self-reported vote data because the analysis is of a single cross-section for which use of the validated vote data makes the most sense. However, the results reported here differ little from those obtained using the self-reported vote data.

71. It is interesting that these results on the partisanship of voters versus the entire electorate are virtually identical to those reported in Wolfinger and Rosenstone 1980, chap. 6. Because their estimations were based on a 1972 data set, whereas I use data from 1988, this suggests that the results reported here are quite robust and not a peculiarity of the survey year employed.

TABLE 3-10. *Validated Voters and Nonvoters, by Partisanship and Issue Positions, 1988*

Percent

Partisanship or position	Nonvoters	Voters	All
Partisanship			
Strong Democrat	13.8	20.4	17.6
Weak Democrat	19.5	16.6	17.9
Independent–Democrat	13.2	10.9	11.9
Independent	18.9	7.3	12.2
Independent–Republican	13.9	12.5	13.1
Weak Republican	12.6	14.7	13.8
Strong Republican	8.3	17.6	13.6
Should abortion be allowed?			
Never	14.3	11.4	12.6
Only if rape, incest, etc.	33.7	33.5	33.6
Only if clear need	15.6	20.5	18.4
By choice	36.4	34.6	35.4
Opinion on federal spending to assist blacks			
Increase	26.2	23.3	24.5
Stay same	49.7	55.5	53.0
Decrease	22.8	19.9	21.1
Cut out entirely	1.4	1.4	1.4
Opinion on federal spending on environment			
Increase	60.4	65.6	63.4
Stay same	36.1	32.3	33.9
Decrease	3.1	2.1	2.5
Cut out entirely	0.4	0	0.2
Mean on 7-point issue scale			
Government guarantee jobs	4.18	4.55	4.39
Government help minorities	4.46	4.50	4.49
Try to get along with Russia	3.78	3.76	3.77
Defense spending	3.94	3.91	3.92

SOURCE: Author's tabulations of National Election Study data.

partisan in general than the current electorate, as the sharp decline in strong partisans illustrates (down 7 points from the current electorate).

Thus full mobilization of nonvoters would not by itself decisively change the partisan leanings of the electorate. And judging from the rest of the data in table 3-10, full mobilization of nonvoters would be even less likely to change the policy preferences of the voting electorate substantially. A fully mobilized electorate would be slightly more likely (up 1 point) to favor outlawing abortion, slightly more supportive of increased federal spending to assist blacks (up 1 point), and slightly less supportive of increased federal spending on the environment (down 2 points). In addition, based on the first 7-point[72] issue scale displayed, a fully mobilized electorate would be slightly more liberal toward the government guaranteeing jobs and a standard of living to individuals (moving 0.16 in the liberal direction).[73]

These differences are obviously quite small and by no means all in the same direction politically.[74] Moreover they are quite a bit smaller than the *demographic* differences between voters and the overall electorate shown in tables 3-7 and 3-8. This shows that demographic differences do not translate in anything close to a one-to-one way into policy differences. Apparently policy skews by SES group in the United States—although they clearly exist and are of some significance politically—are simply not strong enough for such a relationship to obtain.

These findings are quite consistent with the literature on the comparative policy preferences of voters and nonvoters.[75] The studies, which look at a variety of issues across a variety of years, all tell a similar story: nonvoters are somewhat more liberal than voters on policy issues concerning the economic role of government and somewhat less liberal on defense, the environment, and social issues such as abortion.[76] And all agree that the magnitude of these differences is not large and that therefore the absence of nonvoters from the voting pool probably has little immediate effect on the policy output of government.

72. On these scales, 7 is the most conservative viewpoint and 1 is the most liberal viewpoint. Therefore the *lower* the average score, the more liberal a group is, whereas the *higher* the average score is, the more conservative a group is.

73. The other scales show that the full electorate would be a tiny bit more liberal on government assistance to minorities and a tiny bit more conservative on getting along with Russia and on defense spending. But these differences are so small that they should be treated with a great deal of caution.

74. The mixed directionality of these differences is consistent with what one would expect from reducing the weight of the well-educated in the voting electorate. This is because the well-educated tend be somewhat conservative on the economic role of government, but liberal on social issues, the environment, and national defense. Thus if the relative weight of the well-educated among voters is reduced—as it would be if everyone voted—policy preferences of voters are moved in the opposite direction: more liberal on the economic role of government; *less* liberal on the environment, social issues, and so on.

75. See besides Wolfinger and Rosenstone 1980, Shaffer 1982, Kleppner 1982, Bennett and Resnick 1990, Calvert and Gilchrist 1991, and Gant and Lyons 1992.

76. Several also note that, although the basic pattern of these differences remains about the same, the relative magnitude of the differences may change over time. In particular, 1984 and 1988 are described as years in which there were *larger* than normal differences between nonvoters and voters on the economic role of government. Thus the data in table 3-10, far from showing an isolated year in which the differences between voters and nonvoters were not large, actually shows a year in which these differences, such as they are, were accentuated.

Hence it can be concluded that the difference in policy preferences between voters and nonvoters has only a relatively minor impact on the signals currently sent to policymakers through elections. These signals would change little even if an augmented electorate that included all current nonvoters were to vote. Thus whatever the pernicious effects of low voter participation may be, the communication of skewed and unrepresentative policy preferences should not be numbered among them.

Should We Care about Nonvoting?

If the driving force behind declining voter turnout is a voluntary disconnection from politics—a sort of "why bother?" attitude—rather than any profound rejection of "the system," and if by and large, levels of turnout have little effect on election outcomes or on the policy preferences communicated to elites (as we have seen in this chapter), why should we care? Is it really so bad that many people are withdrawing from politics and tending to their private lives, given that those who do participate provide a pretty fair representation of population-wide electoral and policy preferences? In fact if elections are regarded as polls, voters merely provide a slightly biased sample for these polls, but not biased enough generally speaking to throw the "top-line" of these polls very far off. So what's the problem?

The problem is that elections are *not* just polls. They are the main form of interaction between elites and ordinary citizens and have a great deal of influence on the quality of the link between these two groups. Because of this, levels of turnout may be politically relevant even if in the short run they are largely irrelevant to election outcomes and the communication of policy preferences. Specifically I believe low and declining voter turnout makes the democratic link between elites and citizens difficult in at least two important ways.

First is the problem of democratic legitimacy. As fewer and fewer citizens participate in elections, the extent to which government truly rests on the consent of the governed may be called into question. As a result elites may feel they do not have sufficient legitimacy among citizens to pursue desired policy objectives, and citizens may feel the government is not legitimate enough for them to support these elites and their policy objectives. The result of such delegitimation could range from generalized social and political disorganization to reinforcement of some milder social pathologies already seen today: gridlocked government and a political culture that devalues government and turns talented people away from careers in public service.

Of course, it could be argued that at the current time these delegitimation effects seem relatively modest and pose little to worry about. But how much lower would turnout have to get for delegitimation to become a more serious problem? This would not seem like a social experiment worth conducting if it could feasibly be avoided.

Second, is the problem of agenda setting. Ideally in a democracy, the agenda from which elites select policy alternatives and present them to the public should reflect the needs and interests of the population as a whole. If not, segments of the public may be disadvantaged by the agenda, even if their specific policy preferences within the agenda differ little from those of the rest of the population.[77]

Low and declining voter turnout may contribute to the problem of an unrepresentative policy agenda, because nonvoters and voters do tend to differ systematically from one another in attributes that reflect individual needs and interests, even if their specific policy preferences within a given agenda generally do not. For example, data clearly show that low-SES individuals, who presumably have distinctive needs and interests, are underrepresented among voters (tables 3-7 and 3-8).[78] Moreover this lack of representativeness has become somewhat worse over time as a result of differential turnout decline trend. All this may be contributing to a situation in which, in the short run, the policy decisions of elites accurately reflect the immediate policy preferences of the population, but in the long run the policy agenda set by those elites only poorly represents certain segments of the population.

Data recently collected by Verba, Schlozman, Brady, and Nie[79] accentuate this concern. In a followup to the seminal *Participation in America* study[80] they found that those who participate in political activities that are less common but may have more impact on elites than voting— contacting officials, community activism, campaign giving, and so on— differ even more sharply in needs and interests from nonactivists than voters do from nonvoters. Their analysis suggests that this acute strat-

77. See Verba and others 1992 for a lucid discussion of this point.
78. Verba and others 1992 provide some examples of nondemographic attributes reflecting needs and interests upon which voters and nonvoters also differ substantially. They include having recently felt a financial "pinch" and having received means-tested benefits (for instance, food stamps, medicaid, aid to families with dependent children, and so on).
79. Verba and others 1991, 1992.
80. Verba and Nie 1972.

ification has a great deal to do with the relatively high level of resources (money, skills, time) such alternative forms of participation demand. Those who can afford to devote such resources to political participation are, not surprisingly, a quite unrepresentative segment of the population. But by virtue of such participation, these individuals will be exceptionally visible to agenda-setting elites.

Participation in elections, which requires few resources and is easily practiced by the ordinary citizen, should ideally function as a democratic counterweight to high-impact, resource-intensive activism, exposing elites to signals from a relatively wide array of needs and interests. When nonvoting is widespread, however—and is also significantly class-skewed—participation in elections may fail to play that role effectively. The result may be a gradual erosion of the democratic link between the needs of the overall populace and the policy agenda set by elites.

This problem may be accentuated by the well-publicized activities of organized groups lobbying for particularized agendas (so-called special interests). These activities should be thought of as a form of political participation by these organized groups—participation, moreover, that has been growing over time, according to all accounts. And because this form of participation has a relatively high impact, attempting as it does to directly influence the agenda set by policymaking elites through extensive personal contacts and the dispensation of favors, the need for a democratic counterweight to special interest participation seems compelling. Again widespread nonvoting makes it less likely that electoral participation by ordinary citizens will play that role.

Of course, a number of other reasons could be advanced to support higher turnout. For example, it could be argued that participation by itself is good for individuals in a self-development sense and that therefore more participation is good for that reason. Or somewhat more abstractly, it could be argued that real democracy calls for participation and that therefore more participation means more democracy, which is good.

But I believe these reasons are secondary to the concerns outlined about the quality of the link between elites and citizens. Low and declining voter turnout erodes this link and has an adverse effect on the type of democracy the United States is today and will become in the future. Provided the costs of reform are not too onerous, these concerns should be enough to merit action to increase voter turnout without invoking either the specter of a rotting political system in which the affluent dictate election outcomes or the utopian vision of a democracy in which all citizens participate all the time.

Conclusion

The results of the investigations discussed in this chapter point to six conclusions.

First, turnout decline has not been the responsibility of any one demographic group, no matter how these categories are defined (by income, education, occupation, race, age, and so on). The decline has been, as it were, a collective enterprise with almost all demographic categories participating.

Second, though turnout decline has been generalized across all groups, it has been somewhat more rapid among those groups least likely to vote in the first place (that is, the poor, the poorly educated, those in "lower" occupational categories, the young, and so on). Because turnout decline has not been uniform, turnout rate gaps by income, education, occupation, and age have all widened over time.

Third, these gap-widening trends have generally been moderate and do not appear to have created a dramatic new problem with the representativeness of the electorate. In fact the clearest effect of these trends has simply been to aggravate already existing demographic skews in voting. Thus if a problem with the representativeness of the electorate exists, it is much the same problem that existed in 1960 when the current era of turnout decline began.

Fourth, most electoral outcomes are not determined in any meaningful sense by turnout and are not likely to change through even highly implausible levels of nonvoter mobilization. It appears therefore that nonvoting does not as a rule make much of a difference to election outcomes.

Fifth, it appears that nonvoting not only makes little difference to election outcomes, it also makes relatively little difference to policy outcomes as well—at least in an immediate sense. Policy preferences of voters and nonvoters are simply not large enough to seriously skew the signals sent to policymakers through elections. Thus whatever the pernicious effects of low voter participation may be, the communication of skewed and unrepresentative policy preferences should not be numbered among them.

Finally it was argued that, even if levels of turnout have little effect on election outcomes or on the policy preferences communicated to elites, important reasons still exist to support the goal of higher voter turnout. Specifically it was argued that low and declining voter turnout weakens the democratic link between elites and citizens, particularly in terms of democratic legitimacy and agenda setting. Such problems merit action to increase voter turnout, provided the costs of reform are not too onerous.

4

Making Voting Easier: Registration Reform and Other Possibilities

W hat, if anything, can be done about low and declining U.S. voter turnout? Assuming that higher turnout is a social good—as I have argued—how can this social good be brought about?

Using the basic theoretical framework introduced in chapter 1, the obvious solutions are first to decrease the average costs of voting for citizens or second to increase the average (perceived) benefits. Of these options, decreasing the costs is the easiest to justify and the most straightforward to approach. This is because the U.S. voter registration system imposes artificially and uniquely high voting costs on U.S. citizens, judging from the experience of other countries. Given this, it can be argued that lowering such artificially high costs is its own justification—independent of other rationales for increased turnout—because citizens wishing to exercise the franchise should not have to confront unnecessary barriers to their participation.

In this chapter, I explore in detail this cost reduction approach to increasing voter turnout. This entails, first, an extensive discussion of voter registration reform, including probable effects of registration reform on turnout, pros and cons of specific policy proposals, and possible political effects of increased turnout resulting from registration reform. I conclude with a discussion of alternative methodologies of cost reduction, chiefly those involving the use of advanced technology.

Registration Reform and Voter Turnout

Any discussion of reducing costs to facilitate voter participation must begin with the issue of voter registration reform. As discussed in chapter 1, it is the U.S. system of registration through voluntary, individual initiative that constitutes the chief cost of voting for citizens and marks the U.S. political system as a high-cost arena for voter participation relative to other major industrialized democracies. It seems plausible therefore that reforming or eliminating the current voter registration system would substantially cut the costs of voting for the average American citizen and lead to higher turnout.

Estimating the Effect of Registration Reform on Turnout

But *how much* higher would turnout be? Would registration reform help only a little or a lot? The answer is critical, because if reform would only make a marginal difference, it may not be worthwhile to absorb the transition and other costs of moving to a new system. Conversely if registration reform would make a large difference to turnout, then absorbing those costs may be worthwhile.

One way of estimating the possible effect of registration reform on turnout is to look at the *current* effects of registration laws on turnout and estimate how much liberalizing these laws would change turnout levels.

To do this it is first necessary to determine what the current effects of registration laws on turnout are. This is accomplished through estimation of a multivariate model[1] that includes not only the individual characteristics of a citizen, but also the registration laws of that citizen's state (a method pioneered by Wolfinger and Rosenstone).[2] If a given registration law appears to affect turnout significantly, even in the presence of controls for citizens' individual characteristics—education, age, race, and so on—then one may reasonably conclude the law has an independent effect on turnout (that is, all else equal, citizens in states with "tougher" versions of the law vote less often than citizens in states with "easier" versions of the law).

Once these registration law effects have been estimated,[3] the resulting model can be used to estimate how much turnout would change if

---

1. The basic multivariate model is estimated using the census, rather than NES data. This is because the large census sample sizes allow the effects of state-level variables, such as registration laws, to be estimated fairly precisely, while the small NES sample sizes lead to much less precise and trustworthy estimates. This disadvantage outweighs the NES advantage of being able to control for the influence of both attitudinal and demographic variables. (As a check, however, NES-based registration models were also estimated to investigate possible biases introduced by the omission of attitudinal variables in the census-based model.)

2. Wolfinger and Rosenstone 1980.

3. Details on the model and how it was estimated are contained in appendix B.

registration laws were liberalized. This is done by simply "setting" a given registration law (or laws) equal to the most liberal version(s) extant for all states (for example, making the closing date equal to election day all over the United States), and using the model to calculate the resulting predicted increase in turnout.[4] If the predicted increase is small, one would conclude registration reform is likely to yield only marginally higher turnout levels, whereas if the predicted increase is relatively large, one would conclude registration reform could in fact lead to substantially higher turnout levels.

A variety of registration laws could potentially be included in the model. These are laws that exhibit some variation in stringency across the United States and bear some theoretically plausible relationship to turnout.

One of the most obvious of such laws sets the closing date—the last day a citizen can register before a given election. For general elections, the closing date currently ranges from fifty days in advance (Arizona) to election day itself (Maine, Minnesota, and Wisconsin).[5] Because close proximity to an election provides more stimulus to register as well as more time within which to do so, it follows that the nearer the closing date to the election, the more likely, all else equal, that citizens would register and vote.

Closely related to and sometimes confused with the closing date is the residency requirement—the number of days a citizen must have resided in a state to be eligible to register and vote. For general elections, this ranges from fifty days (Arizona) to no days at all in a number of states (though of course unless there is a special provision, someone who moves into a state with no residency requirement *after* the closing date will still not be able to register and vote in that election). One would expect that longer residency requirements would cut some citizens out of the voting process, thereby tending to promote lower voter turnout.

Other registration laws cover the hours during which registration offices are open. The two key distinctions are whether the offices are consistently open during regular hours and whether the offices have mandated hours during evenings or weekends (or both). Some states'

4. See appendix B for details on simulation procedures (these procedures are similar, in most respects, to Wolfinger and Rosenstone 1980, chap. 4).

5. North Dakota, a special case, has no registration system at all. However, for purposes of analysis the state has been treated as if it had election day registration, as well as the most "liberal" form of other voter registration provisions.

registration offices have both regular business hours and evening or weekend registration; others have neither. It seems logical that the more hours registration offices are open—particularly at convenient times—the more likely, all else equal, citizens would be to register and vote.

Another set of laws covers the removal (purging) of citizens from the registration rolls for nonvoting.[6] Key aspects of purge laws include the number of years nonvoting citizens can remain on the rolls before they can be purged; whether and how citizens are notified that names are being purged from the rolls; and how often jurisdictions are mandated to conduct a purge of their rolls. All could bear some relationship to turnout, though the one with the most plausible relationship—and the only one for which consistent time series data are available—is the purging periods for nonvoting citizens. These periods vary from two years in some states to never in a number of others. Presumably relatively short purging periods eliminate some potential voters from the rolls, leading to lower turnout, other factors being equal in such states.

Other possibly important registration laws cover whether and to what extent mail and absentee registration is permitted. Mail registration allows citizens to register through the mail rather than having to appear at a registration office. Absentee registration allows citizens who are ill, disabled, or out of the jurisdiction to register without appearing in person at any office. Some states permit anyone to register by mail and anyone incapacitated or absent for any reason to register absentee, whereas other states permit neither (with the exception of absentee registration for those in the military or overseas, which is required by federal law). One would expect that the more liberal or universal the provisions for mail and absentee registration, the higher, all else equal, voter registration and turnout should be.

A variety of registration laws cover where registration is permitted, including the location of the main registration offices (county, city, or neighborhood) and whether registration is permitted at social service agencies (agency-based registration) or at motor vehicle bureaus (motor voter). Such provisions vary widely with some states permitting registration only at the county seat and others allowing registration at neighborhood institutions such as firehouses and libraries as well as agencies and motor vehicle bureaus. It seems reasonable to suppose the

6. Not all purging is targeted at nonvoters, however, as I noted in chapter 2 in the discussion on the turnout rate of registrants. Some general address verification purges are also conducted. Little reliable data are available on this type of purging.

more convenient the locations for registering, the more likely citizens would be to register and vote.

Finally registration laws determine whether deputy registrars are allowed. Deputy registrars are ordinary citizens specifically deputized to register other citizens—for example, in shopping centers. Currently about three-quarters of the states have provisions for deputy registrars. One would expect that such provisions facilitate registration, leading, all else equal, to higher turnout in these states.

The question now becomes how can it be determined which of these laws really affect turnout and which only appear to affect turnout because of their interrelationship with demographic attributes or other registration laws or both?

Fortunately the multivariate model mentioned previously makes it possible to estimate the effect of a given registration law while controlling for the influence of both demographics and other registration laws. Based on this model, the following state registration provisions were found to have a consistent and significant relationship to turnout:[7] the closing date (expressed as the number of days between closing and the election); whether the state requires registration offices to be open evenings or Saturdays; whether the state requires registration offices to be open consistently during normal business hours; and the number of years before nonvoting citizens can be purged from the registration rolls.[8] All the other registration provisions lacked the consistent, significant relationship to turnout exhibited by these four and therefore would probably have only a marginal impact on turnout if liberalized.

7. Separate models were initially estimated on three different presidential years: 1972, 1980, and 1984. These are the only three presidential elections for which both adequate census data tapes and an adequate set of registration variables are available (for more details on why available 1976 and 1988 data were not adequate, see appendix A). (I focused on presidential elections exclusively so the difference in dynamics between presidential and off-year elections would not cloud the assessment of registration law effects.) Once it was determined which variables were consistently significant across the three surveys, samples were drawn from each year and combined into a pooled data set (for more discussion of how and why data were pooled, see appendix B). The final model was estimated on this data set, using the variables that demonstrated a consistent relationship to turnout across elections. (Note that the use of 1972 and 1984 data prohibited the use of residential mobility in model specification, because the mobility variable was only included in the 1980 data set. This does not appear to be a problem, however, because analysis of the 1980 data indicated the presence of mobility does not significantly affect parameter estimates for registration laws. For more details on the model specification process and final model, see appendix B.)

8. Each of these provisions had a consistent and significant relationship to registration, as well as turnout. This accords well with theoretical expectations (any variables that affect turnout should also affect registration—though the reverse would not necessarily be true).

One would suppose, however, these four provisions *would* have an impact on turnout levels if liberalized. This does, in fact, turn out to be the case. Model estimations indicate that if the most liberal versions of these four laws were adopted nationwide (that is, if all states had election day registration, evening and Saturday registration, consistent, regular office hours, and no purging), turnout would rise about 7.8 percentage points.[9] If registration laws had been liberalized in this manner before the 1988 election, the model results imply that turnout would have been about 58 percent instead of 50 percent—not a revolutionary change perhaps but still a substantial improvement.

This estimate of turnout increase from registration reform is quite consistent with previous estimations performed by other investigators. These estimates, done by Wolfinger and Rosenstone and by Mitchell and Wlezien showed predicted turnout increases of 9.1 percent and 7.6 percent, respectively, from nationwide registration law liberalization.[10] Given that Wolfinger and Rosenstone, Mitchell and Wlezien, and I all used somewhat different data sets[11] and model specifications,[12] the

---

9. The same model predicts a larger increase in registration: 10.7 percent. Again this accords with theoretical expectations—not everyone who is registered will necessarily vote.

10. Wolfinger and Rosenstone 1980, p. 73, Mitchell and Wlezien 1989, p. 13.

11. All investigators used census data, but different years or sets of years of census data were used to estimate the models. Wolfinger and Rosenstone used 1972 data only; Mitchell and Wlezien pooled data from the 1972, 1978, 1980, and 1982 surveys; I pooled data from the 1972, 1980, and 1984 surveys.

In addition, Wolfinger and Rosenstone used a 10 percent sample of their data. Mitchell and Wlezien used (apparently) 10 percent samples from each of their survey years that in turn were then sampled at a 25 percent rate to form their pooled data set. I used a much larger sample based on combining one-third samples taken within each of my survey years. (See appendix B for more details on data sets and sampling procedures used in the analysis reported here.)

12. All investigators used slightly different sets of demographic controls. For example, Wolfinger and Rosenstone did not include terms for income and labor force status, whereas Mitchell and Wlezien and I did. Another example is that, although all investigators used education and age as controls, Wolfinger and Rosenstone specified these attributes as quadratic terms, Mitchell and Wlezien specified them as linear terms, and I specified them as two different sets of dummy variables. Other differences could be noted, but the most important point is that the simulations of increased voter turnout are not sensitive to these differences in demographic specification. Very similar predictions are produced with virtually any reasonable set of demographic controls.

More important differences lie in the use of somewhat different sets of registration variables. Though all investigators included closing date and evening and Saturday registration in their models, Wolfinger and Rosenstone added regular office hours and the lack of absentee registration, Mitchell and Wlezien added length of purging period, and I added purging period and regular office hours (for details on the model specification used in my analysis, see appendix B). The chief reason for these differences appears to lie in the different choices of years included in the model estimations (some years show stronger effects for certain registration variables than other years).

finding of a substantial but not overwhelming increase in turnout from registration law liberalization appears to be a robust one. More specifically no matter which approach is chosen—and different years, demographic controls, and sets of registration variables were used in each—the resulting turnout increase predicted varies only modestly between 7 and 9 percentage points. This concordance of results enhances the confidence with which the model estimation results presented here can be viewed.

The concordance of results extends to the assessment of the relative importance of different registration reforms. My estimations suggest, as do those of Wolfinger and Rosenstone and Mitchell and Wlezien, that eliminating the closing date would have, by far, the largest effect of any of the reforms considered here. Eliminating the closing date alone accounts for over three-fifths (61 percent) of the predicted increase (table 4-1).[13] The next most important reform, eliminating purging for nonvoting, only accounts for one-quarter of the predicted increase, followed by universal evening and Saturday registration with 9 percent and universal regular registration office hours with just 4 percent.

These findings suggest that should registration reform be pursued, the most important aspect is probably eliminating the closing date[14] or approximating this reform through some other means. Implementing evening and Saturday registration, extending registration office hours, or eliminating purging for nonvoting, by themselves, are likely to have only a comparatively minor impact on turnout levels.

Another key question about the effect of registration reform is the relative impact of such reforms on different demographic groups defined by education, occupation, income, age, race, region, and so on. This can be investigated using essentially the same procedure employed for estimating the aggregate increase in turnout (table 4-2).[15]

13. To decompose the predicted increase in turnout by different registration reforms, it was necessary to compare predicted averages generated by the model under regular and liberalized scenarios. This difference in predicted averages could then be decomposed by contributions from the different registration reforms simulated in the model. These are the figures shown in table 4-1 (see appendix B for details on how these figures were derived).

I also performed this decomposition in a different way, by taking each registration reform separately and seeing how much that reform increased turnout by itself. These predicted turnout increases were then added up, and the relative contribution of each registration reform to that sum computed. Results from this decomposition are virtually identical to results presented in table 4-1.

14. Or coming as close to this as possible without creating serious fraud problems.

15. See appendix B for details on how estimations by subgroup were performed.

TABLE 4-1. *Estimated Percentage of Turnout Increase from Registration Reform, by Type of Reform*

Reform	Percent of predicted increase
Election day registration	61.3
Eliminating purging for nonvoting	25.6
Universal evening and Saturday registration	8.9
Universal regular registration office hours	4.2
Total	100.0

SOURCE: Author's computations based on model in appendix B.

These projected increases display a clear and interesting pattern. For every demographic group the projected turnout increases are largest for *underrepresented*[16] groups and smallest for *overrepresented* groups. For example, liberalized registration is projected to increase turnout by 9.9 percentage points among those with eight years or less of education but only by 4.5 percentage points among college graduates. Similarly turnout is projected to rise 9.6 points among those with less than $7,500 in family income and just 5.4 points among those with $60,000 or more in family income. Thus one by-product of registration law reform would be to correct, at least somewhat,[17] the currently skewed demographics of the voting pool.

There are two reasons why the estimated effects of registration reform tend to be highest among those least likely to vote in the first place. The first and generally less important[18] reason is that there is a positive relationship between certain low-turnout demographic attributes (such as low education, living in the South) and restrictive registration laws. Thus liberalization will have a disproportionate effect on some low-turnout demographic groups simply because individuals in these groups are more likely to live where registration laws are most restrictive and hence to experience more liberalization than individuals in corresponding high-turnout groups (such as high education, living outside the South).

16. See table 3-7 for data on under- and overrepresentation of demographic groups among the voting electorate.
17. Though it would come far from equalizing the demographic distribution of the voting pool relative to the overall electorate. This issue is discussed in detail later in the chapter.
18. The exceptions are regional and state-by-state variation in the projected effects of registration reform where this first reason tends to be of prime importance.

TABLE 4-2. *Estimated Turnout Increase from Registration Reform, by Demographic Group*
Percent

Characteristic	Increase	Characteristic	Increase
Education		Age	
0–8 years	9.9	18 to 20	9.9
9–11 years	9.6	21 to 24	9.7
High school graduate	8.4	25 to 34	8.6
Some college	7.0	35 to 44	7.3
College graduate or more	4.5	45 to 54	6.5
Occupation		55 to 64	6.3
Laborers	9.5	65 to 74	6.6
Operatives-craft	9.1	75 or older	8.4
Service	9.1	Race	
Housewives	8.1	White	7.6
Farm	8.0	Black	9.3
Clerical-sales	7.2	Other	8.5
Managerial-administrative	6.0	Region	
Professional-technical	5.3	South	9.7
Family income (1988 dollars)		West	7.6
Less than 7,500	9.6	Northeast	6.7
7,500–14,999	9.1	Midwest	6.3
15,000–19,999	8.8		
20,000–29,999	7.8		
30,000–39,999	7.3		
40,000–59,999	6.2		
60,000 or more	5.4		

SOURCE: Author's computations based on model in appendix B.

The second and generally more important reason is that the effect of *any* given factor on voter turnout tends to be highest on those with relatively low probabilities of voting.[19] This means that even when experiencing identical degrees of liberalization, individuals in relatively low turnout groups (such as those with less than $7,500 in family income) are likely to receive on average a greater boost in turnout than individuals in relatively high turnout groups (such as those with more than $60,000 in family income). For example, projected increases in turnout in California—where the structure of registration and hence the amount of liberalization experienced will be the same for all individuals—are much higher for those with less than $7,500 in income

19. Specifically the effect is greatest on those with about a 50-50 likelihood of voting and substantially less on those already very likely to vote (or very *un*likely to vote). See the beginning of chapter 3 and appendix B for more discussion.

(9.4 percent) than for those with more than $60,000 in income (5.3 percent). Thus the greater effects projected for most low-turnout groups simply reflect, to a large extent, the generic tendency of these groups to experience greater effects on turnout from any given shift in a turnout-related characteristic.[20]

On a state-by-state basis the first thing to note about projected effects of registration reform is the substantial variation in these effects (table 4-3). Projected turnout increases range from a low of zero in North Dakota to a high of 13.7 percentage points in Arizona.

The second thing to note is that—as suggested by the regional data in table 4-2—states in one particular region of the country (the South, where registration laws are generally most restrictive) tend to have relatively large projected turnout increases. For example, Virginia has a projected increase of 12.5 percentage points; Tennessee, 11.8 points; Georgia, 10.3 points; South Carolina, 10.2 points; and so on. In contrast another region, the Midwest, where registration laws tend to be most liberal, has a concentration of states with relatively low turnout increases: North Dakota, 0 points; Minnesota, 1.8 points; Nebraska, 3.4 points; Iowa, 3.6 points; South Dakota, 4.5 points; and so on. Thus, though registration is likely to have an effect in nearly all states, the effect will vary quite a bit from state to state, particularly when states in different regions of the country are compared.

Upper-Bound Estimates of Turnout Increase from Registration Reform

The analysis in the previous section suggests rather strongly that reforming several key aspects of the voter registration system would produce a substantial improvement in voter turnout levels—up to 8 percentage points, according to estimates based on Bureau of the Census data. Although this increase is certainly quite respectable, it is important to stress the possibility that for several reasons this figure could actually *underestimate* the amount of increased turnout that

20. It should be stressed that this differential in increased turnout is purely a reflection of where on the curve individuals within different groups tend to be located (see appendix B). In no way should this be interpreted as implying a special relationship or interaction effect between, for example, income and registration laws. That is, registration laws are not harder on those with low income; rather those with low income simply tend to be placed on the turnout curve in such a way that these laws—and all other independent variables as well—produce greater effects on turnout (see Nagler 1991 for a lucid discussion of this point).

TABLE 4-3. *Estimated Turnout Increase from Registration Reform, by State*

Percent

State	Increase	State	Increase
Alabama	9.3	Montana	9.6
Alaska	9.0	Nebraska	3.4
Arizona	13.7	Nevada	8.3
Arkansas	7.9	New Hampshire	6.0
California	7.3	New Jersey	6.7
Colorado	4.4	New Mexico	9.7
Connecticut	4.9	New York	6.8
Delaware	7.7	North Carolina	8.0
Florida	10.0	North Dakota	0
Georgia	10.3	Ohio	7.5
Hawaii	9.5	Oklahoma	6.0
Idaho	5.2	Oregon	5.0
Illinois	6.7	Pennsylvania	8.1
Indiana	8.1	Rhode Island	7.1
Iowa	3.6	South Carolina	10.2
Kansas	5.2	South Dakota	4.5
Kentucky	9.6	Tennessee	11.8
Louisiana	7.9	Texas	9.7
Maine	2.9	Utah	3.4
Maryland	11.0	Vermont	7.6
Massachusetts	4.9	Virginia	12.5
Michigan	7.5	Washington	9.1
Minnesota	1.8	West Virginia	8.1
Mississippi	10.1	Wisconsin	3.9
Missouri	8.8	Wyoming	9.2

SOURCE: Author's computations based on model in appendix B.

thorough registration reform could produce. There are several reasons for this.

First it is possible some of the registration provisions I looked at have more of an effect on turnout and therefore on increasing turnout, if liberalized, than I was able to uncover. For example, I could not include agency-based registration[21] in most of the models I estimated, because

21. I also had data on "motor voter" (which allows citizens to register at motor vehicle bureaus as they obtain their drivers' licenses) only for 1984 and 1988. But motor voter showed no significant effect on turnout in either year (in contrast to agency-based registration, which showed a significant effect in the only year for which I had data—1988).

However, the motor voter data I had were poor and did not allow me to discriminate well between states where it is only *possible* to register at the motor vehicle bureau and

this development is of very recent vintage (usable data on agency-based registration are only available for 1988). However, if the generous assumption is made that a model based only on 1988 data[22] gives a "true" assessment of this provision's effects on turnout, my estimates suggest making agency-based registration universal across the United States might increase turnout as much as 1.1 percentage points above the 7.8-point increase previously noted. (This estimate should be treated very cautiously, however, because of the relative inadequacy of the data involved.)

The second reason for a possible underestimate of the effects of registration reform is the difficulty of obtaining any data at all on certain registration provisions. Lacking data on these provisions, we have no estimates of their effect on turnout and therefore on turnout levels if liberalized. The problem is most serious for jury duty, a provision of current law[23] in many states that directs that the voter registration lists be used as the basic source for locating prospective jurors. Because selection for jury duty can involve considerable costs—both time and financial—this provision could conceivably act as a deterrent to voter participation.

The only serious attempt to look at this issue, to the best of my knowledge, has been by Knack,[24] who used a data set he himself collected. Though Knack's analysis poses a number of problems and unresolved issues,[25] it does present some suggestive evidence on the

---

states where it is *actively encouraged and facilitated* (presumably the latter would have a far greater effect on turnout). Knack 1992c, who collected his own data on motor voter provisions and was able to distinguish between "active" and "passive" motor voter programs, did find that active motor voter programs worked better. His findings suggested that active motor voter programs raise turnout 5.8 to 8 percent in states that have such programs (though note that this does not tell us how much *more* turnout would go up in the United States as a whole with universal implementation of active motor voter). Although Knack's analysis relies on aggregate data and secondarily on a single cross-section from the relatively small-sample NES, it does provide some hard evidence for the turnout-increasing effect of active motor voter programs.

22. This is particularly a problem because the rest of my registration law data for 1988 is relatively poor—the reason, in fact, why I did not use 1988 data for the model estimates reported in the previous section.

23. This provision dates back to the 1968 Jury Selection and Service Act, which abolished the "key man" system of jury selection.

24. Knack 1991b, 1992b.

25. Knack does not use census data, but relies instead on two separate cross-sections from the NES (1988, and to a lesser extent, 1990) for his individual-level analysis. The small sample sizes here can cause problems with the stability of parameter estimates, particularly with contextual data. Furthermore, the models he specifies do not include several registration provisions known to affect nonvoting (evening and Saturday registration, regular registration office hours, and length of purging period) or any control for the southern low-turnout states (which, judging from Knack's data, tend to be states

turnout-depressing effect of jury duty provisions and on the turnout-elevating effect of eliminating these provisions (7 to 7.5 percentage points). His estimate is almost certainly too high[26]—as he himself acknowledges—but it does suggest the projected effect of registration reform on turnout would probably be higher if the effect of reforming jury duty provisions could be properly captured in the estimations.

The third reason for a possible underestimate of the increase in turnout is that the effect of certain demographic variables on turnout could conceivably be caused by their interaction with registration provisions. It is possible therefore that the estimated effects of registration reform on turnout should also include the effect of eliminating these demographic influences on turnout. This analysis is most defensible in terms of residential mobility,[27] a well-documented predictor of turnout (the more recently one has moved, the less likely one is to vote). The theory here is that the turnout-depressing effect of having moved basically stems from the difficulties of reregistering after the move.

---

using registration lists for jury selection). In addition, his state-level estimations show no effect of jury duty provisions in 1976 as opposed to 1988, an issue that is not satisfactorily resolved in his papers. Finally his model estimations look only at the effects of jury duty provisions on registration and do not directly address the effects of these provisions on turnout. Because of this limitation, his estimations of the projected impact of eliminating jury duty provisions on turnout simply assume the turnout rate of new registrants will match that of current registrants—a highly questionable proposition.

26. Besides basic problems with Knack's model (see previous note), two other observations cast doubt on the magnitude of this estimate. First and less serious, Knack's estimate really applies to the states in which a link exists between jury duty and registration lists—that is, his impact estimates refer to the effect of liberalizing jury duty provisions within such states. Logically, this does not tell us what the overall impact on turnout would be in the United States if such provisions were completely eliminated, because five states already lack such provisions. Therefore the additional increment in turnout from severing the link between jury duty and registration lists would have to be somewhat less than Knack's estimate since there would be no impact in these five states.

Second and more serious, perception of the link between jury duty and registration lists is not widespread among the electorate. According to the 1991 NES pilot survey, only two-fifths of the population believes (mistakenly or otherwise) that there is any link at all between jury duty and registration lists (Knack 1992b). This means that the individual-level turnout-depressing effect of jury duty provisions should be exceptionally strong among this subgroup of the population to generate the overall state-level effects found by Knack (logically, those who do not see a link between registration lists and jury duty—the majority of the population—should experience no turnout-depressing effect at all). Knack's own estimations, however, actually find substantially *weaker* individual-level than state-level effects among those with a perceptual belief in the jury duty–registration link—the reverse of what one would expect.

Oliver and Wolfinger 1992 make a similar point in their review of the 1991 NES pilot study data on jury duty and voter registration. They estimate the turnout-depressing effect of current jury duty provisions at only 2 percent.

27. This argument is made most forcefully by Squire, Wolfinger, and Glass 1987 and Wolfinger 1991, and Wolfinger, forthcoming.

It follows that if registration is reformed in such a way as to allow movers to stay registered[28] when they move (or make it much easier to do so), the turnout-depressing effect of mobility on turnout would be largely removed and overall turnout levels consequently elevated. My estimate of the impact of removing the mobility effect is about 5.5 percentage points over and above the 7.8-point increase directly stemming from registration liberalization. This figure is identical to that from a similar estimation made by Squire, Wolfinger, and Glass.[29]

Skepticism about the size of this estimate is warranted, however. I am doubtful, for example, that all—or even most—of the mobility effect on turnout is truly attributable to the effects of re-registering.[30] But even if only part of the mobility effect on turnout is caused by re-

28. Election day registration would probably help here as would various proposals to use change of address forms, driver's license applications and changes, and so on as ways of automatically updating registration lists. The latter proposals are well represented in current legislation before Congress.

29. Squire, Wolfinger, and Glass 1987 actually give more play to a higher 9-percentage-point estimate of the impact of removing the mobility effect based on an NES model. The difference in the two estimates primarily stems from the fact that the census mobility variable only goes up to six years of residence, whereas the NES variable can be coded to include up to ten years of residence. Because mobility does continue to have an effect up to ten years of residence, there is "more" mobility effect to remove from the NES model and hence a larger predicted turnout increase.

I chose to use the census data because first, I consider the census data and models based on them more trustworthy for this type of analysis; second, I wished to retain continuity with my other estimates; and third, I wanted to see what impact eliminating the mobility effect had *after* taking into account the direct effect of liberalizing registration provisions—an approach for which the census data are far better suited.

30. To a large extent the identification of the mobility effect with reregistration difficulties is an assertion, albeit a fairly plausible one. But direct evidence is noticeably lacking.

Even more troubling perhaps is that the mobility effect continues to increase until one has been in one's residence as long as ten years (in other words, people who have been in their residence as long as ten years are substantially more likely to vote, all else equal, than those who have been in their residences only five years). I find it quite difficult to believe that the problems of re-registering continue to plague individuals for as long as ten years after they move. It seems more reasonable to suppose that a good part of the positive effect of staying—that is, of *not* moving—on turnout has to do with the sense of community "rootedness" that develops with a long stay in the same residence (see chapter 2 for more discussion of the relationship between social rootedness and turnout).

Empirical support for the viewpoint that mobility effects cannot be reduced to re-registration difficulties is provided oddly enough by census-based estimations in the original article by Squire, Wolfinger, and Glass 1987, p. 56. They found that the turnout-depressing effect of mobility was only slightly less in states they categorized as having election day registration (Maine, Minnesota, Oregon and Wisconsin) or no registration (North Dakota). Because re-registration difficulties are presumably far smaller in states with easy registration provisions, significant attenuation of mobility effects should have been observed by their theory. The lack of such significant attenuation suggests their theory does not adequately explain the relationship of mobility to turnout.

registration problems, it still suggests the projected effect of registration reform on turnout would probably be higher if the effects of easing re-registration difficulties could be properly captured in the estimations.

The final and possibly most important reason the model estimation presented in the previous section may underestimate the possible increase in turnout is that registration reform could potentially include new methods of registration. It is impossible, of course, to directly model the effects of completely new methods, because states with such methods cannot be compared to states that lack these methods (by definition, *all* states currently lack a completely new method). The easiest way to think about this is to consider a system in which the state takes the responsibility for registering voters as, for example, in Canada where the government conducts an enumeration to construct voting lists for elections.[31] This makes registration essentially costless and logically should boost turnout even more than the merely cost-*reducing* registration reforms modeled previously. But it is not possible to be more precise than this, because the effects of such a system cannot be directly modeled.

Closer to home, some current reform proposals include provisions for making a driver's license application function simultaneously as an application for voter registration so that citizens applying for or renewing driver's licenses would have to specify that they did *not* want to be registered to vote. This is different enough from the current state practices[32] that typically provide only the *opportunity* to register at motor vehicle bureaus that it cannot be properly modeled with existing data. Hence it is not known how much the simultaneous driver's license–registration application would boost turnout. It can only be speculated that it would probably provide an additional increment to voter turnout, if implemented along with the registration reforms described previously.[33]

31. See chapter 1 for a discussion of state versus individual responsibility for voter registration.

32. Even the so-called active motor programs in a number of states tend to differ in important ways from those called for in reform legislation.

33. Though the extent of this increment might be quite modest because the effect of this reform seems likely to overlap substantially with the effect of election day registration. That is, the type of nonregistrants who might take advantage of low-cost registration through their driver's license applications seem likely to be the same type of nonregistrants who might take advantage of low-cost election day registration. Depending on the amount of overlap in fact, the two reforms may largely be substitutes for one another. I will return to this point later in the chapter.

This discussion establishes the possibility that the census-based projection of increased voter turnout from registration reform could be an underestimate. Therefore it is appropriate to ask: what is the *upper bound* of the increase in turnout that could reasonably be expected even under the most thorough set of registration reforms?

The answer to this question is necessarily somewhat speculative, but several observations can be made. First, it seems unlikely the increase in turnout could conceivably achieve the level suggested by simple addition of all specific estimates given (that is, the original estimate from the census model *plus* the estimate for universal agency registration *plus* the estimate for eliminating jury duty provisions *plus* the estimate from eliminating mobility effects). This is because even assuming all these estimates by themselves tap real effects, a great deal of overlap between them would undoubtedly occur if the reforms were implemented in the real world. (The additional voters from eliminating jury duty provisions would overlap with the additional voters from liberalizing the four registration provisions in the original model.) In addition, even with factors that do not overlap, the effect of any given factor on voter turnout becomes smaller the higher the overall level of turnout, producing a total effect that is not directly additive.[34]

This suggests one should not add together more than two of these estimates at a time and that even this procedure may overstate the case. Thus for example, the original census-based estimate (7.8 percentage points) might be added to the jury duty estimate (about 7 points)[35] to get a combined estimated increase of 14.8 percentage points. But one would not want to go beyond this figure and should treat even it very cautiously.

This 14.8-percentage-point figure is quite similar to Powell's estimate of a 14-percentage-point turnout increase from implementing state-sponsored automatic registration.[36] This further suggests—because the costs of registration cannot be any lower than they would be under an automatic registration system (that is, essentially zero)—that the upper bound for turnout increase from registration reform should not be set any higher than 14 to 15 percentage points no matter how elaborate and far-reaching the set of registration reforms. I therefore conclude that any set of reforms that either includes or goes beyond (or both)

34. See appendix B for more discussion of the nonadditive effects of different factors in a voter turnout model.
35. Knack 1991b.
36. Powell 1986, p. 35.

the four reforms discussed earlier (election day registration, no purging for nonvoting, evening and Saturday registration, regular registration office hours) will produce at most an effect on turnout somewhere in between the 8-percentage-point increase derived from the original model and this upper bound of 14 to 15 percentage points.

Lower-Bound Estimates of Turnout Increase from Registration Reform

Just as the original model estimate of turnout increase from registration reform might be too low at 7.8 percentage points, it might also be too *high*.

There are several reasons this might be so. The first is that some of the registration effects captured in the original model might not be real.[37] If some of the registration laws included in the model do not truly affect turnout, then the projected turnout increase based on the model is probably inflated. I investigated the extent of this possible inflation by successively removing several registration variables from the model.

The logical candidates for removal from the model are registration laws for which estimated effects have been relatively unreliable. The prime suspect here is purging for nonvoting, for which the estimated effect was strongly significant in only two years of the three tested[38] (the other laws in the model described earlier were solidly significant in all three years). Moreover the effect of purging was not uniformly detected by other investigators.[39] Removing this prime suspect from the model (but leaving in closing date, evening and Saturday registration, and regular office hours) reduces the estimated increase in turnout by 1.5 percentage points to 6.3 percent.

The next variable to be removed from the model was regular office hours because not all investigators have found this variable to be a

37. For example, it is always possible that the observed effect of a given registration law on turnout is attributable instead to some other unobserved state-level political peculiarity. This is because state-level contextual data, such as registration laws, function in effect as dummy variables for different groups of states. Thus, the possibility always exists that the groups of states defined by a given registration law coincide with groups of states defined by some other, unobserved turnout-related characteristic. In such a case, a registration law effect would show up in the model, but would be truly attributable to the unobserved characteristic.

38. Though it was still marginally significant in the third year.

39. Wolfinger and Rosenstone 1980, p. 76, did not find a significant purging effect.

significant influence on registration and turnout.[40] Removing this variable from the model (but leaving in closing date and evening and Saturday registration) reduces the predicted increase in turnout only modestly from 6.3 to 5.5 percent, a decline of just 0.8 percentage point.

Finally an argument could conceivably be made that evening and Saturday registration should be removed from the model—despite the uniformity with which it registers a significant impact on turnout—because the estimated effect of this variable on turnout tends to be somewhat unstable across elections. (Closing date, in contrast, is very stable in its effect on turnout.) Removing evening and Saturday registration from the model (and leaving in just closing date) further reduces the predicted turnout increase by 0.7 percentage point to 4.8 percent. This figure of 4.8 percent means that the turnout increase from registration reform could be as much as 3 percentage points lower than originally predicted if the registration laws just discussed are not in fact true influences on voter turnout.

A second reason the original model prediction might be too high is that the election day registration reform simulated by the model—and clearly the most important of the reforms in the model—may not really be feasible under any reform program. This would be true if the problem of election day fraud was indeed insurmountable in larger states with a history of "dirty politics."[41] If this were the case, it might only be possible to limit closing dates to a maximum of seven days before the election (that is, all states must have closing dates seven days or *closer* to an election).

Setting the closing date at a seven-day maximum (but keeping states with less than seven days between closing and election at their current values) lowers the projected increase in turnout from 7.8 to 6.6 percent. Thus the possible impracticality of universal election day registration might lower the increase in turnout stemming from registration reform but only modestly—by 1.2 percentage points.

The final and most important reason the original model prediction of increased turnout might be an overestimate is that the model involved

40. I found this variable to be a significant predictor of turnout and registration, as did Wolfinger and Rosenstone 1980. Mitchell and Wlezien 1989 did not. (An NES-based model did not find this variable to be significant either.)

41. See Smolka 1977 for a thorough discussion of the mechanics of election day registration, the historical experience of Wisconsin and Minnesota with this system, and ways in which the reform can lend itself to election day fraud.

is just that: a model. It is only a very educated *guess* about what might happen if registration laws were liberalized. The model cannot predict definitively what *will* happen in the real world if such a liberalization is undertaken.

In fact some alternative estimates suggest real-world effects could be smaller than the model estimates previously presented. These estimates are typically derived from studying the experience of states across elections as they change their election laws. One example is Smolka, who studied the experience of Minnesota and Wisconsin as they moved to an election day registration system.[42] Smolka's somewhat impressionistic estimate is that the reform boosted turnout levels only 1 to 2 percentage points over what they would have been in these states.

A less impressionistic attempt to look at the effects of registration law changes was conducted by the Committee for the Study of the American Electorate.[43] The committee's study examined all registration law changes over a fairly lengthy period (1960–86) and compared these changes to observed changes in state-level turnout. Based on this comparison, the study reports the effect of the most liberal registration law reform (election day registration) as about 3.8 percentage points,[44] with the possibility that other forms of liberalization could increase this effect.

Although the study has a host of methodological problems,[45] this relatively low estimate provides a useful counterpoint to the model-based estimations (especially as some of the biases in the study would appear to have biased results upward, not downward). The real world may interact with the registration reforms proposed here in such a way as to lessen their impact on turnout levels. In fact if the study's 3.8 percent figure is used as the lower-bound estimate of the increase in turnout from registration reform, this lower-bound estimate is a little less than half (3.8/7.8) of the original projection.

42. Smolka 1977.
43. Committee for the Study of the American Electorate 1987.
44. Author's computation based on raw figures given in report.
45. The study controls neither for the relationship of demographics to registration laws nor for the interrelationships among different registration laws and registration law changes. A proper study of the effects of registration law changes would require a multivariate, longitudinal research design that controls for all this and for state-level changes over time in registration laws. To the best of my knowledge no study has yet done this (though several researchers—Mitchell and Wlezien and Knack—are pursuing research agendas that may lead to such a study).

Conclusions

The data reviewed lead directly to two conclusions. The first is that registration reform no matter how structured is very unlikely in and of itself to "solve" the turnout problem. Even under the most optimistic scenario the turnout increase from registration reform would put turnout in presidential elections only a couple of points higher (50 + 15 = 65) than it was in 1960 at the beginning of the turnout decline era (see table 1-1) and still *15 points lower* than the average among other industrialized democracies. This strongly suggests that a successful approach to the problem of low voter turnout must involve not just lowering the costs of participation—as registration reform would do—but also enhancing the benefits of such participation.[46]

The second conclusion to be drawn from the data is that no matter which estimate one chooses to believe, *any* reasonably thorough registration reform program should provide a serious boost to currently anemic U.S. turnout levels. Whether the impact of registration reform is a 4-, 8-, or 15-percentage-point increase in turnout, this is still a substantial addition of citizens to the voting pool in national elections. (Even a 4-percentage-point increase still amounts to over 7 million voters.) Thus with registration reform the only real question appears to be not *whether* it will work (it almost certainly will), but rather *how much* will it work.

Clearly if increased turnout is viewed as a desirable goal, then serious registration reform efforts should be pursued. In fact the only reason *not* to pursue such efforts would be that the costs in whatever form are deemed too high. These costs could take two forms: financial or political.

The financial costs stem from the simple fact that setting up and administering a new registration system is likely to cost some amount of money. This could obviously be a stumbling block, depending on the magnitude of this amount. However, it does not appear registration reform is intrinsically all that costly, especially when measured against the cost of other nationwide programs.

For example, cost estimates of a bill currently before Congress[47] that include the combined driver's license–registration application system imply that the costs of running this system would be little more (and

46. This issue is addressed in detail in chapter 5.
47. These bills are discussed in detail in the next section.

perhaps less) than current costs, once up-front costs of about $195 million are met.[48] Even the radically different Canadian system of voter enumeration, if transplanted here, would cost only about $90 million a year.[49]

So the financial costs, at least on the surface, do not appear to be terribly onerous. The other cost typically linked to registration reform is political—corruption of the voting process through fraud. Certainly this is a potential problem to be taken seriously. Vote fraud has historically been a particular problem in certain areas and before the implementation of personal registration was apparently a fairly widespread political phenomenon.[50]

However, there are good reasons to believe the political process of today is substantially different from that of a hundred years ago. And no one is advocating replacing the current system with the very loose nonsystem of voter registration in place in that previous era. Furthermore, the one reform that seems most susceptible to the charge of promoting fraud—election day registration—could simply be modified to permit some states to have seven-day closing dates or even replaced with something else that performed an equivalent function (such as nonforgeable voter identification cards). Finally the experience of other nations with different, nonpersonal systems of voter registration hardly suggests that only the U.S. system can prevent voter fraud. Many if not most of these countries appear to have fewer fraud problems than the United States.

Thus from neither source—financial nor political—do the costs of registration appear to be intrinsically and insupportably high. And the probable benefits of registration reform appear indisputable. I therefore conclude that registration reform is a cause that at the least should be seriously addressed by policymakers and appropriate legislation.

Registration Reform and Current Policy

It is useful to preface a discussion of current legislation with a brief review of the tangled history of recent registration reform efforts.[51]

48. Cost estimates for this bill (HR 2190) are discussed in more detail in the next section.

49. Canadian costs are estimated at about a dollar per eligible voter per national election (Gans 1992). For the 180 million voters in the United States, this produces a cost of $180 million; to be divided by two (because national elections occur only once every two years or $90 million.

50. Though the magnitude of vote fraud was probably exaggerated by reformers with their own political agenda. (See the related discussion in chapter 1.)

51. For more detail, see Gans 1991a and Wolfinger 1991, upon which I base much of this discussion.

These efforts really date back to 1977,[52] the year Jimmy Carter became president. Carter took office with the expressed intent of reforming the nation's voter registration system. Key to Carter's approach was legislation that would have made election day registration uniform across the United States.

The election day registration provision led to fairly intense debate in the House of Representatives on the fraud issue. This debate was not satisfactorily resolved, and many members of Congress remained doubtful such a provision could be put into place without running an unacceptable risk of increased fraud. As a result this particular version of registration reform, despite being backed by a Democratic president with large Democratic congressional majorities, was soundly defeated.

Serious registration reform remained off the legislative agenda until the middle of the 1980s. At that time some political openness to the project of registration reform reappeared as a result of increased interest on the part of some elements of the Democratic party and decreased hostility from the Republican camp. Out of this openness developed a sort of bipartisan consensus on two objectives: first, the need to find an alternative to election day registration to accomplish much the same thing in terms of increased voter turnout, and second, the need to establish uniform standards for registration list cleaning that produced accurate, nonfraudulent lists but did not penalize people for not voting.

The eventual result of this bipartisan consensus was a House bill, HR 2190,[53] introduced in 1989, that went some way toward meeting both these objectives. To meet the first objective the bill mandated a strong motor voter system in which a citizen's driver's license application (or renewal or change of address) functioned at the same time as an application for voter registration. To meet the second objective, the bill mandated regular cleaning of registration lists, using either two first-class verification mailings or U.S. Postal Service change-of-address information.[54] But the bill specifically prohibited automatic deletion from the lists for not voting.

HR 2190 progressed fairly easily through subcommittee and committee votes, receiving strong bipartisan support. At that point the bill

52. See chapter 2 for a discussion of the wave of registration reforms that predated the Carter administration.
53. An alternative bill, HR 17, was organized around election day registration. It failed to get off the ground.
54. Specifics on these list-cleaning methods are provided in the next section, where HR 2190 is analyzed in detail.

stalled because of concern in certain quarters, particularly within the civil rights community, that the mandated list-cleaning provisions would be unfair to minorities and the poor. Eventually, however, a compromise was struck and the mandatory list-cleaning period was lengthened from two years to four years. The bill finally passed the House by more than a two-thirds vote in February 1990.

At this point the bipartisan consensus began to break down. Elements of the civil rights community renewed their objections to the legislative thrust of HR 2190 and responses and counterresponses followed along partisan lines. As a result the bill developed in the Senate looked quite different and in some ways weaker than the House bill.[55] In addition—and critically—it lacked the bipartisan support necessary for successful passage through the Senate. Reflecting this, when the bill was called to the Senate floor in September 1990, it faced determined Republican opposition—a filibuster in fact to prevent it from even coming to a vote. The cloture petition to stop the filibuster failed, more or less along party lines, and there the matter rested until 1992.

In 1992 the Senate bill was revived by a coalition of forces (mostly Democrats, but including a handful of Republicans) and managed to pass. The bill was then sent to the House, where it also passed, basically on a party-line vote. The bill was then sent to President Bush, who vetoed it as expected in early July. Although Bush claimed the veto was motivated by concerns about fraud, it was clear that the identification of the bill as a partisan Democratic move made the veto almost inevitable. It is now back to square one, raising the possibility that the House bill in its original form (HR 2190) may eventually be revived. Alternatively, the Senate bill (S 250) may be revived again or possibly some amalgam of the two bills.

The House Registration Reform Bill

With this history as background, I now turn to the specifics of these two main registration reform bills and evaluate their potential benefits and costs.

The centerpiece of House bill HR 2190 is its motor voter provision. Under this provision, an application for a driver's license (or renewal or change of address[56]) would include *on the same form* an application

---

55. Specific differences between the House and Senate bills are discussed in the next section.

56. The renewal and change-of-address aspect of this provision is very important. Otherwise because most citizens originally apply for their driver's licenses at 16, before

for voter registration. Thus a citizen would complete both applications as close to simultaneously as possible. In fact a citizen would actually have to check a special box on the form to *avoid* being registered to vote when obtaining a license.

Another salient provision of HR 2190 is the mandated registration list-cleaning procedures. States would be mandated to clean their registration lists at least once every four years. Moreover they would be specifically enjoined to choose between two methods of attaining this goal.

The first is a method already employed by a number of states: the use of two first-class verification notices. The first notice is not forwardable and, if not returned by the post office, is assumed to indicate that the registrant's address on the registration rolls is correct.[57] If the notice is returned, a second, forwardable notice is sent to the registrant, who must then supply a new address to the registration authorities or be removed from the rolls.

The second method takes advantage of the Postal Service's computerized national change of address (NCOA) data. The NCOA data would be matched against voter registration lists to determine which individuals have moved and to where. If the individual has not moved, nothing is done, and the individual remains on the rolls. If the individual has moved, but has remained within his or her former geographical voting unit,[58] the registration address is simply updated automatically, and the individual remains on the rolls. Finally if the individual has moved out of the geographical voting unit, a notice is sent out informing the individual that his or her registration must be updated. If the individual does not update the registration with the appropriate authorities, he or she is then removed from the rolls.

---

they are eligible to vote, the provision would have little effect. But, because everyone who wishes to keep their driver's license has to eventually renew it or change the license address, this provision should over time reach virtually every citizen who gets a license.

57. This may or may not be a justified assumption. It appears to be the case that in many areas the post office simply delivers any mail that has a valid address to that address. Thus if a registrant has moved, but no longer has an operative change of address with the post office (or has died or never lived there in the first place), the notice may get delivered anyway. This problem clearly deserves some attention if the verification notice system is to work as intended.

58. The term "geographical voting unit" is defined in the bill as a county, municipality, or other geographical area that constitutes a geographical voting unit under state law. The definition is very broad and could potentially cover an area as small as a precinct or as large as the entire state. Because it is uncertain how states would interpret this particular term (though the committee discussion of the bill does recommend using the entire state), I choose an intermediate-sized unit, the county, for purposes of estimating the probable effects of NCOA-match list cleaning.

The bill also specifies that list cleaning, by whatever method, cannot include the automatic deletion of individuals from lists for not voting no matter how long it has been since they voted. On the other hand the bill does allow states to exempt recent voters (that is, individuals who *did* vote in the most recent federal election) from the list-cleaning procedures. In this sense nonvoters are more likely to be subject to list-cleaning procedures (though again they cannot be eliminated simply for not voting).

Another provision of the bill mandates that mail registration be available to citizens in all states. In addition the bill specifies that agency-based registration must be implemented in all states and must cover a wide range of major agencies that have large-scale interaction with the public.

Finally the bill provides $50 million in assistance to states on a 50–50 matching basis to assist them in implementing the list-cleaning provisions of the bill. Though the states can technically use this money as they see fit, the purpose of the appropriation is to help states computerize registration lists and therefore be able to use the NCOA match for list cleaning.

What would be the benefits and costs of implementing such a bill? In terms of benefits there are good reasons for thinking that the effect on voter turnout levels might be substantial.

First the motor voter provision alone seems likely to have a substantial effect on turnout because it comes close to eliminating registration as a separate activity with its own costs. By folding the costs of registering in with the costs of obtaining a driver's license, costs directly incurred from registering to vote are almost zero.

In this sense, the motor voter provision functions very much like election day registration, which also folds the costs of registering into the costs of another activity (voting). In both cases, the marginal costs of registering become very low. This similarity suggests that a reasonable estimate of the effect of the motor voter provision on turnout can be based on the previously derived estimate for election day registration.[59] Because the estimated effect of universal election day registration alone was 4.8 percent, and about 87 percent of Americans of voting age have driver's licenses,[60] this would imply that universal implemen-

---

59. No direct estimate of the effect of the motor voter provision turnout is possible, because the provision is too new and different for appropriate data to be available. The only similar system with any kind of history is in Colorado, and even that one only dates back to 1985.

60. U.S. Congress 1990.

tation of HR 2190's motor voter provision might raise turnout as much as 4.2 percentage points.[61]

Other provisions of HR 2190 might also have a positive effect on turnout. One is the NCOA list-cleaning option. To the extent states are able to computerize their lists and take advantage of this option, it should eliminate the re-registering problem for many movers—particularly those moving within their geographical voting units (here assumed to be their home counties, within which 60 percent of moves take place). This might raise turnout as much as 3.3 percentage points, assuming that much of the turnout-depressing effect of residential mobility is actually because of re-registration problems.[62]

Related to list cleaning, another provision that might have a positive effect on turnout is the elimination of automatic purging specifically for not voting. This reform in fact was one of the four reforms whose projected effects on turnout levels were analyzed earlier in this chapter (see table 4-1). Based on the same model used in those estimations, eliminating purging for not voting might increase turnout as much as 2 percentage points.[63]

The final provision of HR 2190 that might have a positive effect on turnout levels is the mandate for universal agency-based registration.[64] A tentative estimate of a 1.2-percentage-point increment to turnout

61. 4.8 × 0.87 = 4.2. It is possible of course that the real effects of universal motor voter might be higher than those of universal election day registration because having to register *and* vote on the same day may strike some people as onerous, no matter how low the discrete costs of registering are. (This is particularly likely to be a problem where registration on election day involves a trip somewhere other than the local polling place.) In this sense, being able to vote with the costs of registering "prepaid," as would be true under the motor voter system, could constitute a real advantage for this system, and possibly make it more effective than election day registration.

62. In the discussion of mobility effects earlier, I estimated the impact of eliminating the mobility effect at about 5.5 percentage points. Assuming this effect will be eliminated for the 60 percent of voters moving within-county: 0.60 × 5.5 = 3.3 (U.S. Bureau of the Census 1985). I should note, however, that I am skeptical that the entire mobility effect is truly attributable to re-registration difficulties. Therefore I tend to think this 3.3-percentage-point figure is an overestimate and recommend that it be treated very much as an upper-bound figure.

63. It should be noted, however, that the bill also mandates list cleaning at least once every four years, and that this list cleaning is most likely to affect recent nonvoters (recent voters are potentially exempt). The effects of this regular, mandated list cleaning could conceivably work in the opposite direction to the effects of eliminating automatic purging for not voting. However, no good estimate can be made of the strength of this countervailing force, primarily for lack of a good estimate of the effect of *frequency* of purging on turnout (though there are some indications that the effect of higher frequency is generally negative—see Committee for the Study of the American Electorate 1987).

64. The mandate for universal *mail* registration is unlikely to have any effect because studies—including my own—have consistently failed to find a positive relationship between the availability of mail registration and voter turnout levels.

from this reform was advanced earlier in this chapter. It is possible therefore that implementing this provision of HR 2190 would have a similar effect (perhaps more, because agency-based registration, as defined in HR 2190, appears to mandate wider coverage than many states with such systems currently have).

The combined effects of these provisions on turnout levels are difficult to gauge because they are unlikely to be directly additive,[65] and some of the individual estimates may be too high (or too low). Therefore a cautious approach is mandated that puts the projected effect of HR 2190 on turnout levels in relatively nonspecific terms at somewhere between 4 and 10 percentage points.[66] Thus at the low end the bill might add more than 7 million voters to the pool in national elections, and at the high end the increment might approach 18 million voters.

Another potential benefit of HR 2190 also deserves mention. This is the construction and maintenance of more accurate registration lists, which safeguard the integrity of the electoral process. To the extent states choose the NCOA option for cleaning their lists[67]—and the bill's financial provisions encourage states to do so—the result should be substantially more accurate, up-to-date registration lists. This has considerable value over and above the effect of the bill on voter turnout levels.

This discussion suggests that HR 2190, if implemented, would probably deliver substantial benefits (even if their exact magnitude is not entirely clear). But what of the costs? Are they too high to justify the implementation of HR 2190 despite these payoffs?

Estimations made by the Congressional Budget Office (CBO) suggest this is not the case. According to CBO,[68] the chief costs of implementing HR 2190 would come in the first five years after passage. These costs would stem from two sources.

---

65. See the discussion earlier in this chapter.

66. The low-end estimate assumes that nothing other than the motor voter provision has any effect. The high-end estimate is based on adding the individual estimates together, but doing so by translating the probability increments into probit increments. These probit increments can then be added together and the summed probit increments translated back into a probability increase. In this way it is possible to compensate for the reduced impact that changes in turnout-related characteristics have as the estimated level of turnout increases. (See appendix B for more discussion of the relationship between the probit model and predicted probabilities of voting.)

67. For reasons noted earlier in this section, I am skeptical of the efficacy of the two-postcard option in producing clean lists.

68. *National Voter Registration Act of 1989.*

The first source is implementing the motor voter system. CBO estimates the costs to states of setting up motor voter systems as specified in HR 2190 at about $20 million to $25 million a year for the first five years (after that the marginal costs of maintaining these systems should be relatively small). This amounts to $125 million,[69] using the high-end figure.

The second source is computerizing data necessary to implement provisions of the bill efficiently. This would apply to the motor voter provision and especially to the list-cleaning provision if the NCOA match option were selected. Though some states already have their records on computer, others would need to computerize motor vehicle data, voter registration data, or both. CBO estimates that attaining this minimum level of computerization across states would cost $60 million to $70 million.[70] But once computerized, the system should not cost much more than the present one to keep running.

The other costs associated with implementing the bill are comparatively minor and should mostly be offset, according to CBO, by administrative savings from streamlining and computerizing the voter registration system. Thus the estimated up-front costs appear to total less than $200 million, not an insignificant sum but hardly an immense one by today's budgetary standards. Of course it is quite possible this is an underestimate, but even assuming it is way off—say by a factor of two—the costs would still be less than $400 million—an average of only $80 million a year over the five-year phase-in period. This just does not seem like an excessive sum to spend for a fairly large increment in democratic participation.

The Senate Registration Reform Bill

The Senate bill (in its current incarnation, S 250) differs in some important respects from the House bill. To begin with, the motor voter provision is somewhat weaker than in the House bill. HR 2190 specifies that a driver's license application must include on the same form an application for voter registration. In contrast, S 250 allows states to

69. According to CBO, this figure could be partially offset by savings from having to hire fewer part-time registration workers around election time (a savings of $17 million to $24 million in the first five years).

70. Though the bill could technically be implemented without computerization, especially if the two-postcard list-cleaning option were selected, CBO estimates such an approach might double the costs for states in the long run.

provide two separate forms for the different applications if they are presented to the citizen at the same time. Because of this, S 250 links voter registration and driver's license applications less tightly, making registration less automatic than under HR 2190.

A second difference is in the list-cleaning provisions. Here the Senate bill is also weaker than the House bill. S 250 does not specify how often list cleaning must be done, nor does it specify the methods to be used (though it is similar to HR 2190 in prohibiting automatic deletion for not voting). States are simply required to establish a "general and comprehensive" program that makes a "reasonable" effort to ensure clean lists. Among other things this means that the NCOA match system of list cleaning, one of two mandated options under HR 2190 and the one that tends to be favored by the structure of that bill, receives no real push under S 250.[71]

Other provisions of the bill mandate universal mail and agency-based registration, provisions similar in spirit to HR 2190. However, S 250 does not specify as long a list of public places where agency-based registration must be conducted and is therefore in this sense also somewhat weaker than the House bill. On the other hand the language in S 250 designed to guard against discriminatory purging, denial of the right to vote, and so on is quite a bit stronger (and a great deal more complicated) than that in HR 2190.

Finally the funding provisions are quite different in the Senate bill. Under S 250 the only financial support provided for state-level implementation is a postal rate subsidy for necessary mailings. This subsidy (amounting to $21 million to $22 million over five years) would be provided to the states by the U.S. Postal Service, which would then be reimbursed by the federal government. This clearly tends to encourage mail-based list cleaning and registration rather than the level of computerization necessary for NCOA-based list cleaning and genuinely effective motor voter registration.

---

71. Another slight difference between the bills is that the Senate bill uses the term "voting registrar's jurisdiction" rather than "geographical voting unit" when defining the area within which movers would not have to re-register. It is not clear to me that this term makes any real difference, though the committee report does make a point of saying a voting registrar's jurisdiction should be no smaller than a "county, parish, city or town." Although this is an attempt to exclude very small areas from the definition, the fact remains that the final choice is the state's, just as in HR 2190. Thus I assume again that an intermediate level (county) is an appropriate way to approximate how this term might actually be used by states.

In terms of benefits, the effect of S 250 on turnout levels would probably be less than that of HR 2190. First, the mandated motor voter system is less strong (also less likely to be adequately computerized) and therefore likely to raise turnout levels less. Second, the NCOA-based list-cleaning method would probably be lightly used, thereby doing less to raise turnout levels by easing the difficulties of re-registration.[72]

How much less is difficult to say, because the Senate bill leaves a fair amount of discretion to the states on implementation—much more so than the House bill. As a result, state-level implementation could vary from something very close to the general mandates of the House bill to something quite different (and probably weaker for the reasons just outlined). This suggests that the range of impact for the Senate bill should be considered similar to that of the House bill (4 to 10 percentage points), but this estimate should be weighted more toward the lower end of the range.

Another way in which the benefits of S 250 are likely to be less than those of HR 2190 is in terms of maintaining accurate registration lists. Under the House bill, states are very likely to select the NCOA option for regularly cleaning their lists and therefore to derive the considerable benefit of substantially more accurate, up-to-date registration lists. Under the Senate bill this seems much less likely to happen.

In terms of costs, the CBO estimates for S 250 are quite similar to those for HR 2190. Again this reflects the fact that states could choose to implement the Senate bill in a way that looks very much like the House bill. However, it does not seem probable that this will happen, given the structure of the Senate bill and financial support from the federal government that is both less and mail oriented. I would expect the overall costs of the Senate bill to be somewhat lower (at least in the five-year phase-in period), because states will be less likely to choose and spend money on computerization. Thus if the costs of the House bill appear not to be excessive, the costs of the Senate bill should be even less so (but then the benefits are also likely to be less—perhaps substantially less).

72. Possibly, the weaker agency-based registration provision in S 250 also might result in less turnout increase from this source than under the House bill. The difference seems likely to be modest, though, because the Senate bill covers the main public agencies where, presumably, most of the net registration attributable to this method would take place. (In any event, it is not clear from estimations that agency-based registration in whatever form adds a great deal to turnout levels, so minor differences in implementation of this provision are especially unlikely to have much impact.)

Conclusions

Two conclusions follow immediately from this analysis. The first is that either bill implemented in its current form would probably have a positive impact on turnout levels. However, it also appears that provisions of the House bill are likely to have a greater impact on turnout levels than its Senate counterpart's. In addition HR 2190's provisions would probably also do more to ensure accurate, up-to-date registration lists, which are critical to the integrity of the electoral process. Thus if a choice can be made, I believe it would be preferable if the bill finally signed into law looked more like the House than the Senate bill.

The second conclusion is that although either bill would probably have a positive impact on turnout, both bills fall short of what could be done to maximize impact on voter turnout levels. Neither bill does anything about the early closing date issue, shown time and time again to be a deterrent to voter turnout. Even if it is politically unfeasible to mandate universal election day registration, it should still be possible to set closing dates at no more than seven days before an election. The estimations presented in this chapter suggest that even a closing date reform on this level could still provide a substantial boost to turnout levels.[73]

But even adding a closing date reform to the current registration reform packages would still not produce the maximum impact. This is because the maximum impact on turnout levels would logically be derived from cutting the costs of registration by the maximum amount—that is, by replacing personal registration altogether with some form of automatic, state-sponsored registration. A number of models—from the Canadian voter enumeration system to the nonforgeable voter identity cards used in Germany and Belgium—could be considered for use in the United States. None is probably exactly right for the United States, but if the concern is to push as close as possible to the upper-bound impact on turnout levels (about 15 percentage points), serious consideration of these alternative models is in order.

---

73. It must be acknowledged, however, that the additional effect of a closing date reform, in the context of the other reforms in the House and Senate bills, cannot be specified very precisely. To some extent, it probably depends on the substitutability of motor voter and closing date reforms. If the two reforms are largely substitutes for one another, the additional effect of the closing date reform would probably be low. On the other hand if the amount of overlap is small, the additional effect of closing date reform could be substantial.

Political Effects of Registration Reform

Given that general registration reform would probably have a substantial, positive impact on voter turnout levels without incurring excessive costs, one might well ask why more progress is not being made on this front. Why is it so difficult to get past the debating stage to the enacting stage?

This is certainly a complicated question, as the tangled recent history of registration reform efforts suggests. Whatever the nuances, however, it seems fair to say that much of the controversy about registration reform stems from beliefs about the political impact of such reform. Simply put, Democrats tend to believe registration reform will help them, whereas Republicans tend to believe reform will hurt them.[74]

A similar argument was examined in the discussion of nonvoting and election outcomes in chapter 3.[75] As explained there, a certain conventional wisdom holds that nonvoting promotes Republican victories, whereas nonvoter mobilization promotes Democratic victories. But as that discussion showed, it turns out most election outcomes are relatively insensitive to the level of voter turnout and therefore relatively hard to change through increased nonvoter mobilization. Moreover, as chapter 3 went on to show, even *general* (that is, 100 percent) mobilization of nonvoters is unlikely to change election outcomes or even the partisan and issue preferences of the voting pool in a substantial way.

Given that general mobilization of nonvoters does not appear to have a large political impact, it would seem to follow that the relatively modest mobilization of nonvoters under registration reform would also lack such an impact. In fact, one would expect the impact to be a great deal smaller because the voting pool would expand by so much less under registration reform (8 percentage points versus 50 points under general mobilization). However, it could still be argued that registration

74. In addition, many local politicians believe that new voters simply tend to upset the status quo—which, in turn, hurts the local incumbents who *are* the status quo. There may be a kernel of truth here, in the sense that low-turnout elections—which local elections generally are—are more susceptible to the effects of turnout surges than higher-turnout state and federal elections. This is because mathematically a 5-percentage-point increase in turnout will make a larger difference, all else equal, to electoral contests that traditionally draw 20 percent of the electorate than to electoral contests that draw 50 percent of the electorate (see the discussion of this point in chapter 3). This does not mean that a given increment of nonvoters *would* necessarily change local election outcomes, but it does mean that the chances of this happening are somewhat greater at the local level.

75. See "Does Nonvoting Make a Difference?" in chapter 3.

reform will not randomly mobilize nonvoters, and instead will mobilize precisely those elements among nonvoters most likely to skew the voting pool toward the Democrats. This is undoubtedly what some Republicans fear (and what some Democrats hope).

Some support for this argument is provided by the data in table 4-2. These data do indeed show that projected voting rates under registration reform will increase the most among disadvantaged, Democratic-leaning groups—that is, the poor, the uneducated, blue-collar workers, blacks, and so on. But it is impossible to tell from these data how much the composition of the voting pool would really change as a result of differential turnout increases.

To answer this question, it is necessary to look directly at data on the projected composition of the voting pool, both before and after registration reform (tables 4-4 and 4-5). These data are presented under three different scenarios: (1) a "low" scenario, in which turnout only increases about 4 percentage points under registration reform; (2) a "moderate" scenario, in which turnout increases about 8 points (this corresponds to the prediction of the original model presented in this chapter); and (3) a "high" scenario, in which turnout increases almost 16 points.[76]

The story told by the data on the projected demographic composition of the voting pool could not be clearer (table 4-4). The effect of registration reform on the demographic composition of the voting electorate

76. Projections of the composition of the electorate under registration reform were performed using the method pioneered by Wolfinger and Rosenstone 1980. Thus the "actual" voting pool in my comparison, as in theirs, is a *predicted* actual voting pool, not the voting pool in the sample.

The "low" and "high" estimations were performed by simply halving and doubling, respectively, the estimated individual increments in voting probability under the basic model reported in appendix B. Thus, the low and high estimations assume that, whatever the overall impact on turnout, the relative distribution of individual effects will be the same as under the moderate scenario (the basic model). This is equivalent to assuming that, whether there is a little or a lot of liberalization, liberalization will have the most effect in states with stringent registration laws and the least effect in states with loose registration laws (and none at all in North Dakota, where registration does not exist). I believe this is the most plausible approach to take, given the lack of specific models for these alternative scenarios.

Finally, these projections are based on 1984 data, because this is the last year for which I had adequate registration data (see appendix A for a discussion of registration data sources). The use of 1984, as opposed to 1988, data should not have much effect on the object of interest here—the change in composition from enlarging the voting pool. The 1984 census voting survey is used for table 4-4, whereas the 1984 NES survey is used for table 4-5. The same model was used for both data sets, however, on the theory that the census-based model provides the most accurate estimates of the impact of registration laws on turnout.

More details on these estimations and associated issues may be found in appendix B.

TABLE 4-4. *Estimated Composition of Voting Pool under Registration Reform, by Demographic Group*
Percent

| | | Projected | | |
Characteristic	Actual	Low estimate	Moderate estimate	High estimate
Education				
0–8 years	8.6	8.9	9.2	9.6
9–11 years	9.8	10.2	10.5	11.0
High school graduate	39.1	39.3	39.6	39.9
Some college	20.5	20.3	20.1	19.8
College graduate or more	22.0	21.3	20.7	19.7
Occupation				
Laborers	1.7	1.8	1.8	1.9
Operatives-craft	13.1	13.4	13.6	14.0
Service	7.9	8.1	8.2	8.4
Housewives	17.6	17.6	17.6	17.7
Farm	1.8	1.8	1.8	1.8
Clerical-sales	19.0	18.8	18.7	18.5
Managerial-administrative	8.9	8.7	8.6	8.3
Professional-technical	12.7	12.4	12.1	11.6
Family income (1988 dollars)				
Less than 7,500	8.7	9.0	9.3	9.8
7,500–14,999	15.2	15.5	15.7	16.1
15,000–19,999	9.8	10.0	10.1	10.3
20,000–29,999	19.3	19.2	19.2	19.2
30,000–39,999	16.3	16.2	16.1	16.0
40,000–59,999	18.6	18.3	18.0	17.5
60,000 or more	12.1	11.8	11.5	11.1
Age				
18 to 20	4.3	4.5	4.7	5.0
21 to 24	7.2	7.4	7.7	8.1
25 to 34	22.3	22.5	22.8	23.1
35 to 44	19.3	19.2	19.1	18.9
45 to 54	14.8	14.6	14.4	14.1
55 to 64	15.1	14.8	14.6	14.2
65 to 74	11.2	11.0	10.9	10.6
75 or older	5.8	5.9	5.9	6.0
Race				
White	88.8	88.6	88.5	88.2
Black	9.6	9.8	9.9	10.2
Other	1.6	1.6	1.6	1.7
Region				
South	31.8	32.4	33.0	33.9
West	19.2	19.1	19.1	19.0
Northeast	22.4	22.2	22.0	21.6
Midwest	26.6	26.3	26.0	25.5

SOURCE: Author's computations based on model in appendix B.

TABLE 4-5. *Estimated Composition of Voting Pool under Registration Reform, by Partisanship, Ideology, and Selected Issue Positions*
Percent

		Projected		
Characteristic	Actual	Low estimate	Moderate estimate	High estimate
Partisanship				
Strong Democrat	17.0	17.1	17.1	17.2
Weak Democrat	19.7	19.7	19.7	19.8
Independent/Democrat	10.5	10.5	10.6	10.6
Independent	10.5	10.7	10.8	11.1
Independent/Republican	13.7	13.6	13.5	13.4
Weak Republican	15.1	15.1	15.0	14.9
Strong Republican	13.5	13.4	13.3	13.1
Ideology				
Extremely liberal	1.4	1.4	1.4	1.5
Liberal	8.2	8.2	8.1	8.0
Slightly liberal	10.2	10.2	10.1	10.1
Moderate	24.3	24.2	24.1	24.0
Slightly conservative	16.2	16.0	15.9	15.6
Conservative	14.8	14.6	14.5	14.3
Extremely conservative	1.5	1.5	1.5	1.5
No placement	23.4	23.9	24.3	25.1
Should abortion be allowed?				
Never	10.9	11.1	11.2	11.4
Only if rape, incest, etc.	29.5	29.6	29.7	29.9
Only if clear need	21.1	21.1	21.0	20.8
By choice	38.5	38.3	38.2	37.9
Too much pushing for equal rights?				
Agree strongly	18.2	18.2	18.3	18.3
Agree somewhat	26.3	26.3	26.3	26.3
Neither	11.9	11.9	11.9	11.8
Disagree somewhat	21.4	21.4	21.4	21.4
Disagree strongly	22.2	22.2	22.2	22.2
Should government see that everyone has job and good standard of living?				
Government should help	26.0	26.2	26.4	26.8
Middle-of-road	21.1	21.0	21.0	20.9
People get ahead on own	41.5	41.1	40.8	40.2
No placement	11.4	11.6	11.8	12.1

SOURCE: Author's computations based on model in appendix B.

is likely to be *negligible*. Not surprisingly this inconsequential impact is especially noticeable with the low-turnout increase scenario, in which overall turnout would increase about 4 percentage points. The proportion of high school dropouts in the voting pool would increase just 0.7 percentage point, while the proportion of college graduates would decline by the same meager amount. Similarly the proportion of those with very low family income (less than $7,500) would go up only 0.3 percentage point, while the proportion of those with relatively high income (more than $60,000) would go down the same amount. Finally the proportion of blacks in the voting pool would go up a minuscule 0.2 percentage point.

All of these changes are certainly in the direction that should, all else equal, help the Democrats. But it is very difficult to believe changes of this magnitude would have any real impact on the relative fortunes of Republicans and Democrats. In all likelihood, these changes are simply too small to enter into the determination of election outcomes.

Nor does this impression change a great deal when the moderate 8-percentage-point increase is examined. The projected increases are as follows: for high school dropouts, 1.3 points; the very poor, 0.6 point; and blacks, 0.3 point. The projected decreases for college graduates and those with high incomes are 1.3 points and 0.6 point. Again these differences appear to be too small to justify the level of political paranoia (and fantasy) attached to them.

Finally even under the high-increase scenario, which reaches the estimated upper bound for the impact of registration reform (no matter how radical) and yields a 16-percentage-point overall increase, the changes in demographic composition are still relatively minor. The projected increases are as follows: for high school dropouts, 2.2 points; the very poor, 1.1 points: and blacks, 0.6 point. The projected decrease for college graduates reaches 2.3 points and that for the high-income group reaches 1 point. Thus even the education category differences—which are generally the largest among all the demographic groups—remain small, while the income differences are even smaller and racial differences smaller still.[77] It therefore appears that no matter how radical and far-reaching the program of registration reform, the resulting

77. This pattern was also observed by Wolfinger and Rosenstone 1980 in their analysis of projected demographic differences from expanding the voting pool. This underscores the robustness of the findings presented here on compositional change in the voting pool because Wolfinger and Rosenstone's analysis was based on a different data set and a (somewhat) different model.

pool of voters is likely to differ—at least in demographic terms—only marginally from the current pool of voters.

But perhaps nonvoters mobilized by registration reform are likely to differ from current voters primarily in their attitudes, rather than their demographics. If this were true, the data by demographic category in table 4-4 could be hiding substantial effects on the voting pool from newly mobilized nonvoters. However, an analysis of the projected composition of the voting pool by partisanship, ideology, and key issue positions for the three different registration reform scenarios shows that the demographic analysis does not understate the amount of change from registration reform (table 4-5). In fact these data suggest registration reform would change the attitudes of the voting electorate even *less*, not more, than it would change the demographics. For example, under the moderate (8-percentage-point increase) scenario the proportion of the electorate with some partisan tie to the Democrats increases just 0.2 percentage point[78]—hardly enough to justify the popping of champagne corks down at Democratic headquarters.[79] And, even under the radically optimistic high-increase scenario, in which the numbers of newly mobilized nonvoters are doubled, the total Democratic windfall is still only 0.4 percentage point.

The rest of the data in the table tell a similar story. Registration reform would have very little impact on ideological leanings among the voting pool—and would certainly not move voters in a definably liberal direction. (The biggest change is a slight increase in the proportion professing no ideology.) Nor would registration reform have more than a trivial impact on issue positions. Under the moderate scenario slightly more voters (0.3 percent) would want abortion completely outlawed, slightly more (0.4 percent) would want the government to see everyone has a job and a good standard of living, and (very) slightly more (0.1 percent) would think there has been too much pushing for equal rights. (And these tiny figures do not get much larger when the upper-bound, high-turnout increase scenario is tested). All these changes are minuscule

78. Again the basic results are very similar to those of Wolfinger and Rosenstone 1980, p. 85, who found that just a 0.3 percent increase in Democratic sympathies from registration reform. Thus the finding of a minimal impact on partisan leanings from registration reform also appears robust.

79. Wolfinger and Rosenstone 1980, p. 86, illustrate this point with some simple estimations of the impact of a slightly different partisan distribution on state races. They found that the amount of partisan change they measured (which was actually slightly more than in my estimations) would probably have changed only one outcome out of 200 state races between 1964 and 1976.

and seem highly unlikely to have any discernible effect on the character of the voting pool, much less change actual election outcomes.

The conclusion seems inescapable: registration reform, under virtually any conceivable scenario, will have negligible partisan impact. The Democrats will not be significantly helped, and the Republicans will not be significantly hurt. The tremendous partisan concern about the impact of registration reform is therefore profoundly misplaced and should be put aside in the interests of moving ahead on the reform packages discussed in the previous section.

Other Approaches to Cutting the Costs of Voting

So far this chapter has been basically concerned with the issue of registration reform, because reforming the personal registration system appears to be central to cutting the costs of voting for U.S. citizens. But, though registration reform is the most obvious, and probably the most effective, way to cut the costs of voting, it may not be the *only* way. This section investigates this possibility by briefly considering some alternative approaches to cutting the costs of voting.

One alternative approach to cutting the costs of voting periodically receives legislative attention in Congress (though it rarely gets anywhere). This is the concept of making election day a holiday on the theory that simply making it to the polling place on a workday is a substantial cost for many people, so this cost should be eliminated by making election day a "free" day for everyone. In this way, people can simply vote at their leisure on the election day holiday, leading presumably to higher turnout.

I am skeptical of this analysis. To begin with, most polling places are open for a substantial period after (and before) work, so most people who work could presumably vote at those times, if they were so motivated. Second, it is not clear that having more free time necessarily makes the expenditure of time on voting less onerous. Third, it is at least possible that the gain in turnout from hard workers who could not vote may be canceled out by the loss in turnout from citizens who decide to engage in holiday activities not conducive to voting (such as going out of town, "partying"). Finally, the election day holiday does no good whatsoever for those who are not already registered,[80] so most

---

80. Except in states that have election day registration, so that citizens could theoretically take advantage of the election day holiday to register and vote at the same time.

nonvoters are not likely to benefit from this reform. For all these reasons I think the election day holiday should be placed fairly far down the list of possible cost-cutting reforms.

Another alternative goes the election day holiday proposal one better. According to this approach, the problem is not making it to the polling booth on a workday, the problem is making it to the polling booth, *period*. The theory here is that the very act of getting out of the house (or workplace) and traveling to the polling place is a substantial cost in and of itself and constitutes a serious obstacle for many people. This cost should therefore be eliminated by replacing polling places with remote electronic voting that can be done at people's convenience in their homes or workplaces (or perhaps even in their cars for people with the appropriate high-tech equipment).

This argument certainly has some theoretical merit. Getting to the polling place is indisputably a real cost of voting, albeit a fairly modest one for most individuals. It follows that eliminating this cost should have a positive effect on the likelihood of voting, all else equal.

But all else might *not* be equal. It is at least possible that some of the expressive benefits associated with voting may be linked to the physical act of casting a ballot at a collective gathering place. This would particularly be true to the extent people are motivated to vote by the support of others (or fear of their disapproval), a factor that would be attenuated by not having to show up in a public place. The more these factors are pertinent, of course, the more turnout gains from cutting the physical costs of voting would be counterbalanced by turnout losses from lower levels of citizen motivation.

Evidence from the field further suggests the problematic nature of this approach. Abramson, Arterton, and Orren, in one of the only reviews of available evidence on remote electronic voting, report that low turnout is more the rule than the exception in the various experiments conducted with "televoting."[81] Of course these experiments have not been conducted with any election on the scale of a presidential election, so it is not certain that televoting would not have a strong turnout-promoting effect in the proper context. Still the lack of success so far with this approach does strike a note of caution about this particular method of cost cutting.

It would seem caution is further advised when the tremendous cost

81. Abramson, Arterton, and Orren 1988.

of providing electronic access to voting for all Americans is considered. Perhaps several decades from now these costs will be trivial, but at the present they would certainly be very high (not to mention all the security difficulties universal electronic voting would pose). This suggests that—especially considering the uncertain payoff in terms of higher participation—remote electronic voting should also be put fairly far down the list of cost-cutting reforms.

Some of the same criticisms could be made of another approach to eliminating the trip to the polling place, though here the problems seem less severe. This is the extension of absentee voting to all registered voters—so-called no excuse or unrestricted absentee voting.[82] Under such a system, individuals need not qualify for absentee ballots by being absent on election day or sick or disabled (as is the current practice in all but a handful of states[83])—they can vote absentee simply because they prefer to do so. All they need do typically is request an absentee ballot in writing, which can then be filled out in their own home and mailed back to the registrar.

Thus just as with remote electronic voting, citizens voting absentee save the cost of the trip to the polling place but also lose whatever benefits accrue from the communal act of voting at a polling place. In addition the individual cost savings derived from voting at home should be weighed against the additional costs of having to request the absentee ballot (the balance of these cost additions and subtractions is not clear). Moreover, monetary cost problems may crop up as well—though not as severe as with remote electronic voting—because evidence exists that absentee balloting is substantially more expensive than conventional balloting.[84] Finally no reliable evidence has been found yet that unrestricted absentee voting actually has a positive effect on turnout rates.[85] For all these reasons I believe that unrestricted absentee

82. A related development is so-called early voting, currently being implemented in Texas, where citizens can vote for 17 days prior to elections at special polling places in grocery stores, shopping malls, and so forth, rather than having to vote at their polling place on election day. For useful—albeit excessively optimistic—summaries of this and other relatively new approaches to voting, see Christe and Cooper 1991.

83. States that allow unrestricted absentee voting include Alaska, California, Kansas, Oregon, and Washington (League of Women Voters 1988).

84. Estimates from Florida and California suggest that absentee balloting is roughly three times as expensive as conventional balloting (Christe and Cooper 1991).

85. Though these programs do tend to be relatively new (all appear to be less than ten years old), so there may not have been enough time for the impact on turnout to develop.

voting, though more technically feasible than remote electronic voting, should also be placed fairly far down the list of possible cost-cutting reforms.

Thus it appears that registration reform, while not the only logical possibility for cutting costs, is far and away the most straightforward, the most feasible, and the most likely to be effective. The alternatives discussed above would certainly not do as substitutes for registration reform and may not even be useful as supplements to such reform. These alternatives should therefore be deemphasized until such time as the registration issue has been dealt with effectively. It may then be appropriate to reconsider the efficacy of these alternatives, but at the present time I believe more attention to them would be unproductive, if not diversionary.

Conclusion

This chapter has investigated the possible efficacy of cutting the costs of voting as a route to higher turnout levels. Three main conclusions have been reached from this investigation.

First, one particular way of cutting voting costs—the reform of the personal registration system—would probably have a strong, positive effect on turnout levels. This effect is estimated at about 8 percentage points, though different approaches to registration reform, as well as various imponderables concerning the effects of real-world implementation, might make that figure as low as 4 percentage points or as high as 15 percentage points.

Second, the current bills before Congress—particularly the House bill, HR 2190—show significant promise of realizing this potential turnout increase if passed and effectively implemented. Moreover this turnout increase from registration reform is likely to be realized without any significant impact on the partisan balance of forces, thereby removing one of the chief objections to progress on these bills.

Finally, registration reform, no matter how structured, is very unlikely (in and of itself) to "solve" the turnout problem. Even under the most optimistic scenario, the turnout increase from registration reform would put turnout in presidential elections only a couple of points higher ($50 + 15 = 65$) than it was in 1960 at the beginning of the turnout decline era. This level of turnout—an improbable outcome, it should be stressed, even if registration reform *is* implemented—is still 15 points lower than the average among other industrialized democracies. This strongly suggests that a successful approach to the problem of low voter turnout must involve not just lowering the costs of participation but also enhancing the benefits of such participation.

5

Conclusion:
The Problem of
Voter Motivation

Chapter 4 demonstrated that cutting the costs of voting through registration reform would help increase turnout levels in the United States. But I also showed that the extent of this improvement would be limited—no more than a 14- to 15-percentage-point increase in turnout at the maximum with an increase half that being more plausible. This suggests that if U.S. turnout is ever to reach respectable levels by international standards, enhancing the perceived benefits of participation, not just cutting the costs, will be necessary.

This in turn means that the problem of voter motivation must be confronted directly. Somehow citizens' motivation levels must be increased so that participation in an election seems like a meaningful exercise rather than a pointless chore, and therefore provides citizens with expressive benefits of some reasonable magnitude. If this is not done, simply removing the structural barriers to participation (for example, through registration reform) will be only a partial fix for the low-turnout problem. The "motivational barriers" will remain intact.

Consideration of the research results presented in chapter 2 gives this reasoning added force. If it is true that the decline in turnout since 1960 is primarily attributable to an evolving disconnection from politics that has eroded voter motivation, then lowering the costs of voting does nothing by itself to address the root cause of declining voter turnout. Hence it is possible that, even were registration reform to be implemented and to produce immediate increases in turnout levels, the decline in turnout might soon resume, resulting eventually in turnout

148

levels as low or lower than they are today. Thus not only is registration reform by itself unlikely to produce high turnout levels, but it also may not even produce a lasting increase in turnout levels unless the problem of voter motivation is adequately addressed.

But how can this be done? Two limitations immediately present themselves when a person attempts to think through and justify possible solutions to the voter motivation problem. The first is that trying to solve the voter motivation problem requires more justification than lowering voting costs through registration reform. Though it can be argued that everyone has a right to exercise the franchise without incurring unreasonable and artificially high costs, it is more difficult to argue that everyone has a right to be motivated. Therefore, the costs of increasing voter motivation must be weighed carefully against the benefits that could accrue from increased voter turnout to ensure that proposed solutions can be adequately justified.

This becomes a particularly important consideration to keep in mind when it is recalled that nonvoting is not nearly as pernicious a phenomenon as many people suppose. Because low voter turnout does *not* currently produce a situation in which the affluent dictate election outcomes—as is frequently asserted—then increasing voter turnout will not have the compelling payoff of eliminating this situation. Instead the payoff lies, as I argued earlier, in less dramatic improvements in the quality of political life—particularly in terms of the democratic link between elites and citizens. Now these improvements may be important—I believe they are—but it does not necessarily follow that they justify substantial tinkering with the political system simply on this basis. Tinkering inevitably involves costs, and it should be reasonably certain that the benefits of such tinkering will outweigh the attendant costs.

This suggests it will be easiest to justify reforms to increase voter motivation that would have other desirable effects on the political system beyond increasing voter turnout. Such reforms may make it possible to kill two birds with one stone, generating both higher turnout *and* a generally improved political process with the same set of reforms. This would avoid the necessity of having to justify fairly substantial changes in the conduct of American politics in the name of higher turnout alone.

The salience of this point is underscored by the second limitation constraining attempts to think through the voter motivation problem and how to solve it: it is far more difficult to estimate the impact on turnout of reforms designed to increase voter motivation than it is to estimate the impact of reforms designed to cut voting costs. As discussed earlier, because states vary in the stringency of their registration laws, the impact of registration laws (and their liberalization) on turnout can be modeled fairly cleanly using existing data. No such analogous geographical variation exists in the realm of voter motivation factors, however, so existing data[1] do not allow the turnout impact of most voter motivation–oriented reforms to be estimated with any precision.

Indeed existing data generally provide at best only hints about what sort of reforms *might* have an impact on turnout, not definitive judgments about *whether* these reforms would have impact or *how much*. This uncertainty further suggests the desirability of a multipurpose approach to the voter motivation problem rather than one rooted narrowly in the objective of higher turnout levels.

The purpose of this chapter then is to examine possible solutions to the voter motivation problem within the limitations just outlined. First I consider some general approaches to increasing voter motivation and assess their relative plausibility and usefulness. Then I outline some specific methods for increasing voter motivation based on what I believe is the most plausible approach. I conclude with some observations about the possible effectiveness of these methods and the general future of American voter turnout.

General Approaches to Increasing Voter Motivation

One approach for increasing voter motivation flows from the analysis presented in chapter 1, which showed that the U.S. political system—in terms of the legal structure of voting, the structure of electoral competition, and the level of party mobilization—is generally organized so as to generate a relatively low level of perceived benefits for voters. In other words the U.S. system is set up so that voter motivation is "naturally" low relative to motivation in other countries. A logical solution then is to change the U.S. system so that, in terms of legal, electoral competition, and party mobilization characteristics, voting

---

1. This is not to say that such precise estimates are theoretically impossible. Given, for example, exactly the right survey questions asked over a sufficiently long period or a sufficiently complex social experiment, such estimates could be made. But given existing "real world" data (such as the NES, the census, and so on), they cannot.

looks more like it does in other countries. This method of increasing voter motivation might be called the big fix approach.

The Big Fix Approach

First consider possible alterations in the legal structure of voting. The legal structure of voting in the United States is generally unfavorable to electoral participation chiefly because the personal registration system has a large effect on the *costs* of voting. Thus changes in the legal structure of voting are generally thought of as ways to cut voting costs, not increase voter motivation.

However, it is also possible to affect voter motivation through changes in the legal structure of voting. One way of doing this would be through implementation of a compulsory voting law, such as those in effect in Australia, Belgium, and Italy. Under such a law the avoidance of punishment for not voting becomes a "benefit" and therefore a motivation for voting. Of course these laws tend to be very lightly enforced, but even the threat of enforcement may be enough to affect voter motivation substantially.

A related approach is actually to pay people for voting—or perhaps provide the opportunity to win some sort of lottery through their participation. To the best of my knowledge, this is not currently practiced in any *legal* way in any industrialized democracy, so no models or examples can guide such an approach. On a theoretical level, however, the logic seems compelling: to increase voter motivation, the most direct and effective way may be to simply put cold hard cash in people's pockets.

Another possible big fix would be to alter the structure of electoral competition. I have shown that a variety of different aspects of the structure of electoral competition impinge on the expressive benefits of voting and therefore on voter motivation: the extent to which electoral districts are competitive, especially on a national level; the extent of electoral disproportionality; whether the legislative system is unicameral or bicameral; and the extent of multipartyism.[2] On each of these characteristics, except for multipartyism, the U.S. electoral competition structure tends to depress the benefits of voting, so clearly some potential exists here for increasing voter motivation.

This potential could be realized in two main ways. The first would be through abolishing the bicameral structure of the U.S. Congress,

2. See the discussion in chapter 1.

replacing it with a unicameral structure. In practical terms this would amount to abolishing the Senate and making the House the sovereign legislative body.

The second way would be through abolishing the single-member, winner-take-all structure of U.S. elections. In terms of the House,[3] this could be done by abolishing the one-member-per-district system, replacing it with multimember districts covering entire states or large subdivisions of states.[4] These members could then be allocated to different parties in proportion to the votes cast over the entire district. Such a proportional representation system would presumably make minority parties more competitive in areas currently dominated by one party, as well as reduce the extent of electoral disproportionality.

In terms of the presidency, the winner-take-all structure could be altered most directly by abolishing the electoral college, replacing it with simple, direct election of the president by popular vote. A less direct approach would be to keep the electoral college but allocate electoral votes within a state, proportionally based on some standard such as popular vote,[5] number of congressional districts won, and so on. Either the direct or indirect approach should make minority-party candidates more competitive within states currently dominated by one party.[6]

The final big fix for the voter motivation problem would be to change existing levels of party mobilization. As discussed in chapter 1, relatively low levels of party mobilization appear to play a key role in depressing the perceived benefits of voting in the United States. It follows that increasing party mobilization levels to levels common in other countries would do much to raise these benefits and increase voter

3. The Senate is not included in this discussion because it would be quite difficult, if not impossible, to distribute the two-senator-per-state allocation on other than a winner-take-all basis.

4. Arguments for this approach, as well as more details on how such an approach might be implemented, may be found in Cossolotto 1991, 1992; and Amy 1992.

5. In general allocating electoral votes proportional to the popular vote within a state should be roughly equivalent to having national direct election of the president while keeping something called "the electoral college." This is because under such a system the proportion of the popular vote for a given candidate and the proportion of electoral college votes for that candidate should be very close to one another. It is mathematically unlikely in fact that these proportions would differ substantially from one another.

6. Some differences should be noted, however. Simple direct election of the president would presumably make mobilization throughout a state important, because every vote would count the same. In contrast allocating electoral votes proportional to congressional districts won within a state would make mobilization unlikely in those districts where the party balance is too lopsided, because minority votes in those districts would not really count.

motivation.[7] This increased mobilization could be accomplished through the development of dense and penetrative party organizations along European lines and much stronger party linkages to social groups and organizations.

How should the big fix approach be evaluated? On the positive side cross-national analyses indicate that such an approach, considered strictly in terms of turnout impact, would probably increase voter participation levels. For example, if laws were passed and implemented that punished nonvoters or materially rewarded voters, U.S. turnout in all likelihood would increase.[8] Or if laws were passed and implemented that abolished the Senate and established proprortional representation for the House and established direct election of the president (or at least abolished the winner-take-all system for allocation of electoral votes), turnout levels in the United States would probably go up.[9] Or if U.S. parties suddenly developed levels of mobilization akin to those in European countries, U.S. voter participation levels would probably rise.[10]

Now, these cross-national analyses are based on very small samples and should be treated very cautiously—much more cautiously, in my view, than the large-sample analyses of registration reform presented in

7. It is also possible that increased levels of party mobilization could reduce voting costs. Most directly, parties could provide more physical assistance to citizens in registering and getting to polling places. Less directly, increased party mobilization might reduce the amount of information citizens have to gather independently to make a voting decision, thereby reducing information costs.

8. Exactly how much is difficult to say. The model in Jackman 1987 implies that compulsory voting adds 13 percentage points to a country's turnout rate. In my view this estimate should be treated as an upper-bound estimate because his model technically does not apply to the United States (or Switzerland) and his compulsory voting variable is, in effect, a dummy variable for Australia, Belgium, and Italy, so it could be capturing effects caused by some other trait(s) these countries share in common. No data of any kind are available on the effects of paying people to vote, so no estimate of the impact of adopting this practice can be offered.

9. The magnitude of the probable effect on turnout is difficult to gauge. Based on the models in Powell 1986 and Jackman 1987, unicameralism could add as much as 6 percentage points to the turnout rate, whereas some combination of proportional representation and abolishing the electoral college (that is, direct election of the president or eliminating winner-take-all distribution of electoral votes) might add from 5 to 12 percentage points to overall turnout. Again I believe these estimates should be treated very much as upper-bound figures because: (a) these models may apply only poorly to the United States; (b) the variables in the models may be capturing effects of other, unobserved turnout-related traits with similar cross-national distributions; and (c) these reforms may promote multipartyism, which should *depress* turnout, according to Jackman's model (the negative effect could be as much as 4 percentage points).

10. The estimate in Powell 1986, p. 34, is that bringing U.S. party mobilization levels up to the level in an average democracy would increase turnout about 10 percentage points.

chapter 4. However, they do provide some empirical support for the idea that these big fixes—whatever their other effects—might actually increase voter turnout. This is clearly a point in favor of implementing one or several of these big fixes, if Americans wish to see higher turnout levels.

But these big fixes have obvious and serious negative aspects as well. Some may be virtually impossible (such as making U.S. political parties like those in other countries). Some are unconstitutional (such as abolishing the electoral college). Some are antithetical to American values (such as forcing citizens to vote or paying them to vote). Some might cause political disruption of unknown magnitude (such as instituting proportional representation). And all involve very large changes in the structure and functioning of the American political system. Can such large changes really be justified simply in the name of increasing voter participation?

I do not think so. With such radical changes—even assuming one could overcome political and other obstacles and implement them— one runs a real risk of having the cure be worse than the disease. And nonvoting, as I stressed earlier in this chapter, is simply not harmful enough by itself to the body politic to justify taking such a substantial risk. It appears therefore that the search must go farther afield for a reasonable approach to the voter motivation problem.

Fortunately I believe a moderate alternative to the big fix approach exists—one that, though less straightforward, could provide benefits both in the form of increased voter turnout *and* general improvements in the conduct of U.S. politics. That is, this approach would have positive value in and of itself and need not be justified solely in terms of its impact on turnout. Moreover, this approach has relatively little downside risk and does not involve a chimerical quest to make the U.S. political system look and act like those in other countries. Instead the approach is based on a "more like us" orientation that accepts and builds on the unique nature of American politics.

Reconnecting Americans to Politics

As discussed in chapter 1, the individual-level characteristics of U.S. citizens are a key positive influence on the perceived benefits of voting—one of the *only* positive influences, in fact, within a political system that tends to produce low voter motivation. In chapter 2 it was shown that voter motivation from this source has been declining over time as a result of ongoing processes of social and political disconnection, and that this decline in voter motivation has played a critical role in bringing down U.S. turnout levels. This suggests that the individual attributes of Americans could be a source of enhanced voter motivation for citizens—and indeed these attributes may need to be strengthened at the current time to counter the influence of recent trends.

Of course, not all the individual characteristics of citizens can reasonably be viewed as candidates for improvement—at least in any conscious way. This is particularly true of those characteristics believed to tap different aspects of social connectedness,[11] such as age, marital status, church attendance, residential mobility, and so on. These are characteristics whose levels among the population are set by either natural demographic processes[12] or personal decisions inappropriate for conscious social intervention. Clearly people cannot (or should not) be made to get older, get married, attend church, or stay in the same place. Thus changing individual characteristics tapping social connectedness does not appear to be a promising route toward enhancing voter motivation.[13]

Changing individual characteristics tapping *political* connectedness,[14] however, has a great deal more potential. No one can mandate, of course, that Americans feel more psychologically involved in politics, believe more in the responsiveness of government, care more about the political parties, know more about the positions of parties and candidates in elections, and so on. But all of these characteristics should, at least potentially, be susceptible to changes in the political environment. And the political environment should, at least potentially, be susceptible to changes (structural or voluntary) in how campaigns are conducted and how government, parties, candidates, and the media organize their relationships with voters. This suggests that if proper changes are made in the conduct of campaigns and the behavior of various actors in the political process, it may be possible to counter trends of the last three decades and *reconnect* Americans to politics.

11. See chapter 2 for a discussion of these characteristics.
12. The age distribution is already changing in a turnout-promoting way, anyway, as the baby boom generation moves through the life cycle.
13. Because of this the implication of analyses—such as Knack 1991a, 1992a, and Pomper and Sernekos 1989, which blame the post-1960 decline in turnout on the decline in social connectedness—is that little can be done to reverse the decline in turnout. As explained in chapter 2, however, I believe these analyses overestimate the role of social connectedness in turnout decline and, therefore, underestimate the possibilities for improvement.
14. See chapter 2 for a discussion of these characteristics.

In turn, this should lead to an increase in voter motivation and therefore to increased voter turnout.

Possible Methods for Reconnecting Americans to Politics

But *how* can Americans be reconnected to politics? And what are the most important characteristics to concentrate on when attempting to reforge these links? The first step in answering these questions is to reconsider the evidence presented in chapter 2 concerning turnout decline and the erosion of political connectedness.

The model-based evidence presented there (see table 2-6) showed that not all characteristics tapping political connectedness played equal roles in the turnout decline phenomenon. Instead sharp decreases in citizens' psychological involvement in politics and citizens' sense of government responsiveness played the key roles in bringing down turnout levels. This suggests that attempts to reconnect Americans to politics should focus especially on ways to encourage psychological involvement in politics and promote a sense that the government is responsive to the ordinary citizen.

The evidence presented in chapter 2 also showed that some other aspects of political connectedness that affect turnout—partisanship, concern over the election outcome, perceived difference between the parties, and knowledge of parties and candidates—played, as a group, only a modest role in turnout decline, primarily because levels of these characteristics changed only moderately over time. This makes these characteristics a less obvious focus for attempts to reconnect Americans to politics. Still the well-documented relationships between these characteristics and turnout[15] suggest increasing levels of these characteristics could potentially be important and, therefore, should not be ruled out completely.

Furthermore I believe that the information-oriented nature of two of these characteristics (perceived difference between the parties and knowledge of parties and candidates) points in a valuable direction for the general project of reconnecting Americans to politics. Though it may be implausible to expect a characteristic like party identification (partisanship) to increase much in intensity, because the salience of parties has been generally declining in American society, it is quite plausible, it seems to me, to expect levels of information-oriented char-

15. See model B-1 in appendix B.

acteristics to increase, because the role of information in society has grown steadily and continues to increase. In other words citizens' *affect* toward parties and candidates may have some quite serious limits, but I can see no such limits on citizens' *information* about these parties and candidates. Information, at least, is something U.S. society can supply to its citizens in abundance.

One final characteristic should be taken seriously even though that characteristic could not be included in the estimations presented in table 2-6: citizen duty. As discussed in the last section of chapter 2, levels of citizen duty, a powerful influence on turnout, appear to have declined sharply in the 1980s. If these data are accurate, raising levels of citizen duty—at least, perhaps, returning citizen duty to levels existing at the beginning of that decade—may also be an important part of efforts to reconnect Americans to politics.

This discussion suggests a short list of changes to focus on in attempting to reforge the links between Americans and politics: increasing citizens' psychological involvement in politics; increasing citizens' sense of government responsiveness; increasing citizens' election-relevant information about parties and candidates; and increasing levels of citizen duty. The question now becomes how the political environment can be altered to promote these changes.

A number of proposals can be entertained along these lines, but two points need to be made. The first is that the likely effectiveness of these proposals in promoting these changes is generally not known. Existing data simply do not permit quantitative estimations of this sort to be made. Thus though there is reasonable certainty that reconnecting Americans to politics would increase turnout, there is no certainty that the reforms proposed here would succeed in reforging these political links. This does not mean these reforms will *not* succeed—far from it—but it does mean that relative uncertainty would accompany the implementation of these reforms, in contrast to implementation of the registration reforms discussed in chapter 4, where hard data can be used to evaluate the probable outcome.

The second point is that, because increased turnout is desirable but not essential and because the effectiveness of reforms designed to increase political connectedness (and therefore voter turnout) is uncertain anyway, it follows that these reforms should have possible payoffs that go beyond simply putting more bodies in the polling booths on election day. Otherwise, it seems to me, the efforts necessary to reform the political environment substantially cannot be justified.

Fortunately many of the reforms proposed below do have such pay-offs. Indeed I believe a consensus is evolving in this country that the political process should become more substantive, less manipulative, more accessible to the ordinary citizen, less money-driven, more competitive, and so on. The proposals considered here fit squarely into that consensus for political reform. They are, in fact, political reform possibilities that would have a good chance of both increasing voter turnout *and* improving the political process.

The proposals I have in mind may be divided into two basic groups. The first consists of proposals that would have to be implemented from the top down, generally through legislative mandate, to alter the structure within which the political process takes place. The second consists of proposals that would be implemented from the bottom up, through voluntary effort by the media, parties, institutions, and other key actors to improve the political process directly. I believe that both types of changes will probably be necessary—both to increase voter turnout and to further the broader goals of political reform.

Structural Reforms (from the Top Down)

The structural reforms that should be considered for implementation may be roughly divided into those that deal specifically with the media and those that deal with overall campaign finance.

Media reform proposals are usually animated by concerns that either the money involved in media—primarily television—advertising or the content of that advertising (or both) is subverting the contemporary political process. The money concerns are driven by increased expenditures on television advertising that are, at the minimum, a major contributing factor to rapidly escalating campaign costs.[16] Escalating campaign costs are believed, in turn, to make politicians excessively responsive to fund-raising sources ("special interests") and to make competitive challenges of incumbents relatively difficult.[17] Finally, the need to spend heavily on media may make it difficult for campaigns and parties to allocate funds to grass roots activities and direct citizen mobilization.

---

16. See Gans 1983; Committee for the Study of the American Electorate 1984; Nahra 1984; Sabato 1989, chap. 3; Progressive Policy Institute 1990; and Magleby and Nelson 1990, chap. 3.

17. The trend toward reduced competitiveness is mostly pertinent to congressional (especially House) races, not presidential races, because of the very different way in which presidential races are financed.

The concerns about content are driven by the perception that "spot" political advertising on television (that is, the now ubiquitous campaign commercial lasting 90 seconds or less) is having a strongly deleterious effect on the quality of the contemporary political process. The standard indictment asserts that political advertisements, elaborately produced, frequently negative in content, and scientifically designed to manipulate the emotions of prospective voters, are alarmingly poor vehicles for the communication of political information. Typically much of the information conveyed is distorted, designed to provide a factual gloss on the true purpose of the commercial: the construction of an emotionally laden image favorable to the candidate (or unfavorable to the candidate's opponent). The constant barrage of such commercials, virtually impossible for prospective voters to avoid, tends to leave citizens rather cloudy about candidates' and parties' actual positions on campaign issues and doubtful about the stakes involved in the election (other than furthering the careers of the politicians involved).

One does not have to buy this entire indictment to believe that it contains considerable truth.[18] Citizens may need stimulation, some of which these commercials provide, to pay attention to campaigns and to vote. But surely some kinds of stimulation are more effective than others in promoting political involvement. It is hard to believe campaign commercials, at least in their current configuration, provide optimal stimuli in this regard. This suggests at the minimum that the political process might benefit from some change in the *types* of campaign advertisements offered to the public.

Both these concerns can be dealt with in one obvious way: simply abolish paid political advertisements on television. In one stroke both the excessive cost and deleterious content attributed to campaign commercials would be eliminated. And such a step would not be unprecedented—most democracies in fact do not allow paid political advertising during campaigns.[19]

But I believe that such a move would be excessively drastic and antithetical to the "more like us" orientation previously recommended. It is even conceivable that a lack of advertisements might *depress* turnout, because commercials do provide some stimuli and information to voters. It seems more reasonable to accept a continued, large role for television advertising in campaigns and structure that role in ways that

18. See Popkin 1991a, 1991b, for a contrary opinion on this issue.
19. Taylor 1990, p. 272.

speak to the money and content concerns just outlined. Fortunately a variety of media reform proposals fit this description.[20]

These proposals typically deal with the money issue by calling for either free[21] or reduced-rate television time. Sabato recommends that every television (and radio) station be obliged to make eight hours of free time available each year for political advertising.[22] He further recommends that the time be given to the political parties, not individual candidates, and that the time be split equally between national and state parties. Finally he specifies that this time be granted in relatively short spots (ten seconds to five minutes) and be readily available during weekday prime time (half of total time) and during September, October, and November of election years (two-thirds of total time).

In contrast Magleby and Nelson recommend that time be made available on a reduced-rate basis.[23] Specifically, they recommend that a "lowest unit rate" (LUR) be charged candidates for time that is nonvariable (that is, the rate cannot be bid up by other advertisers) and nonpreemptible (that is, the time bought at the rate cannot be preempted by the station and given to a higher-rate advertiser).[24] They further recommend that this arrangement be in effect for sixty days prior to general elections and forty-five days prior to primaries.

Turning to the content issue, media reform proposals typically advocate the use of a "talking heads" format (that is, the candidate or other political personage—no actors—speaking into the camera) in place of the elaborate production formats used in contemporary campaign commercials. Proposals vary, however, in terms of the extent to which this format must be used. Gans' proposal calls for application of this format to all paid political advertisements,[25] whereas Taylor's pro-

20. In what follows, as well as in my discussion of campaign finance reform, I do not discuss all the relevant proposals and pieces of legislation—they are too numerous. Instead I confine my discussion to generally representative reform approaches that seem to illustrate the basic choices involved in formulating effective reform legislation.

21. Free television time is also a component of the "five-minute fix" proposal in Taylor 1990, pp. 268–69. However, Taylor's proposal is basically content oriented, so I cover it below in that portion of the discussion.

22. Sabato 1989, pp. 29–30.

23. Magleby and Nelson 1990.

24. Technically the LUR is available to candidates right now. However, because the LUR is highly variable and time bought at an LUR can be preempted anyway, its practical usefulness for candidates is almost nil. As a result most campaigns are forced to purchase time at standard commercial rates. Magleby and Nelson 1990, pp. 207–08.

25. Gans 1991b, p. 22.

posal calls for this format to apply only to five-minute blocks of free time made available by stations.[26]

Gans's proposal is simple and straightforward: require that production materials be eliminated from all paid political advertisements so that talking heads are the only available format. The restriction would apply to all political advertisements, whether sponsored by candidates, political parties, or interest groups.

Taylor's proposal (which he refers to as the "five-minute fix") is considerably more elaborate. To begin with, the talking heads format is only mandated for free time donated by television (and radio) stations to candidates or parties. For a presidential race, all stations would have to donate this time in simultaneous five-minute blocks to different presidential candidates on alternate nights (that is, Republican candidate one night, Democratic candidate the next night) in the five weeks leading up to the election. For state and local races all stations would have to donate five-minute blocks of time to different state parties on alternate nights covering a similar time period. The parties would then dole out the time to their candidates as they saw fit.

All these proposals—money oriented and content oriented—have problems of one kind or another.[27] However, these proposals also have obvious strengths. The money-oriented proposals should help reduce campaign spending on television, and the content-oriented proposals should at least *encourage* a more informative, less manipulative discourse between candidates and voters. This suggests that the logical course of action is not to favor one type of proposal over another, but rather to incorporate the basic flavor of both types of proposal into prospective legislation. Hence media reform legislation should include both a provision for free or at least nonvariable, nonpreemptible, LUR political advertisements and a provision requiring or at least structurally encouraging increased use of the talking-heads format.

Such legislation would, I believe, both further some broad goals of political reform (more informative and less manipulative political discourse; less money-driven and more competitive campaigns) and have a reasonable chance of contributing to higher turnout. The contribution to higher turnout could come about in several ways. Most clearly a

---

26. Taylor 1990, chap. 11.
27. These problems include, but are not limited to, determined opposition from broadcasters, fairness of rules to third parties, logistics of dealing with local races, and even constitutionality (as applied to mandated free time and especially to format specification).

more informative political discourse should help citizens become more psychologically involved in the political process and improve their knowledge about parties and candidates and what they stand for. In addition it is possible that over time less money-driven, more competitive elections might increase the influence of ordinary citizens (real or perceived) in the electoral process, leading to an enhanced sense of government responsiveness.

I now turn to legislative reforms dealing with overall campaign finance. These reforms are typically motivated by concerns about either campaign expenditures or contributions (or both). The expenditure concerns are driven by the simple fact that campaign costs have risen astronomically in the recent past. For example, between 1972 and 1988 general election expenditures by candidates for the House and Senate rose from $66 million to $407 million.[28] These expenditures represented, respectively, 456 and 600 percent increases in House and Senate campaign costs. These huge increases are believed to make successful challenges of incumbents very difficult, leading to elections that are substantially less competitive and issue oriented.

The concerns about contributions are driven by the perception that those who contribute to today's money-dependent campaigns wield undue influence over officeholders. Because of this, these contributors ("special interests") are said to decrease the influence of ordinary citizens in the political process.

One obvious way to deal with both expenditure and contribution concerns is simply to eliminate the role of private financing in political campaigns by replacing the current system entirely with public financing. Again this seems excessive and not in line with a "more like us" orientation. Moreover it seems quite possible that having campaign spending compete with already underfunded social programs for budgetary support would result in not just lower campaign spending, but campaign spending too low to stimulate public interest adequately. Thus, it seems more reasonable to accept a continued large role for private money in campaigns and to structure that role in ways that speak to the concerns just outlined.

But it turns out to be relatively difficult to structure the role of private money without creating perverse effects. For example, spending limits could favor incumbents, because it is difficult for a challenger to overcome the advantages of incumbency without spending a fair amount of

28. Magleby and Nelson 1990, p. 28.

money.[29] Political action committee (PAC) limits could also increase the difficulties of challengers by cutting off a potentially important source of funds, as could out-of-state contribution limits in certain areas of the country. Soft-money limits could cut funds available for non-television, grass roots–oriented campaign activities. And individual contribution limits—those now existing and certainly anything more stringent—could make it hard for people without individual wealth to run for office and would do nothing in and of themselves to encourage the small, "ordinary citizen" contributor.

So "the more limits the better" is not a good guideline for evaluating these approaches and might actually work against achieving the desired political reform and higher turnout objectives. In fact, if these objectives are put first in evaluating the approaches just outlined, the following, somewhat different, set of guidelines is suggested: (1) if campaign spending is to be limited, limits should be flexible and set high enough to ensure adequately competitive campaigns; (2) partial public financing should be considered as a way of ensuring that challengers have a base level of funding with which to launch competitive races; (3) contribution limits should be cautiously set, so as not to further advantage incumbents and deter grass roots activities, and some limits, particularly for individuals and party committees, should probably be raised to counter the influence of personal wealth and special interests; and (4) tax credits should be provided for the small individual contributor so as to encourage more ordinary citizens to become involved in the political process.[30] Such a reform approach would not necessarily produce *cheaper* elections—though hopefully it would make it more difficult for elections to be "bought," particularly by incumbents—but it would, in my view, produce better, more competitive elections.

Campaign finance reform along these lines would clearly, I think, further the broad goals of political reform. Elections would become more competitive and vigorously contested, reducing the advantages of incumbency and enlarging the potential role for ordinary citizens.

29. Indeed Cox and Munger 1989 present an analysis based on aggregate data that shows high-spending elections, all else equal, tend to have higher turnouts than low-spending elections. This presumably reflects the fact that money tends to be spent more heavily in competitive elections, which generate more voter interest and involvement to begin with, as well as the fact that high spending itself may promote a more stimulating and information-rich political environment.

30. For a series of very detailed proposals that fit reasonably well into these guidelines, see Magleby and Nelson 1990, chap. 11.

In terms of reconnecting Americans to politics, I think the big payoff would come in enhancing the perception that the government is responsive to ordinary citizens. This should follow both from reducing the incidence of lopsided noncompetitive elections where money appears to dominate and from increasing the opportunities for ordinary citizens to play a role in politics.

Voluntary Reforms (from the Bottom Up)

For political reform to have the maximum possible impact, simply changing the rules of the game with the structural reforms just proposed will not be enough. It will also be necessary for the players in the game—political parties, the media, and other relevant institutions[31]—to volutarily adopt different standards and practices in their political work. In other words, actions from the top down must be supplemented with actions from the bottom up.

Of course virtually an infinite number of such voluntary reforms could be adopted, depending on the institution of interest and the focus of desired change. Because of this I present here three case studies of reform practices without pretending to offer a definitive program for from-the-bottom-up reform action. Rather these case studies are simply useful models, illustrating how certain institutions have pursued a voluntary reform course with some degree of success. They by no means exhaust either the spectrum of current practice or especially the range of future possibilities.

The first case study concerns the role of the media. The media, by all accounts, have come to play an increasingly prominent role in modern campaigns. In fact a good argument can be made that the media have, to an astonishing extent, taken over basic communicative and evaluative tasks that were formerly the province of political parties.[32] One need not believe that therefore political parties have become ir-

31. I do not include individual candidates here because I consider candidates, with their short-term, individualistic orientation toward the political marketplace, an unlikely source of independent, voluntary reform. This is not to say candidate practices are not capable of change—I believe they are. But I believe that such changes are likely to come about as candidates adapt to a new political environment, not through a proactive effort on the part of candidates to be "nicer" or "more substantive." Because of this I believe that appeals such as "Candidates [should] pledge to conduct clean campaigns"—found in Markle Commission on the Media and the Electorate 1990, p. 10—are essentially quixotic and not a viable focus for voluntary reform.

32. See Orren and Mayer 1990 for a strong argument along these lines.

relevant (as some accounts have it) to view this as a development of some significance. It underscores just how important media practices are to defining the character of modern campaigns.

Television and newspaper coverage are clearly the most important aspects of this media presence in modern campaigns. Survey data suggest, however, that of the two, television coverage probably affects the largest number of citizens. This is shown by both data on news consumption in general (more people regularly watch the news on television than regularly read a newspaper; more people mention television as their primary source for news than mention newspapers)[33] and data on campaign news consumption in particular (more people follow campaigns on television than in the newspapers).[34]

Thus the news television purveys to the public is of particular salience to how citizens experience campaigns. And just what are citizens experiencing about campaigns through their television viewing? It is not much of an exaggeration to say sound bites and images. According to Adatto, the average length of sound bites shrank rapidly from 1968 to 1988 (from 42.3 seconds to an incredibly short 9.8 seconds), whereas in the same period, time devoted to visual images of candidates, unaccompanied by their words, increased by 300 percent.[35]

That style of coverage—rapid-fire succession of sound bites and images—is no doubt familiar to anyone who has absorbed even a small amount of recent television campaign coverage. Also familiar should be the trememdous emphasis on analyzing and critiquing how campaigns interact with the media—that is, describing in great detail how and with what success candidates have attempted to manipulate the media through the staging of events, construction of sound bites, spin control, photo opportunities, and so on. This peculiar form of self-referential "theater criticism" has now assumed a dominant role in television campaign coverage, having increased, according to Addato, from 6 percent of campaign reports in 1968 to 52 percent in 1988.[36]

How much time does this leave for direct coverage of the issues in the campaign? Not much, as one would guess from the above figures. According to a media content study of the 1988 campaign conducted

33. See Times-Mirror 1990a for recent data; see Stanley and Niemi 1988, chap. 2, for historical data.
34. See table 2-5.
35. Adatto 1990, p. 20.
36. Adatto 1990, p. 21.

by the Markle Commission on the Media and the Electorate, less than 10 percent[37] of television campaign story content could be described as about campaign issues per se. Another small proportion of story content—also less than 10 percent[38]—concerned the positions of candidates on those issues. Even allowing for the substantial measurement error that sometimes bedevils content analyses, these are very low figures indeed.

Now, none of this is to say that campaign coverage could (or should) be composed entirely of issue analysis or that theater criticism, horse-race analysis, and so on, could (or should) be completely eliminated from that coverage. But considering that television campaign coverage affects the largest number of citizens and, for many of them, is their main source of information about politics, the current mix of coverage does seem alarming. The average citizen is receiving less and less substantive information about campaign issues and candidates' and parties' actual positions on them and more and more quick sound bites, visual images, horse-race polls, and—perhaps the final insult—detailed analyses of how the candidates they are being asked to vote for are attempting to manipulate them.

Consider now the role of newspapers in campaigns. First it is important to stress just how important this role can be, despite the pervasive influence of television. About three-fifths of the adult population still reads a newspaper on a daily basis, with Sunday readership even higher and almost nine in ten reading a newspaper at least once a week.[39] Thus though newspaper readership and particularly newspaper circulation are not what they once were, it is simply not the case that television has driven newspapers from American homes.

Moreover as discussed in chapter 2,[40] the consumption of newspaper campaign coverage has a substantially stronger relationship to turnout than consumption of television campaign coverage. That is, someone

37. As described in Buchanan 1991, table 4-1. The content actually may be substantially less than 10 percent, because this figure includes both print and broadcast sources included in the study. But it is not known how much less, as Buchanan's discussion of the study's results indicates only that broadcast sources were much less likely than print sources to cover issues but does not specify the extent of this differential.

38. Calculated from data in Buchanan 1991, tables 4-1, 4-2, and 4-4. Again the true figure for television campaign is probably substantially lower for the reasons outlined in the previous note.

39. At least according to Times-Mirror 1990a. Other sources give different figures—sometimes higher, sometimes lower—though they do tend to fluctuate around the 60 percent figure (see Stanley and Niemi 1988, Knight-Ridder Newspapers 1989, and Times-Mirror 1992).

40. See also the model in appendix B.

who follows the campaign in the papers is more likely, all else equal, to vote than someone who only follows the campaign on television. This reflects, in my view, two notable strengths of newspaper, compared to television, campaign coverage. First, newspapers tend to provide more substantive and detailed campaign information than television, so citizens who are more involved in the campaign are particularly likely to turn to newspapers for coverage. Second, precisely because newspapers provide more substantive and detailed information and because citizens must make more effort, relative to television, to consume that information, the very process of following the campaign in the papers tends to engender *increased* campaign involvement. This suggests that newspaper campaign coverage, despite being less popular than television campaign coverage, plays a very important role indeed in how citizens interact with campaigns.

And just what are citizens currently experiencing about campaigns from their newspaper reading? On the positive side, newspapers cannot do sound bites and visual images in the way television can, so newspaper coverage has not evolved (and probably cannot evolve) to the same extremes that now characterize television coverage. Moreover newspapers, relative to television, do continue to provide more coverage that is substantive and issue oriented.[41]

That is the good news. The bad news is that newspaper campaign coverage has otherwise evolved in ways that are similar to television campaign coverage. Newspapers now carry, just as television does, a tremendous amount of horse-race coverage, theater criticism, and other campaign analysis relatively unlikely to provide prospective voters with useful information. Thus it appears that newspaper coverage differs more quantitatively than qualitatively from television coverage.

The general reform course suggested by this review of television and newspaper campaign coverage is fairly obvious. The media should alter their coverage mix so that more useful information is conveyed to citizens. Such a change would entail a deemphasis of the sound-bite, visual-image, horse-race, and "theater criticism" type of campaign coverage and a reemphasis of substantive issue coverage and analysis.

The payoffs of such a reform course also seem obvious. In terms of broad political reform goals, campaign coverage of this nature should go far toward establishing a more substantive and less manipulative political discourse. In terms of reconnecting Americans to politics and

41. Buchanan 1991, pp. 57–60.

increasing turnout, this style of coverage should, given the central role of the media in modern campaigns, greatly facilitate citizens' psychological involvement in these campaigns. Moreover substantive, issues-oriented coverage should also do much to increase levels of election-relevant information about parties and candidiates, another key aspect of reconnecting Americans to politics.

The difficult question here of course is: what would be the mechanics of such an altered mix? How might television and newspaper campaign coverage be altered to convey more issue substance without turning currently detached media consumers into simply bored media consumers? In terms of television, relatively little experimentation has been done with innovative forms of campaign coverage, so it is difficult to describe very concretely what this altered mix might look like. In terms of newspapers, however, some very interesting experiments have been conducted, and it is to one such experiment I now turn—the practices of the *Wichita Eagle* newspaper during two political campaigns, the general election of 1990 and the municipal Wichita elections in 1991.[42] Although the *Wichita Eagle* model is applicable most directly to newpaper campaign coverage, I believe many of the principles elucidated here would also apply, with some modification, to television campaign coverage.

The Wichita experiment was initiated by Knight-Ridder Newspapers in 1990, in conjunction with the editorial leadership of the *Wichita Eagle* (a Knight-Ridder newspaper), as a conscious effort to use newspaper resources to facilitate citizen interest, involvement. and participation in politics. The motivation stemmed from the perception that newspaper coverage had become increasingly tangential to the real issues of political campaigns and needed substantial reorganization and direction to capture readers' imaginations and play a positive role in these campaigns. To further these goals, Knight-Ridder decided to use upcoming political campaigns as "natural laboratories," in which various methods of stimulating citizen awareness and participation could be tested and results tracked up to and through elections. The project was confined to one medium-sized city (Wichita) so that a number of techniques could be experimented with and their effects tracked relatively easily.

42. The *Eagle* also plans similar efforts around the 1992 general election. But because the 1992 election postdates the publication of this book, no analysis of these efforts could be included here.

The project was implemented in the fall of 1990 (for the November general election) and again in the spring of 1991 (for the May Wichita municipal election).[43] For each election campaign, the project had essentially two components. One component was survey research to provide baseline information on the local electorate and track the progress and ultimate effectiveness of project efforts.[44] This research included two surveys taken in each election (for a total of four in all), a baseline preelection survey, and a final postelection survey.[45]

The baseline surveys were designed to draw detailed political portraits of the local electorate before each election in the dimensions pertinent to the project. Thus data were gathered concerning people's feelings about politics and politicians, their level of clarity on campaign issues, their levels of political interest and involvement, and their past political behavior, including participation (or lack of it) in previous elections. These surveys also obtained detailed information on respondents' media consumption habits, particularly the different ways in which they used newspapers and television to follow politics. Finally the baseline surveys were used to "test market" themes and action plans deemed potentially useful for project activities.

The postelection surveys were taken right after each election and were designed as final report cards on the project in that campaign. Respondents were asked whether they voted, whether they were clear on key campaign issues, whether they believed the results of the election would really matter on these key issues, whether they followed the special campaign coverage in the newspapers (and if so what types of coverage they read and what they thought about the coverage), whether they were aware of other project activities and themes (and what they thought of them), and a number of other campaign-related items.

The other component was a series of newspaper-initiated actions designed to kindle citizen involvement in politics and facilitate voter participation. Most of this activity, naturally enough, centered on re-

43. I participated in this project as a research advisor and analyst. I had chief responsibility for designing and analyzing the surveys used to gauge the overall success of the project and the relative efficacy of its different components. Results from these analyses are reported here with permission of Knight-Ridder and the *Wichita Eagle*.

44. Four focus groups were also conducted in March 1991 to provide qualitative data on the relationship between newspaper coverage of political campaigns and the process of citizen involvement (and noninvolvement) in these campaigns.

45. Details on interviewing dates, sample sizes, and so on for these surveys are found in appendix A.

structuring the mix of coverage provided by the *Eagle* to its readers. Along these lines the *Eagle* deemphasized horse-race coverage and "theater criticism" and concentrated on stories and features designed to make it easier for newspaper readers to understand relevant issues and involve themselves in the campaigns as they unfolded. These stories and features included, for example, summary boxes (boxes that provided quick, cogent summaries of candidates' positions on key campaign issues and tracked candidates' positions as they changed over time), "truth" boxes on campaign advertising, in-depth articles highlighting the difference campaign issues might make to a voter's daily life, and "You be the city council [or governor]" features that attempted to make the stakes of political decisions clear for voters. Finally the *Eagle* attempted to tie all campaign coverage together with a common logo ("Your Vote Counts," with a graphic of a marked ballot) and common approach that emphasized issues, both in the coverage presented to readers and the questions posed to politicians.

In addition the *Eagle* attempted to involve other community institutions in their efforts to promote citizen awareness and participation. For example, the *Eagle* convinced a local television station to show specially produced commercials promoting voting in the weeks leading up to the election. The *Eagle* also worked with local educational and literacy programs to distribute "easy reader" guides covering the election (including information on candidates, issues, and the mechanics of voting) to those with low reading skills.

The results of this experiment were very encouraging. Of course by the very nature of a local and uncontrolled experiment, it cannot be known for sure that successful aspects of the *Eagle*'s campaign coverage would generalize to other areas[46] or, especially, that the *Eagle*'s innovations, even where successful, had any tangible, independent, impact on levels of voter turnout.[47] Nevertheless I believe certain aspects of

46. Though survey results do indicate that the Wichita electorate, in terms of differences between nonvoters and voters, is quite similar to the rest of the country. In addition a recent analysis of census data by *American Demographics* magazine/Donnelly Marketing Information Services (Lohr 1992) ranked Wichita the sixth most "typical" city (among 555) in the United States. All this suggests that the dynamics of participation in Wichita may be fairly representative and therefore enhances the probability that research results can be generalized.

47. It simply cannot be said for sure that levels of turnout-related characteristics and, therefore, turnout, would not have been the same had the *Eagle* never changed its campaign coverage. However, though the effect of project activities on overall turnout levels is problematic, much valuable information was nevertheless gained about the relationship between the *kinds* of characteristics the *Eagle* was attempting to promote (for example, citizen clarity on issues) and voter turnout, as detailed later in this section.

the *Eagle*'s experience hold valuable lessons for those in the media seeking an alternative approach to campaign coverage.

To begin with the *Eagle* found a tremendous market for issues-based coverage, provided it was done in the right manner. The biggest success story here was the summary boxes, a feature that appeared in every Sunday's paper in the weeks leading up to an election.[48] These boxes summarized candidates' positions on all important issues in that election in a read-at-a-glance format. The theory was that, though many citizens might not have the time or motivation to pore over long campaign stories, they still wanted to understand campaign issues and have some sense of the election's significance.

Survey results indicated that this was in fact the case. These summary boxes were easily the most widely read component of the Eagle's campaign coverage, followed by 70 to 80 percent of readers who consumed any campaign coverage at all. Moreover judging from both survey and anecdotal evidence, readers found these summary boxes exceptionally helpful in understanding the bottom-line significance of the election.

The *Eagle* also had success with an issues-oriented voter's guide, published as a separate pull-out section on the Sunday before each election. The guide identified the candidates, provided summary box—type information on their issue positions, and gave basic specifications on how and where to vote.[49] The guide, even though it only came out once on the Sunday before elections, was the second most widely read campaign feature and, along with the summary boxes, was judged the most helpful by readers in understanding the significance of the election.

Finally the *Eagle* was able to generate fairly high readership levels even for its longer, in-depth stories on particular issues. Though not as

48. Running this feature on Sunday is important because nonvoters are much more likely to read the Sunday paper than the daily paper. Surveys, in fact, revealed that two-thirds of nonvoters *regularly* read the Sunday paper (that is, three to four times a month), making it an ideal vehicle for reaching this group.

This finding assumes additional importance in light of focus group research that suggests nonvoters tend to start following a campaign in the papers because a story "catches their eye," not because they were interested in the campaign to begin with. Thus attracting a potential nonvoter's attention in the Sunday papers with a feature like the summary boxes may be crucial to getting such an individual to follow the campaign at all.

49. It is this attempt to crystallize the issues of the election in the summary box format that most distinguished the *Eagle*'s guide from traditional newspaper voter's guides. Traditional guides typically provide basic information about the election (such as who is running for what offices, how to vote) and only the sketchiest of substantive information about the campaign. A typical practice is simply to print campaign statements by the candidates—information of questionable reliability and value.

high as for the summary boxes and voter's guides, readership levels were higher than expected and higher than for several other, more standard components of coverage, such as stories about day-to-day campaign events. Success here was attributed to keying the stories to issue logos popularized through the summary boxes and using questions and answers, lists of pros and cons, and other "reader friendly" devices to highlight basic information on the issue and make the story easier to digest.

Thus, research results based on the *Eagle*'s experience indicate that issue-based coverage, if approached imaginatively and with a realistic appreciation of readers' time and motivation constraints, can actually be widely read and even appreciated. But what, more specifically, should such coverage strive for, other than to be "read"? Here the Wichita experience also provides some useful hints and, in the process, underscores a critical way in which changes in media practices can help reconnect Americans to politics.

Modeling results, based on the survey data collected in Wichita, indicate that the *clarity* with which a citizen apprehends the different positions of candidates on key issues in an election and the extent to which a citizen believes the election outcome will actually make a *difference* on those issues are important determinants of that citizen's likelihood of voting. This is true even when a citizen's other individual characteristics are controlled for, such as education, age, income, political efficacy, partisanship and even level of campaign newspaper reading.[50] All else equal, a citizen who is clear on the main issues in an election and believes the outcome of the election will make a difference on those issues will be more likely to vote than a citizen who is unclear and believes the election will make little difference.[51]

Thus election-relevant information of this nature has an important impact on citizens' likelihood of voting. At the same time it is a type of election-relevant information that the media are well positioned to

50. Although the set of controls used in this model was not as extensive as that used in the turnout model in appendix B, it was still fairly elaborate because I tried to include a number of the most important turnout-related items from the NES. Thus though I cannot say for sure that the relationship between turnout and, say, issue clarity would not "disappear" with a larger set of controls, I am fairly confident that this would not happen.

51. This relationship certainly seems intuitively plausible and accords well with the theoretical perspective sketched in chapter 1: the more the issue stakes of an election are clear and meaningful, the higher the instrumental expressive benefits of voting should be and therefore the likelihood of participation. However, to the best of my knowledge, the Wichita data are the only data that allow this concept to be tested so directly.

provide to citizens, because the pronouncements of candidates and parties themselves are generally designed to sway voters to their side, not clarify issue positions or election stakes. All this suggests that one of the key ways in which the media can play a role in reconnecting Americans to politics is to consciously strive—as the Wichita paper did—to raise levels of this kind of information during campaigns. In doing so the media may lay the basis for an "information age" voter, who, forced to rely less on traditional cues like party, is still able to derive enough motivation from consideration of available information to participate on election day.

Given this perspective the goals of issue coverage become clearer. Coverage should strive to make candidates' relative positions on key issues as clear as possible for citizens (one of the strengths of the summary box format, for example) and illuminate for potential voters what difference, if any, the outcome of the election will really make to them on those issues. The latter goal is a particularly difficult one, since it is sometimes very hard to draw out how, in terms of a particular issue, the outcome of an election will affect a citizen personally. But focus group and other research indicates that getting issues down to that personal level is important for citizens and a critical aspect of what they are looking for (and usually not finding) in campaign coverage.

The Wichita experience is also instructive on what useful campaign coverage should *deemphasize*. First, stories about political polls, though an increasingly prominent part of campaign newspaper coverage nationwide, were relatively poorly read and rated very negatively by readers in terms of helpfulness in understanding the campaign (over half gave these stories the most negative rating they could). This is not to say that such stories should be eliminated but simply to suggest readers do not find them particularly helpful and would probably be happy to see less of them.

Second, stories analyzing television commercials were the most poorly read of all campaign stories. Moreover they were rated very negatively in terms of helpfulness—just about as poorly as stories on political polls. Now, these "truth squad" type stories have become a fad in contemporary newspaper coverage and are touted by some papers as a real public service contribution to the quality of campaigns. But, did anyone stop to ask whether ordinary citizens really *like* these stories and, in fact, want to see them?

The results from Wichita suggest that they do not. Moreover, recent national data strongly confirm that this distaste for television commercial analysis is general, not a quirk of the Wichita electorate. According to a Times-Mirror poll taken in late 1991, the type of campaign coverage people wanted to see *least* of was "analyses and commentary on campaign commercials," with almost three-quarters (73 percent) wanting to see less of this type of coverage and only 15 percent wanting to see more. This compares with tremendous (80 percent) sentiment in favor of seeing more issue coverage.[52]

It is hard to avoid the conclusion that the sudden interest in analyzing campaign commercials reflects more the media's fascination with analyzing itself than any real demand on citizens' part to actually see such analyses. Again this does not necessarily mean such stories are completely useless and should therefore be eliminated. But it clearly indicates there should be fewer of them and they should be done carefully, because the interest of the reader cannot be taken for granted. Along these lines, results from Wichita do indicate that the more such stories concentrate strictly on the truthfulness of claims made in the commercial and avoid extended analysis of how the commercial is cleverly manipulating the viewer, the more favorably these stories are received.

A final lesson from the Wichita experience is that a newspaper can act as a community catalyst for efforts to promote voter interest and participation.[53] During the 1990–91 voter participation project, for example, the *Eagle* involved a local television station (which donated time for airing voter participation spots), local election officials, local literacy and educational programs, and various local individuals in organizing and publicizing the project. Moreover, the level of community involvement grew over time, as the *Eagle* has succeeded in recruiting additional volunteers, individual and institutional, to work on a 1992 version of the project.[54] For example, graduate students from the local university are now contributing their time to conduct in-depth interviews with citizens about their issue concerns, their expectations of the political system, their level of community and political participation, and so on, which will be used to structure the *Eagle*'s coverage of the 1992

52. Times-Mirror 1991.
53. Actually a great deal more could be said about the Wichita experience, since the experience was such a rich one. But I have restricted my account here to only the most important lessons of the project and, moreover, the ones that seem like they would generalize the best. For more details on the project and attendant research findings, see Teixeira 1991 and Guzzo 1991.
54. At the time of this writing, the 1992 version of the project was under way and scheduled to continue at least through the presidential election of 1992. In addition Knight-Ridder was sponsoring another, similar 1992 project in Charlotte, North Carolina, built around efforts of the *Charlotte Observer*.

campaign. Thus newspapers can not only work on their own to increase citizen involvement in campaigns (by improving coverage and so on), but they can also spark general community efforts in that direction.

The second case study concerns the role of political parties. Much has been written about the declining salience of political parties in America[55] and practically as much about how to reverse this decline. As a result a great number of possible party reform actions exist to choose from. Some in fact were mentioned earlier in this chapter during the discussion of structural reforms: tax credits for individual contributions to parties; increased donation limits for party committttee contributions; party control over free television time; and so on.

Others are more along the lines of the from-the-bottom-up reforms being considered here. Sabato, a strong advocate of party renewal, provides a lengthy list, including (1) promoting "old-style" parties by designating party "ombudsmen" in key constituencies and establishing mobile party offices; (2) providing party members with nonpolitical services and rewards; (3) expanding party fund-raising capacities, campaign services to nominees, and candidate or volunteer worker recruitment; (4) promoting party institutional advertising, both during and in between campaigns; (5) undertaking a bipartisan educational campaign to convince voters and the news media that strong parties are desirable; (6) empowering party policy commissions during presidential interregnums so as to increase party capacity for policy formation; (7) having parties sponsor presidential debates; and (8) increasing the number of unpledged delegates to both party conventions.[56]

This is certainly a long list of reforms, many or all of which might produce useful improvements in the performance of today's political parties. However, with the possible exception of the first two reforms on Sabato's list, most of these changes would act only indirectly on the rank-and-file citizen.[57] Given that the central objective, as defined here, is to reconnect the ordinary citizen to politics, it would seem to be preferable for reform to act directly on the link between parties and citizens.

One way of doing this would be to strengthen the role of direct party-citizen contact during campaigns to counter the trend toward

55. Though note, as discussed in chapter 2, that a decline in raw party *organizational* strength does not seem to be a problem.

56. Sabato 1988.

57. Indeed some of these reforms seem likely to simply increase raw party organizational strength, *not* currently a problem for American political parties.

impersonal political contact through the media. Such a course of action could have several payoffs. In terms of broad political reform goals, a stronger role for direct party-citizen contact during campaigns would provide one way of increasing the accessibility of the political process to ordinary citizens. And to the extent intensified party-citizen contact lessens dependence on media-based campaign tools, the campaign process could become less expensive as well.

In terms of reconnecting Americans to politics and increasing turnout, more direct party-citizen interaction during campaigns should promote more psychological involvement in politics, as well as (given the close relationship between parties and government) increase perceptions of government responsiveness. Moreover intensified party-citizen contact should increase basic knowledge about parties and candidates and may even lead to stronger affect toward parties (for instance, stronger partisanship) because direct, personal contact, more so than media "blitzes," tends to facilitate emotional identification.

But is it really feasible to strengthen the campaign role of direct party-citizen contact given the nature of modern campaigns and the resources of local political parties? An experiment conducted by Research Strategy Management, Inc., for the Republican National Committee during the 1988 presidential election illustrates how this may be done.[58] This experiment was specifically designed to increase registration and turnout among young adults (eighteen to thirty-four years old) via a party-directed effort.

Two matched counties were selected for the experiment—one the target (experimental) county, the other the control county.[59] A baseline survey of 500 eighteen- to thirty-four-year-olds was then conducted in the target county. Based partially on this survey, simple, people-intensive voter registration and turnout programs were set up in the target county to be run by the local party organization and staffed by volunteers. These programs were monitored throughout the campaign and finally evaluated through postelection surveys and other research conducted in both the target and control counties.

58. Research results reported here are based on RSM, Inc. 1989, which was released to the author with the permission of the Republican National Committee.
59. The two counties were Peoria and Macon counties in Illinois. The criteria on which they were matched included no special attention for the county from the 1988 Republican presidential campaign; a population of 20,000 to 50,000 young voters; at least one four-year college and at least one community college or business school; similar past records of voter turnout and Republican presidential voting; and a relatively strong local Republican organization.

The programs themselves were staffed almost entirely with volunteer labor. Volunteers were used to draw up lists of nonregistrants; conduct telephone banks to canvas nonregistrants; register potential voters—particularly party supporters, of course—on campus, at shopping malls, in grocery stores, and door-to-door in precincts; recontact potential new voters by phone right before the election; and participate in a massive get-out-the-vote effort that included these potential new voters. According to project researchers, the local party organization had little problem obtaining the requisite volunteer labor and was able to run the entire registration and turnout program fairly easily through normal party channels.

The results were encouraging. First the programs turned out to be very inexpensive, so other local party organizations could presumably muster the resources to implement similar programs. This is important both from a feasibility standpoint and from the standpoint of containing, and possibly even reducing, campaign costs.

Second, registration and turnout for young adults did appear to go up significantly in the target county, based on both project research and election returns in precincts where younger voters dominated. Though it is impossible to know for sure that project activities were truly responsible for these gains, the relatively careful and controlled design of the project provides reasonable grounds for believing this was so.[60] Thus not only was the project fairly easy to set up and inexpensive to run, but it also seemed to accomplish its stated objectives.

The third case study concerns the role of schools. Schools have a natural role to play in reconnecting Americans to politics because we know that (a) preadult experiences can strongly affect adults' political attitudes and (b) cohorts are entering the electorate with very low turnout rates (table 3-5), suggesting their preadult impressions of the political system have not been positive ones. It would be desirable therefore for schools to give students a more positive impression of politics *before* they reach voting age and add to the low turnout problem.

One obvious approach would be to improve the content of the civics courses that most U.S. students take. But relatively little is known about

---

60. Of course the design was not fully controlled, in the traditional, scientific-experiment sense of term, because individual counties may vary from one another in too many ways for investigators to even begin to control all of them. Still the sort of design used by these researchers comes a great deal closer to that ideal than most studies on these topics do, and they should be applauded for this.

what works and does not work in civics courses. Moreover the evidence is ambiguous that civics courses have a particularly strong influence on students' political atttitudes in general, much less on those most pertinent to voter participation.[61] Perhaps this should come as no great surprise, given that civics courses typically have to cover much ground and cannot focus tightly on voting participation per se.

This suggests that an approach deliberately focused on voting participation might serve a useful function, especially if that approach engaged students in the substance and issues of political campaigns, not just the mechanics of voting. From a broad political reform standpoint, such an approach might—at least over the long run—contribute to a more substantive political discourse by training students to take politics seriously. In terms of reconnecting Americans to politics, a substantive, issues-oriented promotion of voting participation should help increase students' psychological involvement in politics as well as their sense of civic duty.

A promising approach along these lines is that of a program known as "Kids Voting." This program, originally based in Arizona but now spreading to other states, specifically involves students from kindergarten through the twelfth grade in the voting process.

Prior to an election, students learn about the democratic process, how to become an informed voter, and the mechanics of registration and voting. During this period, homework assignments include having discussions with their families about pertinent campaign issues and the relative merits of different candidates. On election day students accompany their parents to the polling place and cast simulated votes on the same candidates and ballot initiatives that their parents do. Results of these simulated ballots are not thrown away, but are tabulated and distributed to the press (though, of course, they do not count in the real election).

Several aspects of this program are worth emphasizing. The program does not simply tell students they *should* vote, but rather encourages them to become involved in the campaign, understand the issues and candidates, and vote on that basis. Moreover the program involves interaction between students and their parents, thus encouraging parents as well to become involved in the campaign. Finally the program has students go through the actual act of voting in a polling place, which

61. See Niemi 1992 for a good overview of the evidence on the effects of civics courses.

seems likely to generate more expressive benefits for the student than just reading about it or voting in a classroom (and perhaps providing a positive association for the time when the student can actually cast a legal ballot). All this seems well designed to move these prospective voters—and perhaps their parents, as well—toward stronger connections with the political system and a higher likelihood of voting.

This is the theory. But how has it worked out in practice? Has it, for example, increased turnout in Arizona? Here, I think the claims of the program's supporters that Kids Voting has already increased Arizona turnout must be viewed skeptically. Specifically, these supporters claim that the program directly increased turnout by 4 percent in Arizona in the most recent election—1990.[62]

It is true that turnout increased by about that amount in that election relative to 1986. However, the research purporting to show a direct link between this increase and the Kids Voting program is simply too weak to be credible.[63] This is especially true in light of the fact that the 1990 election also featured a very controversial ballot issue on the Martin Luther King holiday. This ballot issue seems a much more plausible source of increased voter interest and turnout than the Kids Voting program.

That said there are still definite indications that the program is doing well and is having a positive effect. First, the program has caught on very rapidly. Starting from a pilot project involving 30,000 students in metropolitan Phoenix school districts and election precincts in the 1988 election, the program in 1990 included 675,000 students statewide, 131,000 of whom cast simulated ballots at polling places. Areas covered by the program included 93 percent of all Arizona political precincts and 86 percent of all school districts.

Second, the program has generated a great deal of community support, including numerous individuals who provide volunteer labor at the local level as well as various banks, corporations, universities, and community organizations. In addition the Tribune newspaper group has been very active in publicizing Kids Voting (the Tribune papers were a charter sponsor) and distributing pull-out sections and other information specifically keyed to participation in the program. Given

62. Merrill 1991.
63. A great deal of it rests on adult respondents' self-reports that Kids Voting was what motivated them to come to the polls. I simply do not believe questions like this are reliable enough to be taken as real evidence of a program's effects. It is too easy for respondents to give a normative answer to a direct query of this nature.

how important the catalyzing role of a newspaper can be (as in the Wichita experience), the participation of these newspapers in Kids Voting seems particularly promising.

Third, the program has high recognition among the public and is very popular. A survey conducted of 800 registered voters after the 1990 election revealed that more than nine in ten (92 percent) claimed to have heard of the Kids Voting program.[64] And, of this group, support for the program was almost unanimous: 91 percent had a favorable impression of the program, and 96 percent recommended the program be continued in the future. Even allowing for normative bias these are very high figures.

Finally the program was rated highly by those who participated in it. Among the students (grades four through twelve) who participated, almost three-fifths (58 percent) said their interest in voting had increased, and nine in ten (91 percent) thought the program should be continued in their school. Among the teachers who participated, almost all thought the program worthwhile (44 percent very worthwhile; 51 percent somewhat worthwhile) and deserving of continuation (95 percent). And among the parents, almost all (92 percent) had a favorable impression of the program, with more than three-quarters (77 percent) reporting that children initiated political discussions at home, and almost nine in ten saying their children were enthusiastic about the program (60 percent very enthusiastic; 29 percent somewhat enthusiastic).[65] Again even allowing for normative tendencies to overreport positive feelings about this kind of program, these are high figures.

Thus though attributing Arizona's relatively high 1990 turnout to Kids Voting is probably going a bit too far,[66] the record of the program is still a good one. The program has spread rapidly, has involved many, many students and parents in the voting process, and has broad community and popular support. It appears therefore that the basic idea of

64. All research results reported here are based on Merrill 1991.
65. All of the parents in the survey had school-age children, though judging from the description of the survey, not all of them *necessarily* had children in the Kids Voting program. However, given the high level of coverage of the program, it is probable that a strong majority of these respondents actually did.
66. The program, after all, should have much if not most of its turnout-promoting effects on students. These effects will not be felt for a number of years until students who have experienced Kids Voting enter the electorate in large numbers. This is not to say that the program may not have turnout-promoting effects on adults right now or in the near future. This is certainly possible (though yet to be demonstrated, as I have argued). But I believe that too much emphasis on an immediate turnout "payoff" (which is quite difficult to measure anyway) could detract from the long-term promise of the program as a youth socialization mechanism.

Kids Voting is not just a good idea but a *workable* idea that could be feasibe in a variety of locales.[67]

These three case studies concerning the role of the media, political parties, and schools illustrate just some of the ways in which political reform could be pursued from the bottom up. Combined with the more conventional top down reforms, I believe such approaches could make a real contribution to reconnecting ordinary citizens to politics, while at the same time furthering some of the broad goals of political reform. If so, the end result would be highly desirable: both increased turnout *and* an improved political process.

Of course even assuming these reforms have their desired effects, what they can achieve is probably limited without eventual changes in the substance of American government and politics. In the long run a government that seems to respond to problems with real solutions and parties and politicians whose positions on issues are easily identifiable and meaningful to the average voter would probably make the largest impact both on turnout levels and on the general quality of the political process. Unfortunately these long-run changes in government and politics seem unlikely to happen, given the political dynamic that has developed over the last several decades.

But here also—especially given recent changes in the political environment—I think the reform approaches I have discussed could make a real contribution. Stirrings at the grass roots, for example, suggest that citizens are actively searching for a political model that is different from the one that dominates today. And surely one of the messages of the 1992 Perot phenomenon was about that search: citizens are tired of the way government, parties, and politicians have been conducting themselves and want more responsive, more substantive, and less manipulative politics.

The political reforms discussed here might fall on fertile ground, then. If so, one of the effects of this reform approach might be precisely to help establish a new political dynamic and move government, parties, and politicians in the long-run direction mentioned above. Thus if the reforms recommended here work as intended, not only should they produce some short-term improvements in turnout and the political process, but they should also increase the probability of having truly

67. The exact form in which this idea is implemented, of course, could (and probably should) vary from locality to locality. The idea is the important thing here, and the specific organizational forms devised by Kids Voting may or may not be appropriate in other localities and school systems.

responsive government and principled parties and politicians in the long run.

Political Reform and the Future of American Voter Turnout

No certainty exists that political reform will generate any of the desired results, particularly in terms of higher voter turnout. As I stressed at the beginning of this chapter, data limitations preclude the kind of "hard" estimates of turnout impact I was able to make for registration reform. Therefore political reform of the kind recommended here (or any other type for that matter) would have to go forward in a climate of relative uncertainty as to its ultimate effects.

Moving forward on the political reform front remains a good idea for several reasons despite this uncertainty. First, a broad need for reform of the political process exists, regardless of the ultimate effect on turnout. Thus, if the reforms presented here help produce a political process that is more substantive, less manipulative, more accessible to the ordinary citizen, less expensive, more competitive, and so on, their implementation can be justified even if turnout levels remain flat.

Second, if reform efforts are confined to registration reform, turnout levels would at most recover to about 1960 levels. And even this would require hitting the upper-bound estimate of possible turnout increase from registration reform—an improbable outcome. A more likely outcome would be a rise in (presidential) turnout to 57 to 59 percent, which is still quite low and far, far behind most other democracies.

Third, if registration reform alone is pursued, nothing will be done to turn back the forces currently eroding U.S. turnout levels. That is, if U.S. turnout has been declining since 1960 primarily because of the weakening ties between citizens and the political system, simply making it easier to vote will not alter this basic dynamic. It is therefore possible that registration reform could temporarily push up turnout levels, only to have turnout sink back again to current levels (or lower) for the very same reasons that it has declined for the last thirty years.

Fourth, if registration reform is the only type of reform implemented, hope must be abandoned of ever reaching the levels of turnout (70 to 90 percent) exhibited by other democracies. This is derived from the simple mathematical fact that the United States is too far behind these other democracies to plausibly make up this deficit through registration reform alone. Therefore registration reform must be combined with additional sources of increased turnout if the United States is even to have a chance of closing the turnout gap separating it from other countries.

Finally given the desirability of supplementing registration reform with an attack on the problem of voter motivation, I know of no more plausible way to do so than with the type of political reforms outlined here. Thus even though the turnout impact of political reform cannot be reliably estimated, the chances of lowering motivational barriers with alternative approaches (particularly maintaining the status quo) are probably even worse. In other words, political reform may not be a *sure* bet to solve the problem of voter motivation, but it is the best bet. It follows that ignoring political reform simply because its ultimate impact is uncertain would be a considerable mistake.

What can be said about the future of American voter turnout, given adoption of the registration and political reform program recommended here? The worst-case scenario is that only the registration reform part of the program works at all, that is, produces an increase in voter turnout. This would still mean an increase of perhaps 8 percentage points in turnout[68] combined with improvements in the political process that for whatever reason do not happen to show up in turnout levels. As worst cases go this does not seem so bad.

The best-case scenario is that both components of the program work and work well. In terms of the effect of registration reform, this would mean at least an 8-percentage-point gain in turnout, perhaps several points more given the upper-bound increase discussion in chapter 4. It is harder to gauge what might constitute working "well" for political reform.

One approach is to say that political reform would work well if it not only halted the ongoing erosion of Americans' ties to their political system, but also enabled Americans to regain ground lost in this respect in the last three decades. In other words however much Americans have become disconnected to politics in the recent past, political reform would enable them to reconnect to politics by the same amount in the future.[69]

This effect of this level of change can be estimated by taking the 1988 electorate and simulating a 1960 level of political connectedness

68. Though the forces currently eroding U.S. turnout levels might negate all or part of that gain over time.

69. However, no technical reason bars levels of political connectedness from rising even more than this amount. But at least this amount of change is known to be possible because the United States has experienced that much of a shift in the opposite direction since 1960.

within that electorate. This entails holding the demographic character-istics (education, age, income, marital status, and so on) of the electo-rate constant at their 1988 values, but setting the levels of political efficacy, partisanship, campaign media involvement, campaign interest, and so forth equal to those that prevailed among the electorate in 1960. Model estimations conducted in this fashion indicate that, if political reform was successful to this extent, turnout would rise about 7 to 10 percentage points.[70]

This suggests that, under a best case scenario, in which both regis-tration reform and political reform generated strong turnout-promoting effects, an increase in turnout of around 20 percentage points may be possible (coupled presumably with an improved political process as a result of the political reforms). This figure has implications for future levels of U.S. voter turnout, relative to those of other countries. To begin with, given that the 20-point increase incorporates some genuinely optimistic assumptions, I think turnout levels exhibited by high-end countries such as Germany, Australia, and Belgium, where average turn-out rates are in the high 80 percent or low 90 percent range (see table 1-2), can be safely ruled out. Turnout increases of around 40 points would be required—far larger than the most optimistic figure esti-mated. Indeed I would go so far as to say, given the basic system of representation and political culture in the United States, such high turnout rates are not attainable under any circumstances.

A more reasonable target, I believe, would be the turnout levels exhibited by low-end countries such as Japan and Canada (68 to 72 percent). This is about the level that results from adding the 20-per-centage-point "best case" turnout increase to current U.S. turnout lev-els (50 percent + 20 percent = 70 percent). Thus an appropriate and potentially attainable national goal might be to join the Japans and Canadas of the world in the lower tier of the turnout hierarchy (leaving Switzerland without any serious competition for the cellar).

Of course even a rise in turnout to the 70 percent level would still leave U.S. voter participation below average—though *respectably* below average as opposed to *abysmally* below average where the United States now is. Would it be possible then to move out of below-average status to actually being average by world standards (with about an 80

---

70. The estimate is closer to 7 points if model B-1 in appendix B is used and citizen duty is excluded from the estimations. It is closer to 10 points if citizen duty is included in the estimations.

percent turnout)? I do think this is technically possible, though this level probably represents the absolute upper bound for U.S. turnout, even under the best of circumstances. Reaching this upper bound would probably entail eliminating the personal registration system and replacing it with some form of automatic, state-sponsored registration and transforming today's political universe into one in which the links of Americans to politics are even stronger than they were in 1960.[71]

In light of the heroic nature of such changes, I think the 70 percent level makes a more reasonable goal at the present time. If this is our goal, then our priority should be to get moving on the kind of registration and political reform program that can make this 70 percent level a reasonable future possibility. Whether we can succeed in transforming this possibility into a reality is, as I have repeatedly emphasized, not certain. But given that the methods outlined for getting there would at the minimum improve our democracy in other ways, I think we have very little to lose from trying.

71. This could perhaps be done through the kind of "type A," partisan-oriented realignment described by Burnham 1991. Note that the last realignment in American politics, according to Burnham, was the nonpartisan "type B" realignment that took place in 1968–72.

Appendix A: Data Sets Used in Study

Much of the analysis in this study relies on two data sets. The first is derived from the American National Election Studies (NES) and the second, from the Bureau of the Census Current Population Survey (CPS), November Voter Supplement File. Other data sets used for analytical purposes include a data set on registration laws by state, collected by Glenn Mitchell and Christopher Wlezien, and a data set on media consumption, voter awareness, and voter participation, collected in Wichita, Kansas in 1990–91. Finally a number of other data sets provided useful descriptive data but did not prove appropriate for detailed analysis. They are listed at the end of this appendix.

Census/CPS Data

Whenever possible I have relied on the census-CPS data because of its much larger sample size and therefore its superior reliability. The CPS is a monthly survey of a sample of approximately 100,000 dwelling units across the United States conducted by the Bureau of the Census in the third week of each month.[1] Its main purpose is to measure unemployment, but since 1964 the survey has included a few questions about registration and voting in the November questionnaire during even-numbered years.

---

1. See table A-1 for the exact sample size of the CPS in the years included in my analysis.

TABLE A-1. *Size of Census and NES Data Sets*

Year	Census		NES
	VAP	Citizens	
1960	. . .	. . .	1,181
1964	. . .	. . .	1,571
1968	. . .	. . .	1,557
1972	93,339	92,049	2,705
1976	89,099	86,430	2,248
1980	123,591	114,944	1,614
1984	109,450	101,477	2,257
1988	102,304	96,098	2,040

That the CPS is not primarily a survey of voting behavior and political attitudes is in many ways an advantage. In November of election years respondents are asked a series of demographic questions and are then asked about their participation in the election. Because the focus of the survey is not on their political behavior, respondents have less incentive to misreport their turnout than when they feel that the interviewer is primarily interested in the political aspect of their lives. Respondents are also probably less embarrassed to admit not voting when politics is only one small aspect of what the interviewer is interested in rather than when political involvement and knowledge are the main focus of the interview.

This is illustrated by the relatively small differentials between the aggregate voting rate and the census-based voting rates. For example, in 1984 the actual turnout in U.S. national elections (based on the voting-age population) was 53.1 percent. The voting rate obtained from the census data is 59.9 percent for that year, a difference of slightly less than 7 percent. Similarly in 1988 the actual turnout was 50.2 percent of the voting-age population. According to the census figures based on responses to the CPS, it was 57.4 percent, a difference of 7.2 percent.

These differences are actually fairly small compared to other data sets available for studying voter turnout. In addition it is worth noting that the time trend on turnout rates in the census data closely parallels what is known to be the "real world" trend in turnout rates. This also suggests that the self-reporting bias in the census data is relatively mild.

But perhaps the chief attraction of the census data set lies in the analytical advantages afforded by its large size. For example, unlike the NES large numbers of people are surveyed in every state, making it relatively easy to analyze the effects of registration laws as they vary across states. In addition because of the large sample size, even small demographic groups (such as farmers, students) are well represented. This allows useful analysis to be conducted of their voting behavior, whereas the NES data would have been inadequate.

Data tapes of the November voter supplement are only available from 1972 onward. The 1964 and 1968 data tapes have been lost, so only hard copy is available for these years. In addition, the 1976 data tape does not include a variable for state of residence, so the data could not be used to estimate the effects of state registration laws.

NES Data

Although the census is an exceptionally useful source of demographic and voting data its very strengths lead to its major defect for the purpose of this study: it does not include any political variables other than voter participation. Beyond the handful of specific questions about registration and voter turnout, no other items of a political or attitudinal nature are included. The American National Election Survey, in contrast, includes a wide range of questions about attitudes and political behavior and thus can support descriptive and multivariate analyses (for example, analysis explaining the decline in voter turnout) that go beyond simple demography. In addition NES data are available going back to the beginning of the turnout decline era (to 1960), whereas most of the census data on voter turnout is not available before 1972.

The NES, of course, is far smaller than the CPS, with approximately 1,200 to 2,700 respondents per year.[2] It consists of two parts, one survey done before the election and a follow-up of the same respondents after the election. This arrangement has some disadvantages, because respondents are extensively questioned about their political attitudes and behavior before the election, which may cause them to think about politics and the election more than they otherwise would. As a result being survyed may enhance respondents' probability of voting over what it normally would have been.

In addition respondents are aware that the interviewer is primarily interested in their political behavior, which may lead them to exaggerate or lie about their political involvement and the frequency of their

---

2. See table A-1 for the exact size of the NES survey in the years included in the model.

voting in order not to appear to be violating social norms. And in fact the turnout rates reported in the NES data are consistently higher than those in the CPS, a fact that is *not* attributable to differences in the sampling universes of the two surveys. For example, for the years 1972 to 1988, the NES shows voting rates 10 to 12 percentage points higher than the census,[3] far too large a difference to be accounted for by sampling universe differentials.

Fortunately this overreporting problem—though clearly something one would wish to avoid, all else equal—has not been shown to bias seriously the type of analysis for which the NES is most useful: descriptive and multivariate analysis of the relationship between political attitudes and turnout.[4] Given the unique advantages of the NES data set for pursuing this type of analysis, use of the data set is therefore well justified despite the overreporting difficulties.

At this point it should be observed that the NES does currently include a validated turnout measure that attempts to solve the problem of overreporting. This voter validation is done by checking a respondent's self-report of voting against local records. Unfortunately the validated turnout data does not start until 1964 and then skip twelve years to 1976, which makes the data difficult to use in a time series context.

In addition close scrutiny of the validated data reveal they are susceptible to fairly serious biases that would at least partially offset the advantage of eliminating self-reporting bias. Most serious is that the methodology of NES voter validation has changed quite substantially from 1964 to 1988,[5] so that observed changes over time in validated voting rates are likely to reflect both changes in the real world *and* changes in NES procedures. This further limits the usefulness of the validated data when analyzing changes over time.

For these reasons most analyses conducted in this study used the self-reported data. However, analyses run on the self-reported data were

3. See table 3-1.
4. The issue of demographic differentials in misreporting and how these may bias descriptive demographic analysis using the NES data is a contentious one. I will not enter this debate here, however, because demographic analysis using the NES data is not central to any part of this study. But see Presser, Traugott, and Traugott 1990 for some of the reasons misreporting differentials may not be as severe as sometimes supposed.
5. Traugott 1989. Traugott mentions among other things that the NES staff simply do not know how the validation study was conducted in 1964, that the 1980 study was beset with administrative problems, that a substantial tightening up of validation procedures took place in 1984, and that the magnitude of the "record check can't be done" category has changed substantially over time (from 15.8 percent of respondents in 1964 to 1.7 percent in 1988).

generally run on the validated data as well—for years available—to check for possible biases introduced by self-reporting.

Registration Data

Data on state registration laws were primarily drawn from a data set collected by Glenn Mitchell and Christopher Wlezien. These data, covering even-numbered years from 1972 through 1984, were collected by Mitchell and Wlezien through direct consultation with state statute books. For this reason I believe the data are more reliable than more commonly used data, such as that obtained from the League of Women Voters.

Unfortunately the Mitchell-Wlezien data set does not include data on motor voter or agency-based registration programs. For data on these laws I was forced to consult other, less reliable sources, chiefly the League of Women Voters and the *Book of the States*. Even with these efforts I was only able to obtain data on motor voter for 1984 and 1988 and agency-based registration for 1988. Though I did some experimental analysis with these data, I believe these results should be treated with caution (as I noted in the text of chapter 4), because of these difficulties.

In addition, for the purposes of some related experimental 1988 analysis, I did collect a full set of 1988 registration data from such sources as the League of Women Voters[6] and *The Book of the States*. Again, the questionable reliabilty of these data means results based on them should also be treated with caution (as noted at an appropriate place in the text).

Wichita Voter Participation Data

Wichita voter participation data were derived from four surveys conducted in Wichita, Kansas, in 1990–91. These surveys, which covered media consumption, voter awareness, and voter participation, were part of a project sponsored by Knight-Ridder, Inc. in conjunction with the local newspaper, the *Wichita Eagle*. I designed the survey instruments, which were administered by The Research Center, a survey house in Wichita.

---

6. League of Women Voters 1988.

All surveys were conducted by telephone with respondents eighteen years old or older in Sedgwick County, Kansas. The two 1990 surveys were conducted before and after the November general election, whereas the two surveys in 1991 were conducted before and after the April Wichita municipal elections. Specific sample sizes and interviewing periods for the four surveys were as follows: (1) 600 respondents, September 25 to October 1, 1990; (2) 937 respondents (including 432 respondents from the first survey), November 7 to December 3, 1990; (3) 500 respondents, February 18 to February 23, 1991; and (4) 502 respondents, April 3 to April 8, 1991.

Other Data

Data sets that provided some descriptive information, but were not used for data analysis purposes include but are not limited to the following: Times-Mirror Press, People and Politics surveys, 1987 and 1990; People for the American Way Democracy's Next Generation survey, 1989; Citizens' Political and Social Participation survey (conducted by Norman Nie, Sidney Verba, Kay Schlozman, and Henry Brady), subset, 1990; Research/Strategy/Management, Inc., Registering Young Adults case study, 1988; and Markle Commission on the Media and the Electorate surveys, 1988.

Appendix B: Modeling and Estimation Procedures

This appendix discusses, both generally and in relation to the two main data bases (NES and Bureau of the Census), the modeling and estimation procedures used in the study.

Probit Modeling

The question of how the relationship between turnout and individual characteristics is to be modeled is, at root, a theoretical question having to do with how one believes such characteristics affect an individual's probability of voting. In other words what is the general shape of the curve that plots the relationship between the probability of voting (the dependent variable) and the values of the variables that tap individual characteristics (the independent variables)?

The first possiblity is a straight line. The idea is simple and corresponds to the kind of curve that would be generated were ordinary least squares (OLS) regression used to model this relationship. A unit increase on the independent variable (IV) generates a uniform increase on the dependent variable (DV) equal to the regression coefficient of the IV in question, no matter where on the curve the individual is located.

This procedure presents two problems in modeling voter turnout. The first is that because of the nature of the OLS procedure, values outside the 0–1 interval can be generated for the DV. But because the DV in the model was the probability of voting, this is clearly an undesirable property. Predicted probabilities greater than 1 or less than 0 are meaningless, and hence I wanted to avoid them in my modeling procedure.

The second problem is that the increases in probability are uniform, regardless of location on the curve. This is equivalent to assuming that the effect of a particular variable is the same for all types of people— probably not a warranted assumption. Although the benefits, costs, and resources pertinent to voting undoubtedly accumulate, they may do so in a nonadditive way. Therefore their marginal effect on the probability of voting is not likely to be constant across individuals.

For example, for people almost certain not to vote, the marginal effect of a variable will be small. That is those for whom the costs of voting seem high and the benefits low will be relatively unaffected by a marginal change in costs or benefits. The task of voting will still seem arduous and pointless. But as the balance between costs and benefits becomes more equal, it will take less to tip the individual in the direction of voting.

A second threshold is reached when the individual is 50 percent likely to vote. After this point the effect of marginal changes in costs and benefits will begin to decrease. This continues until the individuals who are almost certain to vote are reached. As with those almost certain not to vote, the marginal effect of characteristics will be small. An individual for whom the benefits of voting are already high and the costs low is not likely to be much more inclined to vote by making the benefits somewhat higher.

Hence, the college-educated, high-income professional who reads the paper every day and feels highly efficacious will not derive much additional motivation from a high level of partisanship. For the working-class, middle-income voter with a high school education who seldom reads the paper and feels only somewhat efficacious, the same high level of partisanship may be the crucial motivation for going to the polls. This seems more reasonable than assuming that both voters would be equally affected by their level of partisanship.

Thus the OLS curve both generates uninterpretable predictions and generates predictions in a manner that probably does not correspond to the real world. A curve that corrects these problems is an S-shaped curve, where the predicted probability asymptotically approaches 1, as the value of the IV goes to + infinity, and asymptotically approaches 0, as the IV's value goes to − infinity. This means, of course, that the predicted probability never goes under 0 or over 1, no matter what values are assumed by the IV. And as is obvious from the shape of the curve, the effect of the IV on the likelihood of voting varies, depending on the location on the curve.

The S-shaped curve, then, has the properties of never predicting probabilities of voting less than 0 or greater than 1 and of describing a functional relationship between voting probabilities and individual characteristics that seems theoretically and practically plausible. Both of these properties are in direct contrast with the undesirable OLS properties outlined previously. This suggests that the S-shaped curve is an appropriate model for analyzing the relationship between turnout and various attitudinal and demographic traits.

The question now becomes: what form of statistical analysis can be used to model this relationship in the desired fashion? The two basic choices are probit analysis and logit analysis. These two methodologies are those typically used by social scientists and others when analyzing a discrete dependent variable, as in the preceding example.[1] In terms of the shape of the curve that links the DV with the IVs, there is little difference between probit and logit, with the probit function approaching 0 and 1 probabilities just a little bit faster than the logit function.

For my analysis, the probit model was used. This was not because probit had any advantages, technically speaking, over logit for this investigation. On the contrary the results produced by either method, in substantive terms, are likely to be virtually identical.[2] Probit was chosen primarily because it has been used in so many other previous studies of turnout, including my own previous work.[3] The use of probit therefore promotes ease of comparison with earlier analyses as well as the accessibility of this particular study to other researchers on the subject.

The first thing that must be understood about the probit model (and the key difference between it and OLS regression) is that the prediction derived from the IVs is not of the DV itself (that is, a probability), but rather of a "probit." What this probit really represents is the distance from 0 in a standard normal distribution. This number is then transformed into a probability by taking the area under the curve up to that distance from the origin (that is, from minus infinity to that point on the x-axis). This area under the curve may range from 0 to 1 and is

1. See Hannushek and Jackson 1977, pp. 179–216, for a clear and thorough discussion of both forms of analysis.
2. Hannushek and Jackson 1977; Mare 1983.
3. Teixeira 1987. I also find the standard normal distribution more intuitive than log-odds, but this is not a central consideration.

simply the value of the cumulative standard normal distribution for the probit value under consideration. This is why the cumulative standard normal distribution is referred to as the "link function," because it links the predicted probit—in theory, the linear part of the DV—to the DV itself (here the probability of voting). Further the existence and nature of this link function make it clear why predictions directly based on the values of the IVs may range from minus infinity to plus infinity, just as in OLS, but the predicted probabilities will range only from 0 to 1.[4]

NES Model Building Procedure

This section of the appendix will discuss how specific NES-based models were constructed to study turnout decline.

Before technical details are dealt with, however, the purpose of the NES model-building process should be examined. The examination begins with a basic idea: that an investigation seeking to explain change over time in the level of voter participation implicitly starts with a simple model already in place. This model includes only one variable, time, and accurately plots changing turnout levels. The problem is that this model explains nothing in substantive terms, because to ascribe change over time *to* time is tautological. The simple model, with no variable but time, then, represents a state of complete ignorance about the real cause of turnout decline.

And this state of ignorance was really where the investigation started. The idea was to transform this ignorance into knowledge by adding terms to the model that would capture the variation associated with time in the beginning model. This was the basic purpose of the model-building process.

The first step of the process was to estimate the "simple" model. This could easily be done by running a weighted probit model (data must be weighted because turnout levels by year change significantly without weights) that included only the seven dummy variables necessary to represent the eight time points in the data set (that is, one dummy each for 1964, 1968, 1972, 1976, 1980, 1984, and 1988).

The next step was adding variables to the model that were believed to be relevant to the question of turnout decline. The first variables

---

4. See Baker and Nelder 1978 for a more extensive and technical exposition of link functions and how they relate to the generalized linear model, of which the probit model is one variant.

added were education, occupation, and income. This is because (see chapter 2), the effect of socio-economic status change on turnout levels should have been to promote, rather than dampen, participation. Thus adding these variables to the model actually increased the coefficients of the time dummies, because "more" turnout decline had to be explained (and no other factors in the model could do this explaining). Another way of saying this is that education, occupation, and income— especially education—act as suppressor variables on time, so adding SES to the model allowed the "true" effects of time to be discerned.

Other theoretically appropriate variables were then inserted into the model to discover the origins of this SES-adjusted decline represented by the (now larger) coefficients of the time dummies. As these variables were added the ways in which the time coefficients changed were observed. If these coefficients were significantly decreased by the addition of a given variable, this was a sign that distributional change on that variable had a substantial role in turnout decline. Further if the addition of a certain number of variables resulted in the substantial attenuation or elimination of the time dummies as significant factors in the model, this suggested that distributional change on these variables could plausibly account for the fall in participation over the twenty-eight-year period. This latter eventuality was a desirable result, because it provided a simple and easily interpretable explanation for turnout decline.

But how was it decided which variables from the additive procedure were worth retaining—and categories of these characteristics if they were considered categorical within the framework of the model? There is no hard and fast way of making these determinations. No one statistical test (or tests) can be mechanically relied upon for such judgments. Thus, my decision to include a particular term in the model, or to collapse over certain categories for a variable was informed by criteria of theoretical plausibility and analytical importance, not just the results of statistical procedures.

Nevertheless two statistical tests were of invaluable assistance in making these decisions. The first is the familiar t test, in which the coefficient of the variable is divided by its standard error to see whether that coefficient differs significantly from 0 (at a level of significance designated by the investigator). If it does not this is good evidence the relationship between the variable in question and the DV is not important.

The second test is considerably less familiar. It is used to test the relative usefulness of a model but is quite different from the *F*-tests used in OLS regression. *F*-tests are based on the difference in explained sums of squares between models. In probit analysis, however, the explained sum of squares is not a meaningful quantity, because this is not the basis upon which parameter estimates are derived. Instead these estimates are maximum likelihood estimates (MLEs) based on probabilistic criteria.[5]

The relevant question for a model based on MLEs is how well the model fits, relative to other models, not explained variance. This may be answered, approximately, with a likelihood statistic with the somewhat unwieldy name of $-2 \times$ log-likelihood ratio (called the log-likelihood here, for purposes of brevity). The log-likelihood measures the goodness-of-fit of the model in likelihood terms. The test statistic is produced by subtracting the log-likelihood of the full model from that of the simplified, reduced model. (The models must be hierarchically nested.) This difference is distributed asymptotically as chi-square with degrees of freedom equal to the difference in degrees of freedom between the models.[6]

Just as with a *t*-test or an *F*-test, the level of significance for this statistic is set by the investigator. The value of the statistic is then compared with the appropriate test chi-square value at this level of significance. Lack of significance indicates that relatively little information has been lost by simplifying the model, considering the degrees of freedom that were saved in the process. This provides a reasonable basis for asserting that the relationships between the DV and the variables or categories deleted from the model were not particularly important and thus can be left out of further analysis.

The NES Model

I constructed the data set from which the NES model was estimated by pooling the NES data for presidential years, 1960–1988, and creating a new variable to indicate in which year the respondent was inter-

---

5. See Bishop, Feinberg, and Holland 1975, pp. 57–122, for a discussion of MLEs and how they are estimated.
6. See Baker and Nelder 1978, sec. 5, and Bishop, Feinberg, and Holland 1975, pp. 123–31, for discussions of this statistic and its strengths and weaknesses.

viewed. Whenever possible I took variables for analysis from the *American National Election Studies Cumulative Data File, 1952–1988*. For several of the variables however, I wanted more information than was contained in the cumulative file.

I did this by merging some data from individual year studies into the data set from the cumulative file. In this way I was able to obtain more detailed measures of family income, occupation, campaign newspaper reading, campaign television viewing, residential mobility, and several other characteristics.

Pooling the data in the manner described had two advantages. First it enabled me to examine directly the effects of time as the data were analyzed. This was desirable because the aim of the NES modeling procedure was essentially to see if the time trend in turnout could be explained through the influence of variables other than time. This, of course, could not be done unless time could be included as a variable in the models under consideration.

The second advantage was that parameter estimates could be based on a much larger number of cases (about eight times as many), hence considerably enhancing their reliability. Admittedly it could be objected that the nature of the respondents in some years may have been substantially different than in others, thereby making the estimates based on the pooled data severely biased. But given that the NES samples are independent, probability samples of the entire U.S. population for each of the years in question, no compelling theoretical reason appears to sustain this objection. In fact the only way in which the samples should systematically differ is that they were taken at different points in time. This of course, was controlled for by the addition of the time variable to the data set. In addition where appropriate, it can be determined through statistical tests (discussed earlier) whether differences over time in the effects of variables exist. For all these reasons therefore pooling the data in the research process seemed a legitimate and useful procedure.

Based on these pooled data and the model-building process, I arrived at the final model displayed in table B-1. Two aspects of the variables and categories used in the model should be immediately noted. First a number of variables are not included in this final model that appeared, at first glance, to be of theoretical pertinence to the decline in turnout. This is basically because regardless of the strength of the relationship on the bivariate level, these variables proved to have no significant effect on turnout in a properly specified multivatiate model. Examples of such variables include all of the political cynicism characteristics discussed in chapter 2 (see table 2-1).

Second I started out with more categories for some of the variables in the final model than appear in table B-1. These categories were collapsed to the levels shown in table B-1 for the reasons described above in the section on model building. However, I list all the categories used in the original coding of these variables in appendix C.

The specific pattern of parameter estimates in the model deserves some brief comment. To begin with education and age are both better predictors of voter turnout than income. This is shown both by the relative magnitude of the estimates and the fact that additional income ceases to have much effect once the $40,000-and-above level is reached.

Also, although education and age are better predictors of turnout than income in this model, the education and age parameter estimates are not nearly as strong as they are in a bivariate model or in a model that includes only demographic or social structural variables. This is because the political and attitudinal variables in my NES model substantially attenuate the effects of education and age on turnout. This relationship is illustrated by the contrast between the education and age parameter estimates in table B-1 and those in the census model in table B-2, where, of course, no political or attitudinal variables are present.

However, in both models—NES and census—the more education one has, the more likely one is to vote. And for age the likelihood of voting increases as one gets older until a threshold is hit at about 75 years. After that the likelihood of voting declines as one gets older, undoubtedly because of the physical difficulties of registering and getting to the polls increase.

Also note that in table B-1, race (nonblack) is a very weak predictor of voter turnout, much weaker than income, or even marital status. Even weaker than race was gender, for which the lack of relationship with turnout was so striking that I simply left it out of the final model.

Interestingly region of residence (non-South) continues to be a good predictor of voter turnout even in a multivariate model, with a parameter estimate of 0.3684. But see the discussion at the end of chapter 2, where the possibility of a change over time in the strength of this effect is considered.

Finally note that campaign newspaper reading is a fairly strong predictor of voter turnout— substantially stronger, for example, than cam-

TABLE B-1. *Probit Model of NES Data*[a]

Variable	Probit estimate	Standard error
Age		
29–36	.2372	.0477
37–44	.2868	.0527
45–64	.4116	.4081
65–74	.6115	.0675
75 or older	.3720	.0812
Church attendance		
Seldom	.2055	.0436
Often	.4432	.0484
Regularly	.5649	.0463
Education		
High school graduate	.2651	.0391
Some college	.4081	.0517
College graduate	.5155	.0670
Family income (1988 dollars)		
7,500–19,999	.1047	.0495
20,000–39,999	.2076	.0550
40,000 or higher	.2809	.0643
Marital status		
Married, spouse present	.1477	.0357
Residential mobility (years)		
2–4	.2436	.0473
5–9	.3886	.0470
10 or more	.5689	.0421
Occupation		
Professional–technical	.3114	.0706
Managerial–administrative	.1446	.0676
Clerical–sales	.3267	.0535
Blue collar–service	.0669[b]	.0401
Farm	.4033	.1073
Student	.1931[b]	.1140

paign television viewing. This is true even after education, age, interest in the campaign, following government and public affairs, knowledge of parties and candidates, and caring which party wins the election are controlled for. The significance of this is commented on in the text.

NES Estimation Procedures

In chapter 2, I discussed the relative contributions of different factors in the NES model to turnout decline from 1960 to 1988. This was based on an estimate of turnout decline generated by the model. Here I clarify how this estimate was made.

TABLE B-1. *Continued*

Variable	Probit estimate	Standard error
Race		
Nonblack	.0857[b]	.0513
Region		
Non-South	.3684	.0340
Important differences between parties?		
Yes	.1385	.0325
Campaign interest		
Somewhat interested	.1634	.0392
Very much interested	.3046	.0486
Campaign newspaper reading		
Some articles	.2541	.0373
Many articles	.3081	.0421
Campaign TV watching		
At least some programs	.1263	.0451
Care which party wins election?		
Yes	.1823	.0334
Following government and public affairs		
At least some of the time	.2310	.0346
Knowledge of parties and candidates		
Low	.2507	.0697
Medium	.3303	.0714
High	.3973	.0764
Very high	.4920	.0808
Partisanship	.2434	.0267
Sense of government responsiveness		
(political efficacy)	.1820	.0189

SOURCES: Author's estimate based on NES data for 1960–88 presidential years.
a. Unweighted N = 9,789; − 2 × log likelihood ratio = 9,079.4.
b. *t*-test is not significant at .05 level.

Predicted turnout decline can be predicted in two ways using the model in table B-1. Briefly put these ways entail taking the average of the predicted probabilities *or* the probability of the predicted average (probit).

Using the average of the predicted probabilities involves computing an individual probit for each respondent, turning it into a probability using the cumulative standard normal distribution function, and then averaging those probabilities over the year or population group one is interested in. This method was used in the section of the text in which I discussed the predicted increase in turnout under registration reform.[7] The drawback of this method is that, though technically more

7. See chapter 4 and also the discussion in this appendix in the section on census-CPS estimation procedures.

TABLE B-2. *Probit Model of Census Data*[a]

Variable	Probit estimate	Standard error
Age		
25–28	.0937	.0182
29–32	.2566	.0190
33–36	.3671	.0202
37–40	.4663	.0213
41–44	.5426	.0223
45–54	.7791	.0176
55–64	1.0038	.0184
65–74	1.1923	.0214
75 or older	.9809	.0245
Education		
9–11 years	.1621	.0166
High school graduate	.5552	.0151
Some college	.8900	.0185
College graduate	1.1590	.0219
Family income (1988 dollars)		
7,500–19,999	.1363	.0150
20,000–39,999	.3288	.0160
40,000 or more	.4619	.0183
Marital status		
Married, spouse present	.2419	.0106
Occupation		
Professional–technical	.2226	.0208
Managerial–administrative	.1091	.0211
Clerical–sales	.1991	.0149
Blue collar	−.0890	.0132
Farm	.1307	.0324
Student	.2741	.0291
Unable to work	−.5695	.0356
Retired or other	−.0466	.0179
Race		
White	−.1998	.0164
Other	−.4660	.0355
Region		
Non–South	.1393	.0123
Closing date (days)	−.0064	.0005
Hours registration offices open		
Regular business hours	.1036	.0158
Evenings and/or Saturdays	.0557	.0100
Purging for nonvoting	.0109	.0022

SOURCES: Author's estimate based on U.S. Bureau of the Census data for 1972, 1980, 1984.
a. N = 92,469; − 2 × log likelihood ratio = 101,558.1.

correct, there is no way to decompose the change predicted by the model to show how much each variable contributed to it. And because of this, there is no way to show the relative contribution of different factors to turnout decline.

Thus in chapter 2, when I wanted to explain how much each demo-graphic—social structural and political—attitudinal variable contrib-uted to the predicted drop in voter turnout between 1960 and 1988, I used the second method, the probability of the predicted average. (However, either method, it should be stressed, produces essentially the same predicted change in turnout levels across time in this case.) The method was implemented in the following way.

First it was necessary to compute the mean for each variable in the NES model for the years 1960 and 1988 (for categorical variables, this entailed computing the mean for each category of the variable).[8] Next the 1960 and 1988 means were multiplied by the coefficient of each variable or category of variable[9] I then subtracted, for each variable or category, the product for 1988 from the product for 1960.

The resulting difference between the 1988 and 1960 products rep-resented, for each variable or category, the amount of (probit) decline predicted by the model that was attributable to the changed mean on that variable or category between 1960 and 1988. (Predicted probit increase was reported as a negative number because the purpose of the table was to explain decline.) I then summed these differences across appropriate variables/categories to obtain the predicted probit decline for each characteristic or group of characteristics displayed in table 2-6.[10]

It was then possible to calculate the percent of predicted decline attributable to each characteristic or group of characteristics in table 2-6. This was done by dividing the predicted probit decline for each characteristic or group of characteristics by predicted decline over the entire model (and multiplying by 100).

It was also possible to calculate the percent of "SES-adjusted" pre-dicted decline. To do this I first subtracted the amount of probit decline

8. I should note here that I used the 1960 means for residential mobility for both 1960 and 1988 because of the coding problems with the mobility variable discussed in appendix C. This essentially holds mobility constant over the 1960–88 period, an as-sumption consistent with Bureau of the Census data. In this way, I "forced" mobility to make no contribution to turnout decline over the 1960–88 period, despite the (probably artifactual) distributional shifts shown in the NES data.
9. See table B-1 for a list of the coefficients used in the model.
10. A little more detail on this method and some simple equations are contained in Teixeira 1987, pp. 71–76.

produced by all the SES variables in the model (education, occupation, and income) from the amount of probit decline produced by all the variables together. Because the SES variables actually produce a negative probit decline (that is, they produce a probit increase), this procedure results in a larger probit decline to be explained. I then divided the probit decline for each characteric or group of characteristics in table 2-6 (excluding the SES variables) by this larger figure to get the percent of SES-adjusted decline explained by each.

In chapter 2, I also discussed the fact that turnout would have gone up in the 1960-88 period on the basis of changing income, occupation, and education, if nothing else had changed during that period. The estimate given in that context was also generated by the probability of the predicted average method with a slight difference in procedure.

This difference was that only the means of income, occupation, and education were allowed to change. All other variables were left (that is, held constant) at their 1960 levels. I then added up the total probit increase produced by the model with only the three variables changed, and used the cumulative standard normal distribution function to translate that probit increase into a predicted change in turnout levels.

The same approach was used later in chapter 2, in which I discussed the effect of the changes in SES, together with changes in social connectedness (that is, changes in marital status, church attendance, and age). Specifically I simply held the means of all variables in the model, other than the six I was interested in, at their 1960 levels and then followed the procedure just described to estimate the change in turnout levels attributable to those six variables alone.

Census-CPS Modeling Procedures

Many of the procedures discussed in the previous sections were also used in constructing the census-CPS model. There were some differences, of course. For example, I did not use time dummies in constructing the census model because the census data were not expected to inform the analysis of turnout decline. Instead I was primarily interested in developing accurate estimates of the effects of demographic characteristics and, especially, registration laws on voter turnout.

Separate models were initially estimated on unweighted data from three different presidential years: 1972, 1980, and 1984. These are the only three presidential elections for which both adequate census data and an adequate set of registration variables are available. (I focused on presidential elections exclusively so that the difference in dynamics between presidential and off-year elections would not cloud the assessment of registration law effects.) Once I determined which variables were consistently significant across the three surveys, samples were drawn from each year and combined into a pooled data set. The data were pooled to enhance the reliability of parameter estimates for registration laws because it is more likely that estimates for one year alone will pick up variation attributable to unobserved state-level political events. The final model was estimated on this data set, using the variables that demonstrated a consistent relationship to turnout across elections.

A few words should be said about the pooled data set. Because each census data set contains approximately 100,000 responses, I could not use the entire data set from each year to construct the final model, as I did with the NES.[11] The combined data set would have simply been too large for our available computer facility. Instead, using a random sampling procedure, I selected one-third of the respondents from each year (1972, 1980, and 1984) and combined them to create a data set approximately the same size as one of the original data sets. The final data set had 101,186 responents of which 92,535 were used for the final probit analysis. (The remaining 8,651 respondents were coded missing on one of the variables in the final model.) This final model is displayed in table B-2.

Census-CPS Estimation Procedures

To estimate the projected turnout increase of selected demographic groups from registration reform, I used the method alluded to earlier as the average of predicted probabilities method. First I computed the probability of voting for each individual in the 1984 data set.[12] I did this by multiplying the coefficients from the model in table B-2 by the appropriate data for each individual in the data set. Then the resulting probit estimate was converted into a probability by evaluating this estimate using the cumulative standard normal distribution function.

11. See appendix A for the exact size of the data set for each year.
12. I used 1984 data because this was the latest year for which I had both the census data and reliable registration law data. Of course, all else equal, it would have been preferable to use 1988 data for these estimates. Unfortunately however, as explained elsewhere, I did not have adequate registration data for 1988. In any event these estimates are likely to look fairly similar no matter which of these years is used, so the use of an older rather than newer census survey should make little substantive difference.

This procedure was then repeated after recoding the registration variables for each individual so that they were at their most liberal setting. That is, a new probit estimate was generated for each individual under liberalized conditions and then converted into a probability. I then simply subtracted the two probabilities—that is, I substracted the probability of each individual voting *under actual conditions* from the probability of that individual voting *with registration laws liberalized*. This created a new variable for each individual (called here "diff") which represented the difference in probability of voting under the two scenarios.

Once I had the predicted change in probability of voting for each individual, those changes could be weighted and averaged over all individuals to generate the predicted change in turnout from registration reform. It was also straightforward to estimate the the projected turnout increase for each demographic group (or state) by simply computing the mean of "diff" for each demographic group (or state).

After estimating the projected turnout increase of selected demographic groups from registration reform as described above, I looked at how the composition of the pool of voters would change under various scenarios of registration reform. Specifically I looked at three possiblities, a "low" increase in turnout, a "moderate" increase, and a "high" increase.[13] The projected voting pool under each scenario was compared to the actual voting pool as described below (and in chapter 4).

For comparison purposes, the "actual" voting pool was really a *predicted* actual voting pool. The reason for this is that, if I had used voters' self-reported turnout to create the actual voting pool, then the differences between projected and actual voters solely from modeled changes in registration laws would become conflated with the individual-level residuals from the model. Using the same procedure to estimate both the "actual" and projected voting pools results in these residuals canceling each other out, leaving compositional change solely attributable to liberalization of registration.

The composition of the predicted actual voting pool was calculated using each individual's predicted probability of voting. (See the first paragraph in this section for a description of how this probability was computed.) I then calculated the percentage of the voters with a given characteristic (for example, living in the South), by (1) adding up the

13. See chapter 4 for a discussion of these three different scenarios.

probability of voting under actual registration laws for each individual with that characteristic; (2) dividing the resulting sum by the sum of the probability of voting under actual registration laws for all individuals in the sample; and (3) multiplying by 100.[14]

The projected composition of the voting pool with a "moderate" increase in turnout from registration reform was calculated by essentially the same method. The only difference was that, instead of summing the probability of each individual voting under actual conditions, I summed the probability of each individual in a given group voting *under registration reform* and then divided this number by the sum of the probability of the entire sample voting *under registration reform* and multiplied by 100.

To compute the projected composition of the voting pool under the "low" estimate of turnout increase (approximately a 4 percent increase instead of the 8 percent projected under moderate reform), I simply divided "diff" by two.[15] I then added each individual's actual probability of voting to this quantity ("diff" divided by 2) to obtain his or her probability of voting with a "low" turnout increase. (Because "diff" represents the difference in probability of voting for each individual under actual conditions and liberalized registration conditions, halving "diff" and then adding to it the probability of voting for a given individual under actual conditions has the effect of halving the projected increase in turnout from registration reform.) I then followed the summation and division procedures described above to calculate the projected composition of the voting pool based on various demographic groups.

The "high" estimate of turnout increase (approximately a 16 percent increase) was calculated in a precisely analagous fashion. I simply multiplied "diff" by 2 and then followed the procedure described above for computing the "low" estimate of turnout increase.

14. This is the same method used by Wolfinger and Rosenstone 1980, p. 139, note 16.
15. See the first paragraph in this section for an explanation of the calculation of the variable "diff."

Appendix C:
Question Wording
for Variables and
Coding Decisions

In this appendix I discuss the coding of the demographic–social structural, political-attitudinal, and registration variables used in my analyses. I also give the original question wording for the political and attitudinal variables. The discussion of the political and attitudinal variables is organized by the tables in which variables appear in the text.

Unless there was a compelling reason to do otherwise, I chose to code and analyze variables as categorical rather than making the interval-level assumption. When variables are treated as categories, meaningful contrasts can be made between the categories in terms of their relationship to the dependent variable. These contrasts are lost when the interval-level assumption is made.

Because categorical variables become unwieldy when too much information is retained (that is, when a large number of categories are used), I attempted to trim the number of categories down to those that captured the most important and significant contrasts. (Technically one could treat every different value of a variable as a separate category—in fact, this is really what is contained within the structure of the data.) I discuss in detail the categories in my original coding in the sections here. Appendix B contains a discussion of why and how some of these categories were collapsed in final model estimations.

Whenever possible I based my coding for the NES on the coding in the *American National Election Studies Cumulative Data File 1952–1988.*

For several of the variables however, I wanted more information than was contained in the cumulative file, so I merged some data from individual year studies into the data set from the cumulative file. In this way I was able to obtain more detailed measures of family income, occupation, campaign newspaper reading, campaign television viewing, residential mobility, and several other characteristics.

NES Demographic and Social Structural Variables

AGE. Age was coded as a series of categories rather than as an interval-level variable such as actual age in years for the reasons discussed above. The categories used for age were 18–24 years, 25–28 years, 29–32 years, 33–36 years, 37–40 years, 41–44 years, 45–54 years, 55–64 years, 65–74 years, and 75 years or older.

CHURCH ATTENDANCE. Church attendance was coded and treated as a categorical level variable. For the years 1960–68 the survey asked, "Would you say you go to church regularly, often, seldom, or never?" The categories used in my model were those given in answer to the question: "regularly, often, seldom, and never." For the years 1972–88 the wording of the question and the possible answers were changed. In those years the NES questionnaire asked, "Would you say you go to (church/synagogue) every week, almost every week, once or twice a month, a few times a year, or never?" Responses to the new question were coded so that a few times a year equalled "seldom," almost every week equalled "often," once or twice a month equalled "often," and every week equalled "regularly."

COHORT. Cohorts were defined by the presidential election in which the respondents were first eligible to vote. However, in 1972 federal election law changed and 18- to 20-year-olds in all states became eligible to vote for the first time. For 1972 I therefore defined two new cohorts, those people aged 21 to 24 who would have been eligible to vote under old laws and those aged 18 to 20 who were only eligible to vote because of the change in the law. I did not use cohorts in my probit analysis, but I traced the turnout rates of each cohort through the years of this study. For a complete listing of all the cohorts examined, see table 3-6.

EDUCATION.   Education was also coded and treated as a categorical variable. The categories used for education were zero to eight years, nine to eleven years, high school graduate, some college, and college graduate or more. I coded education based on the last grade completed by the respondent.

HOME OWNERSHIP.   I coded the home ownership variable 1 if the respondent's family owned their own home and 0 if they did not. "Don't knows" were coded as missing. This question was not asked in 1960.

INCOME.   The data for family income presented a problem as respondents were not asked their exact income but instead were asked to place themselves in one of a series of categories. After adjusting for inflation (all income is presented in the text in 1988 dollars), these categories were not equivalent from year to year. To get around this problem I assigned each respondent a uniformly distributed random number. If their income (after adjusting for inflation) fell into a category that overlapped one of the categories I wished to create, I used those random numbers to assign the respondent to one of the two categories they overlapped.

For example the respondents with incomes of $10,000–$10,999 per year in 1980 dollars have incomes of $14,758–$16,232 per year in 1988 dollars. However, I wanted to use categories of $7,500–$14,999 and $15,000–$19,999 in my analysis. Assuming all respondents in the category were evenly distributed between $14,758 and $16,232, I calculated that 16.4 percent, (15,000–14,758)/(16,232–14,758)100, should be assigned to the lower category, $7,500–$14,999, and the remainder should be assigned to the higher category, $15,000–$19,999. Using random numbers I made those assignments.

The problem with this method is that it is quite likely that respondents are not evenly distributed within each income category, particulary the highest and lowest categories. However, the other reasonable alternative, simply assigning each category in the original data to the category it most closely matched in the categories I wished to create, seemed likely to skew the results even further than assuming even distribution of respondents within categories. In terms of the example above, I could have assigned the entire group of respondents discussed there (those with incomes of $10,000 to $10,999 in 1980 dollars, which became $14,758 to $16,232 in 1988 dollars) to the group most of them fell into—$15,000 to $19,999 in 1988 dollars. However, it seemed likely this would lessen rather than improve, the accuracy of my analyses.

The income categories actually used in my analyses were as follows: less than $7,500, $7,500 to $14,999, $15,000 to $19,999, $29,000 to $29,999, $30,000 to $39,999, $40,000 to $49,999, and $50,000 or more. All categories were in 1988 dollars.

I also divided respondents into sextiles (that is, six equal-sized groups) based on their family income, although I used these sextiles for descriptive purposes only and did not include them in my probit analysis. To do this I calculated the size of each sextile by dividing the weighted number of respondents for each year by six. Starting with the lowest sextile I assigned one category at a time from the original data (beginning with the lowest category in the data) to the first sextile until assigning another category to that sextile would have resulted in the sextile having too many respondents in it. I then used random numbers to assign the correct number of respondents in that category to one of the two sextiles their category overlapped, following the same procedure used above for income categories. In this way I was able to create sextiles with roughly equal numbers of respondents in them.

MARITAL STATUS. The marital status variable was dichotomized between those married and living with a spouse and those who were not. This latter category includes those never married, as well as those divorced, separated, or widowed. Little difference was found among these four groups in terms of their relationship to turnout, a fact that makes sense if the key aspect of marital status is the link to a spouse and the personal interactions and community "rootedness" that it engenders. Thus the particular manner in which individuals lack a spousal link—never married, divorced, and so on—should not be salient. The lack of this link is the important thing, and this is reflected in the dichotomization I used in my coding.

MOBILITY. Mobility was also coded as a categorical variable. The categories used were less than six months, six months to one year, one to two years, two to four years, five to nine years, and ten or more years.

The mobility data presented several difficulties. The first problem originated in the occasional failure of those who design the NES to maintain comparability of interview items from one election year to another. In this case the designers failed to include a question specifically on residential mobility in the 1968 and 1972 surveys. Instead a question on geographic mobility was used—that is, it asked the length of time the respondent had lived in his or her current community. Clearly the lengths of time measured by the two questions need not be identical.

This problem however, is not as severe as it appears at first glance. Although it is true that the lengths of time will not necessarily be identical, it is also true that the length of time at current residence will always be less than or equal to the length of time in current community. In other words someone who has been geographically mobile within two years is certain to have been residentially mobile within that period. Thus the geographic mobility variable may be treated as a residential mobility variable with certain obvious limitations.

The first limitation is that many people who are residentially mobile will not be coded as being so because they were not geographically mobile as well during the two-year time period. Thus the population proportions for being mobile in 1968 and 1972 will considerably underestimate the true population proportions. The second limitation flows from the first. Because the 1968 and 1972 mobility variables code some mobile individuals as nonmobile, this should attenuate the effect of mobility in those years because the contrast between the two categories will be lessened.

The more serious problem with the data for mobility is that the answers were not coded into the same category in each survey. In 1960 interviewers were instructed to put respondents who responded two years into the two-to-four-years category, whereas for the other survey years these instructions were not given and it is likely that some people who responded two years were placed in the one-to-two-years category, while others were placed in the two-to-four-years category. Consequently for 1960 the proportion of the population in the one-to-two-years category may be considerably under-estimated.

In 1976 the lowest category used was one year or less. I coded this as six months to one year, but some of these respondents surely belong in the lowest category, less than six months.

It is also unclear from the NES documentation whether partial year answers were treated the same from year to year. It is possible that in some years a respondent who answered three years and nine months was coded three years, while in other survey years the same respondent would have been coded four years. I did my best to standardize the coding, but the reader should keep the limits of the data for this variable in mind.

Because of these coding problems I did not think this variable would give a good measure of compositional change in residential mobility. In addition census data suggest that the change in residential mobility has been small over the years of this study. Consequently although I used this variable to specify my model, I did not use it when I estimated the effects of distributional change in turnout (see the related discussion in appendix B).

OCCUPATION AND EMPLOYMENT STATUS.   Respondents were originally divided into eleven occupation or employment status categories. Of these eleven, four categories represent people not in the labor force: housewives, students, retired or other, and unemployed or unable to work. (NES data do not allow a clean, consistent distinction to be made between those unemployed and unable to work over the 1960–88 time period.) The occupations of those employed were categorized as follows.

Two categories, operatives-craft and laborers, represent what are traditionally considered blue-collar jobs. Three of the categories, professional-technical, managerial-administrative, and clerical-sales, include what are traditionally thought of as white-collar workers (although clerical-sales jobs generally require less education and are considered less prestigious than professional-technical or managerial-administrative jobs). The remaining two categories are service and farm (the latter, which includes farm owners, managers, and laborers, represents less than 2 percent of the population).

To obtain these coding classifications, I used the occupation coding in the NES cumulative file to code everyone who was currently employed. I then went back to the original coding in the individual-year NES files to form separate categories for service, professional-technical, and managerial-administrative. For respondents who were not currently employed, I used the work status variable in the cumulative file to determine their reason for being out of the labor force.

RACE.   I experimented with different ways of coding the race variable. In the final specifications for my model, race is coded so that 0 = black, 1 = white, other (nonblack). Respondents were also coded into a variable with the categories white, black, and other, which was used in some preliminary analyses.

The problem with this white-black-other variable is that prior to 1980 no specific question on Hispanic ethnicity was asked, so that some Hispanics were probably coded as "other," whereas others were coded as white. For the years 1980–88, in contrast, respondents were specifically asked if they were Hispanic, so Hispanics could be cleanly assigned to either a white or other category. This lack of uniform categorization made me leery of using a race variable more complicated than black and nonblack.

REGION. I created two different region variables, both coded 0 = South, 1 = not South. For the first variable I used the census definition of the South: Alabama, Arkansas, Delaware, the District of Columbia, Florida, Georgia, Kentucky, Louisiana, Maryland, Mississippi, North Carolina, Oklahoma, South Carolina, Tennessee, Texas, Virginia, and West Virginia. For the second variable I defined the South as the former Confederate states: Alabama, Arkansas, Florida, Georgia, Louisiana, Mississippi, North Carolina, South Carolina, Tennessee, Texas, and Virginia.

In my final probit model I used the region variable that defines the South as the former Confederate states. I chose to use this definition of the South both because it had a slightly stronger parameter estimate and because it is the definition most commonly used in the literature on voter turnout. However, the final probit model does not look significantly different in any way when one definition of the South is substituted for the other.

UNION. I coded the union variable 1 if anyone in the household belonged to a labor union and 0 if they did not. "Don't knows" were coded as missing.

NES Political and Attitudinal Variables

In this section I discuss the coding of the political and attitudinal variables that were used in the analysis and give the text of the exact questions from which the variables were derived. The variables are organized by the table in which they first appear in the book.

Political Cynicism

The political cynicism variables in table 2-1 were coded exactly as they were in the original NES data except that answers categorized as "don't know," "both," "other," "depends," and "refused" were coded as missing. The categories are shown in table 2-1. The exact question wording is shown in figure C-1.

FIGURE C-1. *Question Wording for Political Cynicism Variables in Table 2-1*

Can government be trusted?
  How much of the time do you think you can trust the government in Washington to do what is right—just about always, most of the time, or only some of the time?
Is government run by big interests?
  Would you say the government is pretty much run by a few big interests looking out for themselves or that it is run for the benefit of all the people?
Does government waste tax money?
  Do you think that people in the government waste a lot of money we pay in taxes, waste some of it, or don't waste very much of it?
Is government competent?
  Do you feel that almost all of the people running the government are smart people [1958–72: who usually know what they are doing], or do you think that quite a few of them don't seem to know what they are doing?
Is government crooked?
  Do you think that quite a few of the people running the government are [1958–72: a little] crooked, not very many are, or do you think hardly any of them are crooked [1958–72: at all]?

Party-Related Characteristics

The distributional changes in party-related characteristics over the years of this study are shown in table 2-4, which lists all categories actually used in analysis. The exact text of the questions in the NES survey is shown in figure C-2. A discussion of the coding used for each variable is given below.

Party identification (partisanship) was coded as follows. Respondents who identified themselves as strong Democrats or strong Republicans were coded as strong partisans. Those who identified themselves as weak Democrats, weak Republicans, or independents who leaned toward the Democratic or Republican party were coded as weak partisans. Respondents who claimed to be true independents, as well as those who said they were apolitical and did not have a preference, were coded as independents.

"Care which party wins election?" was coded exactly as it was in the original NES data, which put respondents who answered "don't know," "it depends," and other in the same category with those who answered that they did not care very much. See table 2-4 for a listing of the categories.

"Are there important differences between parties?" was coded as follows. I coded respondents who answered "don't know" to this question

FIGURE C-2. *Question Wording for Party-Related Characteristics in Table 2-4*

Party identification
  Generally speaking, do you usually think of yourself as a Republican, a Democrat, an independent, or what? (IF REPUBLICAN OR DEMOCRAT) Would you call yourself a strong (REPUBLICAN/DEMOCRAT) or a not very strong (REPUBLICAN/ DEMOCRAT)? (IF INDEPENDENT, OTHER [1966–88: OR NO PREFERENCE]) Do you think of yourself as closer to the Republican or Democratic party?
Care which party wins election?
  Generally speaking, would you say that you personally care a good deal which party wins the presidential election this fall, or don't you care very much which party wins?
Are there important differences between parties?
  Do you think there are any important differences in what the Republicans and Democrats stand for?
Knowledge of parties and candidates
  Is there anything in particular that you like about the Democratic party? What is that? Anything else?

  Is there anything in particular that you dislike about the Democratic party? What is that? Anything else?

  Is there anything in particular that you like about the Republican party? What is that? Anything else?

  Is there anything in particular that you dislike about the Republican party? What is that? Anything else?

  Now I'd like to ask you about the good and bad points of the two candidates for president. Is there anything in particular about [Democratic presidential candidate] that might make you want to vote for him? What is that? Anything else?

  Is there anything in particular about [Democratic presidential candidate] that might make you want to vote against him? What is that? Anything else?

  Now I'd like to ask you about the good and bad points of the two candidates for president. Is there anything in particular about [Republican presidential candidate] that might make you want to vote for him? What is that? Anything else?

  Is there anything in particular about [Republican presidential candidate] that might make you want to vote against him? What is that? Anything else?

into the same category as those respondents who answered "no," because both groups were unable to identify important differences between the parties.

"Knowledge of parties and candidates" is a variable constructed from the series of eight questions shown in figure C-2. I counted the number of answers to each of the eight questions used to construct this variable to determine a total score for each person. Because the NES survey allowed up to five responses per question, the highest possible score

was 40. However, very, very few individuals attained scores at all this high. This probably reflects the fact that even a relatively knowledgable person could obtain a score of less than 20 if they could volunteer four or five things they liked about one party and that party's candidate but were unable to volunteer much they liked about the other party and the other party's candidate. Therefore I scored 13 to 40 opinions as very high, 9 to 12 as high, 5 to 8 as medium, 1 to 4 as low, and 0 as very low. (Multivariate analysis confirmed that there was little difference in effect on turnout once a certain threshhold of knowledge was reached.)

Political Involvement and Sense of Government Responsiveness

The exact wording for the questions concerning political involvement and sense of government responsiveness is given in figure C-3. Because the wording of several of these questions changed over the years of my study, 1960–88, I had to make a series of fairly difficult coding decisions.

Campaign newspaper reading was asked about in different ways in different years by the NES (figure C-3). Specific coding decisions were as follows:

For 1960–76 I coded responses of "yes, regularly" and "yes, often" as many articles and responses of "no" as no articles. I coded responses of "yes, from time to time," "yes, once in a great while," and "yes (with no frequency)" as some articles. I coded "don't know" as missing.

For 1980–84 I coded responses of "yes, a good many" as many articles and "no" as no articles. I coded responses of "yes, several," "yes, just one or two," and "yes, don't know how many" as some articles. I coded "don't know" as missing.

Both the wording and the placement of this question changed over the years used in this study. As shown in figure C-3, in 1972 the word "much" was added to the question (Did you read *much* about . . . ?"), possibly resulting in a higher number of respondents answering "no" and therefore not being probed about the quantity they read than would have been the case had the question been phrased as it usually was. This may have contributed to the strikingly large proportion in this category in 1972 (see table 2-5).

There is no reason, however, to believe that the proportion of responses coded as "many articles" (regularly, often) should have been seriously affected by this inconsistency. It is unlikely that someone who regularly or often read articles about the campaign would say "no"

FIGURE C-3. *Question Wording for Political Involvement and Sense of Government Responsiveness in Table 2-5*

Campaign newspaper reading
   1960–76. Did you read [1972: much] about the campaign this year in any newspaper? (IF YES) How much did you read newspaper articles about the election—regularly, often, from time to time, or just once in a great while?

   1980–84. Did you read about the campaign in any newspapers? (IF YES) How many newspaper articles did you read about the campaign—would you say you read a good many, several, or just one or two?

   1988. (IF RESPONDENT HAS READ A PAPER IN THE PAST WEEK) Did you read about the campaign in any newspaper? How much attention did you pay to newspaper articles about the campaign for president—a great deal, quite a bit, some, very little, or none?

Campaign TV watching
   1960–76. Did you watch any programs about the campaign on television? (IF YES) How many television programs about the campaign would you say you watched—a good many, several, or just one or two?

   1980–84. Did you watch any programs about the campaign on television? (IF YES) Would you say you watched—a good many, several, or just one or two?

   1988. (IF RESPONDENT HAS WATCHED TV IN THE PAST WEEK) How much attention did you pay to news on TV about the campaign for president—a great deal, quite a bit, some, very little, or none?

Campaign interest
   Some people don't pay much attention to the political campaigns. How about you, would you say that you have been/were very much interested, somewhat interested, or not much interested in following the political campaigns (so far) this year?

Following government and public affairs
   1960. We'd also like to know how much attention you pay to what's going on in politics generally. I mean from day to day, when there isn't any big election campaign going on, would you say you follow politics very closely, fairly closely, or not much at all?

   1964–88. Some people seem to follow [1964: think about] what's going on in government and public affairs most of the time, whether there's an election going on or not. Others aren't that interested. Would you say you follow what's going on in government and public affairs most of the time, some of the time, only now and then, or hardly at all?

Sense of government responsiveness (political efficacy)
   I don't think public officials care much what people like me think.

   People like me don't have any say about what the government does.

when asked if they had read much about the election in the papers and thus be filtered out of the second question. Because the "many articles" proportion also fell drastically in this year (table 2-5), this suggests that the 1968–72 decline in campaign newspaper reading was nevertheless substantial if possibly exaggerated in the "no articles" category.

It is also possible that the different wording for the second question in 1980 and 1984 resulted in some overestimation of the "some articles" category. This is because some people who might have said "often" to the question, as phrased in previous years, and thus were classified as "many articles," replied "several" with the 1980 wording and thus were classified as "some articles." However, because it seems likely that most respondents who often read the newspapers about the election would consider that amount "a good many," the extent of this overestimation should be small—if it exists at all.

The biggest problem for measuring and coding this variable occurs for the 1988 data because the placement of the question in the survey and the wording of the question changed that year. Instead of being asked after the election, as it was in all previous years, it was asked as part of the preelection survey. This must have produced at least some underreporting of the frequency of campaign newspaper reading because at least some respondents presumably read about the election in the newspaper after the survey was conducted but before the election.

Examination of 1988 campaign newspaper reading data by interview completion period, however, suggests that the extent of this underreporting was only modest. For example, those respondents who were interviewed in the last week before the election had campaign newspaper reading levels only a little higher (4 points higher on "many articles," 5 points lower on "no articles") than those interviewed in the middle of September. (Further support for this interpretation is provided by data from surveys taken in Wichita, Kansas, in 1990 and 1991 showing campaign newspaper reading going up by only modest amounts—that is, similar to the amounts quoted above for 1988—during periods running from considerably *before* a given election (more than one month) to periods actually *after* that election (one week).[1]

In addition to question placement the question wording and response categories changed in 1988. Instead of asking, "How many newspaper articles did you read . . . ?" the questionaire asked, "How much attention did you pay to newspaper articles . . . ?" I coded "yes, a great deal" and

1. Research Center 1990a, 1990b, 1991b.

"yes, quite a bit" as many articles and "none" as no articles. It is unlikely that someone who paid "a great deal" or "quite a bit" of attention to newspaper articles only read "some," so this coding is probably fairly accurate.

I also coded "yes, some," "yes, very little," and "yes, don't know how much" as some articles. It is possible that in earlier years some of these people would have been coded into a higher category because of different question wording, but I do not believe the number of such individuals is high. Those who paid "very little" attention to the articles they read is unlikely to have been inspired to have read many articles. And those who paid only "some" attention to the articles they read also probably did not follow the campaign closely and did not read many articles. Again then this leads me to be believe that the exceptionally low levels of campaign newspaper reading reported in the 1988 NES data are largely a reflection of very low campaign involvement in 1988, rather than an artifact of question placement or question wording.

These problems with the data on campaign newspaper reading, though problems that, all else equal, one would not wish to have, were not viewed as serious enough to warrant excluding this known powerful predictor of turnout from analysis.[2] Instead I decided to use the variable in analysis while being careful to keep in mind possible effects of these wording and placement discrepancies. (Notes in the main text alert readers to some of these problems so that readers can make their own decisions on what interpretive weight to accord these problems.)

Campaign TV watching is another variable for which the question wording was changed in the NES over the years of my study (figure C-3). Specific coding decisions were as follows.

For 1960–84 I coded responses of "yes, a good many" as many programs and "no" as no programs. I also coded responses of "yes, several," "yes, just one or two," and "yes (with no frequency)" as some programs.

In 1988 both the placement and wording on the question on campaign TV watching was changed. The question was asked in the pre-

2. I am forced to observe that the NES could make everyone's job a little easier if they simply kept question wording and certain aspects of question placement (that is, pre versus post) uniform from survey to survey. It is hard to see, for example, what was really gained from changing the wording of the campaign newspaper reading question so often and then radically altering the placement of the question. The net result of these activities is to seriously attenuate comparability of items across years, thereby making analysis of change over time—one of the main reasons, after all, we have an NES in the first place—that much more difficult. See Abramson 1990 for a pointed critique along these lines.

election survey instead of in the postelection survey as it had been in previous years. This results in the same potential for underreporting discussed in reference to campaign newspaper reading.

The wording of the question was also changed in much the same way as the wording of the question on newspaper reading that year. Instead of asking about the respondent's quantity of television watching, the 1988 survey asked, "How much attention did you pay. . . ?" This leads to the same coding problems discussed in the section on campaign newspaper reading.

As I did with campaign newspaper reading in 1988, I coded "yes, a great deal" and "yes, quite a bit" as many programs and "no" as no programs. I also coded "some," "very little," and "yes, don't know how much" as some programs for the reasons discussed under newspaper reading. And as was the case with campaign newspaper reading, I felt that, though these wording and placement problems should be kept in mind when interpreting analytical results, they were not serious enough to warrant excluding campaign television watching from my analysis.

Campaign interest is coded exactly as it was in the original NES coding except that "don't knows" are coded as missing. The categories used are listed in table 2-5.

Following government and public affairs is also coded the same as in the original NES coding except that for the years from 1964 on the responses "hardly at all" and "only now and then" are combined into one category, "little of the time" (table 2-5). In 1960 the wording of the question was somewhat different than in the other years of this study (figure C-3), so I equated the responses "hardly at all" with "little of the time"; "fairly closely" with "some of the time"; and "very closely" with "most of the time."

Sense of government responsiveness (political efficacy) is a variable based on the two questions shown in figure C-3. They solicit respondents' opinions about whether they (really, "people like me") have influence over the government and public officials. A three-point interval scale (0,1,2) was used, going from low to medium to high efficacy. Those who disagreed with neither statement were scored as having low efficacy, those who disagreed with only one were scored medium, and those who disagreed with both were designated high.

FIGURE C-4. *Question Wording for Partisanship, Ideology, and Selected Issue Positions in Table 4-5*

Partisanship
  Generally speaking, do you usually think of yourself as a Republican, a Democrat, an Independent, or what? (IF REPUBLICAN OR DEMOCRAT) Would you call yourself a strong (REPUBLICAN/DEMOCRAT) or a not very strong (REPUBLICAN/ DEMOCRAT)? (IF INDEPENDENT, OTHER, OR NO PREFERENCE) Do you think of yourself as closer to the Republican or Democratic party?
Ideology
  We hear a lot of talk these days about liberals and conservatives. I'm going to show you a 7-point scale on which the political views that people might hold are arranged from extremely liberal to extremely conservative. Where would you place yourself on this scale, or haven't you thought much about this?
Should abortion be allowed?
  There has been some discussion about abortion during recent years. Which one of the opinions on this page best agrees with your view? You can just tell me the number of the opinion you choose.
    1. By law, abortion should never be permitted.
    2. The law should permit abortion only in case of rape, incest, or when the woman's life is in danger.
    3. The law should permit abortion for reasons other than rape, incest, or danger to the woman's life, but only after the need for the abortion has been clearly established.
    4. By law, a woman should always be able to obtain an abortion as a matter of personal choice.
Too much pushing for equal rights?
  I am going to read several statements. After each one, I would like you to tell me whether you agree strongly, agree somewhat, neither agree nor disagree, disagree somewhat, or disagree strongly. (RESPONDENT BOOKLET SHOWN TO RESPONDENT) We have gone too far in pushing equal rights in this country.
Should government see that everyone has job and good standard of living?
  Some people feel that the government in Washington should see to it that every person has a job and a good standard of living. Others think the government should just let each person get ahead on his own. And, of course, other people have opinions somewhere in between. Where would you place yourself on this scale, or haven't you thought much about this? (7-POINT SCALE SHOWN TO RESPONDENT)

Partisanship, Ideology and Selected Issue Positions

Table 4-5 lists the categories actually used in analysis. The exact wording of the questions about partisanship, ideology, and selected issue positions is given in figure C-4. An explanation of my coding for these variables is as follows.

Partisanship (party identification) was unchanged from the original NES coding except that I recoded respondents who identified themselves as apolitical with those who called themselves independents, because neither group is affiliated with a political party.

Ideology was also unchanged from the original NES coding.

"Should abortion be allowed?" was unchanged from the original NES coding.

"Too much pushing for equal rights?" was unchanged from the original NES coding.

"Should government see that everyone has job and good standard of living?" was collapsed from the original seven-point scale in which 1 equalled "government see to job and good standard of living" and 7 equalled "government let each person get ahead on own." I recoded 1 through 3 as "government should help," 4 as "middle-of-road," and 5 through 7 as "people should get ahead on their own." Because there were a large number of "don't knows" and no responses on this variable, I retained them in a separate category, "no placement." I felt this would give me a better picture of the actual changing composition of voter sentiments on this issue under various registration reform scenarios.

Other NES Political and Attitudinal Variables

CITIZEN DUTY.   Citizen duty measures come from two variables in the NES. In 1960 and again from 1972 to 1980, the question was asked, "So many other people vote in the national elections that it doesn't matter much to me whether I vote or not." Respondents who agreed with this statement were coded 0 and those who disagreed were coded 1. Respondents who answered "don't know," "it depends," "not sure," and "can't say," along with those who refused to answer or were not asked the question were coded as missing.

In 1960 and again from 1972 to 1988, the question was asked, "If a person doesn't care how an election comes out he (1980, 1984, 1988; then "that person") shouldn't vote in it." Respondents who agreed with this statement were coded 0 and those who disagreed were coded 1. Respondents who answered that they neither agreed nor disagreed with the statement were coded 0 (this response was coded for 1988 only). Respondents who answered "don't know," "it depends," "not sure," and "can't say," along with those who refused to answer or were not asked the question were coded as missing.

VOTING.   Voting was coded as a categorical variable. Only clear answers of yes or no were used. "Don't know," "not available," and refused to answer were coded as missing and not used in the NES model. The question about voting was asked differently in different years. In 1960 the survey asked, "How about you, did you vote this time?" For 1964–70 the question was phrased, "How about you, did you vote this time, or did something keep you from voting?" From 1970 to 1976 the survey asked, "How about you, did you vote in the elections this fall," and 1980 to 1988 it asked, "How about you, did you vote in the elections this November?"

NES Contextual Variables

Several contextual variables used in the analysis were reported at the end of chapter 2. The coding of these variables is discussed in the following pages.

GUBERNATORIAL RACE.   Data on whether a state had a gubernatorial race concurrent with each of the presidential elections in the study was taken from the appropriate volumes of *America Votes, A Handbook of Contemporary America Election Statistics*. This variable was coded 1 if there was a gubernatorial election at the same time as the presidential election in a given year and 0 otherwise.

SPRING PRIMARY.   This variable is coded from information obtained from the appropriate volume of *American Votes, A Handbook of Contemporary American Election Statistics*, and follows the procedures described in Boyd (1989). It is coded on a scale of 1 to 4 and measures the number of contested primaries in the two major parties in each state. A contested primary is defined as one in which at least two candidates appear on the ballot for a given office in a given party. A 0 would mean no contested primaries were held in that state for the year being looked at. A 4 would indicate that contested primaries were held in both parties in all congressional districts, as well as in the senate, gubernatorial, and congressional races. (One point is allocated for congressional primaries, one point for Senate primaries, one point for presidential primaries and one point for gubernatorial primaries.)

For gubernatorial, Senate, and presidential races, each state was given 0.5 points for each contested primary in each major party. For example, if state A had contested primaries in the Democratic party in the gubernatorial and presidential primaries and in the Republican party in the presidential primary only, and state A did not have a Senate primary in the year I was looking at, state A would score 1.5.

To allocate the one point for congressional primaries I added up the number of contested congressional primary races in both major parties in the state and divided the sum by two times the number of congressional districts in the state. Thus if state A had eighteen congressional districts, and primaries were contested in the Democratic party in five districts and in the Republican party in eight districts, state A would obtain a score of 0.36 $[(5+8)/(2 \times 18)]$ for congressional primaries. This would be added to its previous score of 1.5 for a total score of 1.86 for spring primaries.

FALL PRIMARY.   This variable was coded the same way as spring primary.

RUNOFF PRIMARY.   This variable was coded the same way as spring primary.

Census-CPS Variables

AGE.   The age variable was coded as a categorical variable. The categories used were 18 to 24 years, 25 to 28 years, 29 to 32 years, 33 to 36 years, 37 to 40 years, 41 to 44 years, 45 to 54 years, 55 to 64 years, 65 to 74 years, and 75 years or older.

CITIZEN.   Unlike the NES, the CPS data set includes both citizens and noncitizens. I excluded noncitizens from my probit analysis because they are not eligible to vote and including them could have potentially distorted my model of voter turnout. Starting in 1980, the CPS questionnaire specifically asked respondents if they were citizens. Consequently I selected only those who replied "yes" for my probit analysis.

Prior to 1980 however, the question was not asked. Instead, not being a citizen was one of several answers a respondent could give when asked why he or she was not registered to vote. Thus, for my probit analysis for 1972 and 1976, I selected only those respondents who did *not* volunteer that they were not citizens when asked why they did not register. However, I suspect that some noncitizens are included in my analysis for those two years, because isolating noncitizens *after* respondents are asked about voting participation seems less likely to have been a successful device than a direct filter isolating noncitizens *before* respondents are asked about voting (as was the case from 1980 on). It is unlikely however, that the numbers of these "bogus" citizens was great enough to seriously affect the accuracy of my analysis.

COHORT. Cohorts were defined exactly as they were in the NES. See the discussion of cohorts in the section on NES demographic and social structural variables.

EDUCATION. Education was coded in five categories defined by the highest grade completed by the respondent: zero to eight years, nine to eleven years, high school graduate, some college, and college graduate or more.

HOME OWNERSHIP. A question about home ownership was asked by the Census Bureau in 1976 and 1980. I coded the responses 1 if the respondent's family owned the home in which he or she lived and 0 if they did not.

INCOME. Income was coded into the following categories measured in 1988 dollars and based on family, not individual[3], income: less than $7,500, $7,500 to $14,999, $15,000 to $19,999, $20,000 to $29,999, $30,000 to $39,999, $40,000 to $59,999, and $60,000 or more. Income was originally coded by the Census Bureau into a series of categories that I adjusted for inflation so that all incomes were measured in 1988 dollars. Because the categories obtained after adjusting for inflation did not exactly match the categories I wished to use in analysis, I followed the procedure described in the section on income coding for the NES to match respondents to income categories.

For descriptive purposes I also divided respondents into sextiles (that is, six equal-sized groups) based on their income. Again I followed the same procedure for constructing these sextiles described earlier in the section on income coding for the NES.

MARITAL STATUS. Respondents were divided into married and not married. Those respondents who replied that they were never married, divorced, widowed, or separated were coded as not married. The reasons for coding respondents this way were briefly discussed earlier in the marital status coding section for the NES.

MOBILITY. A question about residential mobility was only asked by the Census Bureau in 1976 and 1980. I was therefore able to examine

3. In cases in which the "family" consisted of one individual, that individual's income was considered the family income. In such cases, of course, family and individual income are identical.

the effects of residential mobility on turnout only in these two years. Mobility was coded into the following categories: less than six months, six months to one year, one to two years, three to five years, and six or more years (six or more is as high as the census variable goes).

OCCUPATION AND EMPLOYMENT STATUS. Occupation and employment status was coded in twelve categories: housewives, professional-technical, clerical-sales, operatives-craft, farm, laborers, unemployed, students, unable to work, managerial-administrative, service, and retired or other. These are roughly the same categories used with the NES data, except that the NES data did not allow me to cleanly distinguish between those who were unemployed and those simply unable to work, whereas the CPS data did. (For a discussion of why I used the other categories just given, see my explanation in the occupation coding section for the NES.) Respondents were assigned to occupation and employment status categories by collapsing the census occupational codes for employed workers and then using the census employment status variable to code housewives, the unemployed, students, those unable to work, and retired or other.

RACE. Race was divided into three categories: white, black, and other. I followed the categories used in the original CPS data and did not attempt to separate out Hispanics and include them in the "other" category or a separate Hispanic category. A separate variable about Hispanic ethnicity was not included with the 1972 census data file, and I wished to make my data as consistent as possible from year to year. Therefore, Hispanics were left as originally coded in terms of "white," "black," and "other." In practice this means that Hispanics are overwhelmingly coded as white (over 90 percent) in the data used in my analysis.

REGION. Region is defined in the same way as in the NES data set.

UNION. A question about union membership was asked of a subset of the respondents in the CPS in 1984 and 1988 only. I coded them 1 if they were a member of a union and 0 otherwise. Note that this variable is not the same as the union variable in the NES data set, which asked if anyone in the *household* belonged to a union. The CPS asked only about the union membership of the person being surveyed.

VOTING. The voting variable was coded in two different ways in the census data set. For the purpose of descriptive analysis of the population in the tables in the text, two categories were created, definite voters and everyone one. This follows the procedures established by the Census Bureau in their descriptive publications. The probit model presented in the text, however, distinguishes between voters and non-voters. All others (those who were coded "don't know," "not available," "not in the universe (noncitizens)," or "not reported by the Census Bureau") are coded as missing in the model and thus left out of the analysis. The exact wording of the question asked by the Census Bureau in 1972 is not available in the documentation it provides. In 1972 the Census Bureau asked, "Did . . . vote in the election held on November 2nd?" In 1980 it asked, "Did . . . vote in the election held on November 4th?" In 1984 the CPS survey asked, "In any election some people are not able to vote because they are sick or busy or have some other reasons, and others do not want to vote. Did you vote in the election on November 6th?" In 1988 the question was phrased, "In any election some people are not able to vote because they are sick or busy or have some other reasons, and others do not want to vote. Did . . . vote in the election on November 8th?"

Registration Variables

The Mitchell/Wlezien 1972–84 registration law data set (see appendix A) was my main source of registration law data. For that reason the coding given below for registration laws generally applies to that data set. The two exceptions are for motor voter and agency-based registration, for which the coding applies to data obtained from other sources (see appendix A).

All the states except North Dakota require citizens to register to vote to be eligible to participate in elections. Because North Dakota does not require registration, many of the variables used in my analysis do not apply to citizens of that state. However, when a registration variable did not directly apply to North Dakota, I coded it as the most liberal value possible in order not to exclude North Dakota from the analysis. Because not requiring registration makes it even easier for citizens to vote than liberalizing registration laws does, this seemed to be the best way to code registration laws for residents of this state.

With this in mind the specific coding I used for registration law variables is as follows.

ABSENTEE.   Absentee was coded 1 if anyone eligible to vote could register absentee, if incapacitated or absent for any reason. Otherwise it was coded 0. North Dakota was coded 1.

AGENCY-BASED REGISTRATION.   This variable codes the use of government agencies to register voters. If a state had agency-based registration it was coded 1. Otherwise it was coded 0. North Dakota was coded 1.

CLOSING DATE.   The closing date is the last day on which a person can register to vote before the election. The coding is the actual number of days between closing date and election. North Dakota was coded 0.

COUNTY, CITY, OR NEIGHBORHOOD.   This was measured by two variables. The first variable was coded 1 if registration could only take place at the county level and 0 otherwise. The second variable was coded 1 if registration could take place in local precincts or neighborhoods and 0 otherwise. North Dakota was coded 0 on the first variable and 1 on the second.

DEPUTY REGISTRARS.   The deputy registrars variable was coded 1 if there was any use of deputy registrars. Otherwise it was coded 0. North Dakota was coded 1.

HOURS DURING WHICH REGISTRATION OFFICES ARE OPEN.   The registration office hours variable was measured by two variables. The first variable was coded 1 if state election offices were open during regular business hours and 0 if they were open irregularly (that is, less than forty hours during the business week). The second variable was coded 1 if the state allowed registration during the evenings or on Saturday instead of simply during working hours. If registration could take place only during the work week it was coded 0. North Dakota was coded 1 on both variables.

HOURS POLLS ARE OPEN.   The hours polls are open was coded as the minimum number of hours the polls are required to be open in each state.

MAIL REGISTRATION.   This variable was coded 1 if mail registration was available and 0 if not. North Dakota was coded 1.

MOTOR VOTER.   The motor voter variable was coded 1 if there was a provision for registering while obtaining or renewing a driver's license and 0 otherwise. North Dakota was coded 1.

PURGING.   Purging for nonvoting is the removal of citizens from the registration rolls for failure to vote after a certain number of years. Purging was coded by the actual number of years a state allows to lapse before purging takes place. States with no purging, including North Dakota, which does not require registration, were coded 10.

RESIDENCY REQUIREMENT.   The residency requirement is the minimum number of days a person must have lived in the area before the election. The coding is the number of days required. States with no residency requirement were coded 0.

References

Abramson, Jeffrey, F. Christopher Arterton, and Gary Orren. 1988. *Electronic Commonwealth: The Impact of New Media Policies on Democratic Politics*. Basic Books.

Abramson, Paul R. 1990. "The Decline of Over-Time Comparability in the National Election Studies." *Public Opinion Quarterly* 54: 177–90.

Abramson, Paul R., and John H. Aldrich. 1982. "The Decline of Electoral Participation in America." *American Political Science Review* 76: 502–21.

Abramson, Paul R., John H. Aldrich, and D. W. Rohde. 1987. *Change and Continuity in the 1984 Elections*, rev. ed. Washington: Congressional Quarterly Press.

———. 1990. *Change and Continuity in the 1988 Elections*. Washington: Congressional Quarterly Press.

Abramson, Paul R., Brian D. Silver, and Barbara A. Anderson. 1987. "The Effects of Question Order in Attitude Surveys: The Case of SRC/CPS Duty Items." *American Journal of Political Science* 31 (November): 900–08.

Adatto, K. 1990. "The Incredible Shrinking Sound Bite." *New Republic*. May 28, pp. 20–23.

Aldrich, John H. Forthcoming. "Turnout and Rational Choice." *American Journal of Political Science*.

Almond, Gabriel A., and Sidney Verba. 1963. *The Civic Culture: Political Attitudes and Democracy in Five Nations*. Princeton University Press.

Amy, Douglas J. 1992. "Real Elections: The Case for Proportional Representation in the U.S." Department of Politics, Mount Holyoke College.

Baker, R. J., and J. A. Nelder. 1978. *The GLIM System: Generalized Linear Modelling*. Oxford, England: Royal Statistical Society.

Bennet, Stephen E. 1990a. "The Uses and Abuses of Registration and Turnout Data: An Analysis of Piven and Cloward's Studies of Nonvoting in America." *PS: Political Science and Politics* 23 (June).

———. 1990b. "Some Problems in the Measurement of Psychological Involvement in Public Affairs." Department of Political Science, University of Cincinnati.

————. 1991. "Left Behind: Exploring Declining Turnout Among Noncollege Young Whites, 1964–1988." *Social Science Quarterly* 72: 314–33.

Bennett, Stephen E., and D. Resnick. 1990. "The Implications of Nonvoting for Democracy in the United States." *American Journal of Political Science* 34: 771–802.

Bishop, Yvonne M. M., S. E. Feinberg, and P.W. Holland. 1975. *Discrete Multivariate Analysis: Theory and Practice*. MIT Press.

Boyd, Richard W. 1981. "Decline of U.S. Voter Turnout: Structural Explanations." *American Politics Quarterly* 9 (April): 133–59.

————. 1986. "Election Calendars and Voter Turnout." *American Politics Quarterly* 14 (January-April): 89–104.

————. 1989. "The Effects of Primaries and Statewide Races on Voter Turnout." *Journal of Politics* 51 (August): 730–39.

Brady, Henry, Norman H. Nie, Kay L. Scholzman, and Sidney Verba. 1988. "Participation in America Revisited: A Proposal." Unpublished proposal. University of Chicago.

Brody, Richard A., 1978. "The Puzzle of Political Participation in America." In Anthony King, ed., *The New American Political System*. Washington: American Enterprise Institute for Public Policy Research.

Buchanan, Bruce. 1991. *Electing a President: The Markle Commission Research on Campaign '88*. University of Texas Press.

Burnham, Walter D. 1982. "The Appearance and Disappearance of the American Voter." In Walter D. Burnham, *The Current Crisis in American Politics*. Oxford University Press.

————. 1986. "Those High Nineteenth-Century American Voting Turnouts: Fact or Fiction?" *Journal of Interdisciplinary History* 16: 613–44.

————. 1987. "The Turnout Problem." In A. James Reichley, ed., *Elections American Style*. Brookings.

————. 1991. "Critical Realignment: Dead or Alive." In B. E. Shafer, ed., *The End of Realignment?: Interpreting American Electoral Eras*. University of Wisconsin Press.

Calvert, Jerry, and Jack Gilchrist. 1991. "The Social and Issue Dimensions of Voting and Nonvoting in the United States." Paper prepared for the annual meeting of the American Political Science Association.

Carson, C. C., R. M. Huelskamp, and T. D. Woodall. 1991. "Perspectives on Education in America." Systems Analysis Department, Sandia National Laboratories.

Cassel, Carol A. 1979. "Change in Electoral Participation in the South." *Journal of Politics* 41: 907–17.

Cavanaugh, Thomas E. 1991. "When Turnout Matters: Mobilization and Conversion as Determinants of Election Outcomes." In William J. Crotty, ed., *Political Participation and American Democracy*. Greenwood Press.

Citrin, Jack. 1974. "Comment: The Political Relevance of Trust in Government." *American Political Science Review* 68: 973–88.

Committee for the Study of the American Electorate. 1984. "Non-Voter Study '83–'84: The Role of Television in Increasing Campaign Costs." Washington (February).

———. 1987. *Creating the Opportunity: How Changes in Registration and Voting Law Can Enhance Voter Participation*. Washington.

———. 1989. "Non-Voter Study '88–'89: Only Half the Nation Votes." Washington.

———. 1990. "Non-Voter Study '90–'91: Surges in Local Voting Don't Propel Turnout Upward in Messageless Election." Washington.

———. 1992. "Primary Turnout Down 11.8 Percent; Democratic Vote Down 18.4 Percent." Washington.

Congressional Budget Office. 1988. *Trends in Family Income: 1970–1986.* February.

Converse, Philip E. 1972. "Change in the American Electorate." In Angus Campbell, ed., *The Human Meaning of Social Change*. Russell Sage Foundation.

Conway, Margaret M. 1991. *Political Participation in the United States*. Washington: Congressional Quarterly Press.

Cooper, Jamie, and Ian Christe. 1992. *Policy Alternatives on Voter Participation: A State Report,* vol. 3 (Washington: Center for Policy Alternatives, December 1991).

Cossolotto, Matthew. 1991. "A Competitive Politics." *Christian Science Monitor*. November 21.

———. 1992. "The Representation Deficit." Alexandria, Va: Citizens for Proportional Representation.

Cox, Gary W., and Michael C. Munger. 1989. "Closeness, Expenditures, and Turnout in the 1982 U.S. House Elections. *American Political Science Review* 83 (March).

Crewe, I. 1981. "Electoral Participation." In David Butler, Howard R. Penniman, and Austin Ranney, eds., *Democracy at the Polls: A Comparative Study of Competitive National Elections*. Washington: American Enterprise Institute for Public Policy Research.

Cyr, A. Bruce. 1975. "The Calculus of Voting Reconsidered." *Public Opinion Quarterly* 39 (Spring): 19–38.

Downs, Anthony. 1957. *Economic Theory of Democracy*. Harper.

Edsall, Thomas B. 1984. *The New Politics of Inequality*. Norton.

Erikson, R. S., N. R. Luttbeg, and K. L. Tedin. 1991. *American Public Opinion: Its Origins, Content, and Impact*. Macmillan.

Galston, W., and E. C. Kamarck. 1989. *The Politics of Evasion: Democrats and the Presidency*. Washington: Progressive Policy Institute.

Gans, Curtis B. 1983. Testimony before the Senate Committee on Rules and Administration, on Media and Politics. September 29.

———. 1991a. "Anatomy of a Bill, or the Education of a Student of Politics." In John C. Courtney, ed., "Registering Voters: Comparative Perspectives." Center for International Affairs, Harvard University.

———. 1991b. Testimony on campaign finance before the Senate Committee on Rules and Administration. March 14.

————. 1992. Personal communication citing Jean Marc Hammel, former chief registrar of Canada.

Gant, Michael M., and Norman R. Luttbeg. 1991. *American Electoral Behavior: 1952–1988*. Itasca, Ill.: F. E. Peacock.

Gant, Michael M., and William Lyons. 1992. "Democratic Theory, Non-Voting and Public Policy: The 1972–1988 Presidential Elections." University of Tennessee.

Gibson, James L., Cornelius P. Cotter, John F. Bibby, and Robert J. Huckshorn. 1985. "Whither the Local Parties?: A Cross-Sectional and Longitudinal Analysis of the Strength of Party Organizations." *American Journal of Political Science* 29: 139–60.

Glenn, Norval. 1977. *Cohort Analysis*. Beverly Hills: Sage Publications.

Guzzo, G. 1991. "Lessons of the Wichita Voter Participation Project." Memorandum. Miami: Knight-Ridder Newspapers.

Hanushek, Eric A., and J. E. Jackson. 1977. *Statistical Methods for Social Scientists*. Academic Press.

Herrnson, Paul S. 1988. *Party Campaigning in the 1980s*. Harvard University Press.

Huckshorn, Robert J., James L. Gibson, Cornelius P. Cotter, and John F. Bibby. 1986. "Party Integration and Party Organizational Strength." *Journal of Politics* 48: 976–91.

Jackman, Robert W. 1987. "Political Institutions and Voter Turnout in the Industrial Democracies." *American Political Science Review* 81: 405–23.

Keith, Bruce E., and others. 1986. "The Partisan Affinities of Independent 'Leaners.' " *British Journal of Political Science* 16: 155–84.

Kleppner, Paul. 1982. *Who Voted?: The Dynamics of Electoral Turnout, 1870–1980*. Praeger.

Knack, Stephen F. 1991a. "Civic Norms, Social Sanctions and Voter Turnout." University of Maryland.

————. 1991b. "The Voter Participation Effects of Selecting Jurors from Registration Lists." *Journal of Law and Economics.*

————. 1992a. "Social Connectedness and Voter Participation: Evidence from the 1991 NES Pilot Study." Center for Political Studies, University of Michigan.

————. 1992b. "Deterring Voter Registration through Juror Source Practices: Evidence from the 1991 NES Pilot Study." Unpublished.

————. 1992c. "The Effects of Motor Voter on Turnout and the Vote: An Empirical Analysis of the National Voter Registration Act." School of Public Affairs, American University.

Knight-Ridder Newspapers. 1989. "Readership Trends." Unpublished. Miami.

Lange, Peter, Christine Ridout, and James Cooney. 1978. "Voter Turnout in Advanced Industrial Democracies: A Bibliographical Essay." Washington: Committee for the Study of the American Electorate.

League of Women Voters. 1988. "Vote! The First Steps." July.

Leighley, Jan E. 1992. "Disappearing Elections, Disappearing Voters: Local Voter Turnout and the Substitutibility Thesis." Paper prepared for the Charles

Phelps Taft Memorial Fund conference, "The Disappearing American Voter." University of Cincinnati. April.

Leighley, Jan E., and Jonathan Nagler. 1991. "Socioeconomic Class Bias in Turnout, 1972–1988: Institutions Come and Go, But Voters Remain the Same." Paper prepared for the annual meeting of the American Political Science Association.

Levy, Frank. 1987. *Dollars and Dreams: The Changing American Income Distribution*. Russell Sage Foundation.

Lijphart, A. 1984. *Democracies: Patterns of Majoritarian and Consensus Government in Twenty-One Countries*. Yale University Press.

Lipset, Seymour M., and William Schneider. 1983. *The Confidence Gap: Business, Labor, and Government in the Public Mind*. Free Press.

Lohr, Steve. 1992. "The Media Business; Forget Peoria. It's Now: 'Will It Play in Tulsa?' " *New York Times*, June 1, p. A1.

Magleby, David B., and Candice J. Nelson. 1990. *The Money Chase: Congressional Campaign Finance Reform*. Brookings.

Mare, R. 1983. Lectures on analysis of categorical data. University of Wisconsin.

Markle Commission on the Media and the Electorate. 1990. "Recommendations." New York: John and Mary R. Markle Foundation.

Merrill, Bruce D. 1991. "Evaluating the Impact of Kids Voting in the 1990 Statewide Election in Arizona." Tempe, Ariz.: Kids Voting of Arizona (January).

Miller, Warren E. 1992. "The Puzzle Transformed: Explaining Declining Turnout." *Political Behavior* 14: 1–40.

Miller, Warren E., and Santa Traugott. 1989. *American National Election Studies Data Sourcebook, 1952–1986*. Harvard University Press.

Mishel, L., and D. M. Frankel. 1991. *The State of Working America*. Armonk, N.Y.: M. E. Sharpe.

Mitchell, Glen, and Christopher Wlezien. 1989. "Voter Registration Laws and Turnout, 1972–1982." Paper presented at the annual meeting of the Midwest Political Science Association.

Mitofsky, Warren J., and Martin Plissner. 1988. "Low Voter Turnout?: Don't Believe It." *New York Times.* November 10: A31.

Nagler, Jonathan. 1991. "The Effect of Registration Laws and Education on U. S. Voter Turnout." *American Political Science Review* 85: 1393–1405.

Nahra, Kirk J. 1984. "Non-Voter Study '85–86—Media Spending and Total Expenditures in the Highest Spending Senate Campaigns: 1974–1982." Washington: Committee for the Study of the American Electorate.

National Voter Registration Act of 1989. 1989. H. Rept. 101–243, 101 Cong, 1 sess. Government Printing Office.

Niemi, Richard G. 1992. "The Shape and Determinants of Civics Knowledge among High School Seniors." Unpublished research proposal. University of Rochester.

Oliver, Eric, and Raymond E. Wolfinger. 1992. "Jury Duty as a Deterrent to Voter Registration." Memo to Board of Overseers, National Election Studies.

Olson, Mancur, Jr. 1965. *Logic of Collective Action: Public Goods and the Theory of Groups*. Harvard University Press.

Ornstein, Norman J., Thomas E. Mann, and Michael J. Malbin. 1992. *Vital Statistics on Congress, 1991–1992*. Washington: Congressional Quarterly.

Orren, Gary R., and W. G. Mayer. 1990. "The Press, Political Parties, and the Public-Private Balance in Elections." In L. S. Maisel, ed., *The Parties Respond: Changes in the American Party System*. Boulder, Colo.: Westview Press.

Petrocik, J. R. 1981. "Voter Turnout and Electoral Oscillation." *American Politics Quarterly* 9: 161–80.

———. 1987. "Voter Turnout and Electoral Preference: The Anomalous Reagan Elections." In K. L. Schlozman, ed., *Elections in America*. Boston: Allen and Unwin.

Piven, Frances F., and Richard A. Cloward. 1988. *Why Americans Don't Vote*. Pantheon Books.

Pomper, Gerald M., and Loretta Sernekos. 1989. "The 'Bake Sale' Theory of Voting Participation." Paper prepared for the annual meeting of the American Political Science Association.

Popkin, Samuel L. 1991a. *The Reasoning Voter: Communication and Persuasion in Presidential Campaigns*. University of Chicago Press.

———. 1991b. "We Need Loud Mean Campaigns: Because That's the Only Way Americans Will Pay Attention." *Washington Post*, December 11.

Powell, G. Bingham, Jr. 1982. *Contemporary Democracies: Participation, Stability and Violence*. Harvard University Press.

———. 1986. "American Voter Turnout in Comparative Perspective." *American Political Science Review* 80: 17–44.

Presser, Stanley, Michael W. Traugott, and Santa Traugott. 1990. "Vote 'Over' Reporting in Surveys: The Records or the Respondents?" Paper presented for the International Conference on Measurement Errors, Tucson, Ariz (November).

Progressive Policy Institute. 1990. "Free Media Time for Candidates: Should the Law Require Television and Radio Stations to Make Free Air Time Available to Political Candidates? A Roundtable." Washington.

Research Center. 1990a. "Voter Participation Study, Pre/Post-Election Results." Wichita, Kans.

———. 1990b. "Voter Participation Study, Post-Election Results." Wichita, Kans.

———. 1991a. "Knight-Ridder Voter Participation Study, Analysis of Focus Groups." Wichita, Kans.

———. 1991b. "Voter Participation Study, City Election Results, Pre-Test Versus Post-Test." Wichita, Kans.

Riker, William H., and Peter C. Ordeshook. 1968. "A Theory of the Calculus of Voting." *American Political Science Review* 62 (June): 25–42.

Rosenstone, Steven, and Hansen, John Mark. Forthcoming. *Participation in American Politics*. Macmillan.

Rothenberg, Laurence S., and Richard A. Brody. 1988. "Participation in Presidential Primaries." *Western Political Quarterly* 41: 253–71.

RSM, Inc. 1989. "Registering Young Adults: An Experimental Case Study." Washington.

Sabato, Larry J. 1988. *The Party's Just Begun: Shaping Political Parties for America's Future.* Glenview, Ill: Scott, Foresman.

———. 1989. *Paying for Elections: The Campaign Finance Thicket.* Priority Press.

Scammon, Richard M., and Alice V. McGillvray, eds. 1960–88. *America Votes: A Handbook of Contemporary Election Statistics,* vols. 4–18. Washington: Congressional Quarterly.

Schneider, William. 1992. "'Off with Their Heads': Public Resentment of Professionalism in Politics." *American Enterprise* (July–August).

Shaffer, Stephen D. 1981. "A Multivariate Explanation of Decreasing Turnout in Presidential Elections, 1960–1976." *American Journal of Political Science* 25: 68–95.

———. 1982. "Policy Differences between Voters and Nonvoters in American Elections." *Western Politics Quarterly* 35: 496–510.

Silver, Brian D., Barbara A. Anderson, and Paul R. Abramson. 1986. "Who Overreports Voting?" *American Political Science Review* 80: 613–24.

Smolka, R. G. 1977. *Election Day Registration: The Minnesota and Wisconsin Experience in 1976.* Washington: American Enterprise Institute for Public Policy Research.

Southern Regional Council. 1989. "Winning the South in 1992: An Analysis of the 1988 Presidential Election." Atlanta.

Squire, Peverill, Raymond E. Wolfinger, and David P. Glass. 1987. "Residential Mobility and Voter Turnout." *American Political Science Review* 81: 45–65.

Stanley, H. W., and R. G. Niemi. 1988. *Vital Statistics on American Politics.* Washington: Congressional Quarterly Press.

Strate, John. M., Charles J. Parrish, Charles D. Elder, and Coit Ford III. 1989. "Life Span Civic Development and Voting Participation." *American Political Science Review* 83: 443–64.

Taylor, P. 1990. *See How They Run: Electing the President in an Age of Mediaocracy.* Alfred A. Knopf.

Teixeira, Ruy A. 1987. *Why Americans Don't Vote: Turnout Decline in the United States, 1960–1984.* Greenwood Press.

———. 1989a. "Registration and Turnout." *Public Opinion* (January–February).

———. 1989b. "End of the Rainbow." *New Republic* (April 3): 11–14.

———. 1991. "Wichita Eagle Voter Participation Surveys, 1991–1992." Memorandum to Glenn Guzzo.

Times-Mirror. 1990a. "The American Media: Who Reads, Who Watches, Who Listens, Who Cares." Washington: Times-Mirror Center for The People and The Press.

————. 1990b. "The Press, People and Politics, 1990." Washington: Times-Mirror Center for The People and The Press.

————. 1991. "Times-Mirror Survey, October, 1991." Washington: Times-Mirror Center for The People and The Press.

————. 1992. "Times-Mirror News Interest Index, February, 1992: Public Interest and Awareness of News." Washington: Times-Mirror Center for The People and The Press.

Traugott, Santa. 1989. "Validating Self-Reported Vote: 1964–1988." Paper prepared for the annual meeting of the American Statistical Association.

Traugott, Michael W., and John P. Katosh. 1979. "Response Validity in Surveys of Voting Behavior." *Public Opinion Quarterly* 43: 359–77.

Uhlaner, Carole Y. 1989. "Rational Turnout: The Neglected Role of Groups." *American Journal of Political Science* 33 (May): 390–422.

U.S. Bureau of the Census. 1965. "Voting and Registration in the Election of November 1964." Department of Commerce.

————. 1969. "Voting and Registration in the Election of November 1968." Department of Commerce.

————. 1985. "Geographical Mobility." *Current Population Reports* Series P-20, no. 420. Department of Commerce.

————. 1989. "Voting and Registration in the Election of November 1988." Deptartment of Commerce.

U.S. Congress. 1990. *Congressional Record,* daily ed. February 6, 1990: H254.

Verba, Sidney, Norman H. Nie, and J. Kim. 1978. *Participation and Political Equality: A Seven-Nation Comparison.* Cambridge University Press.

Verba, Sidney, Kay L. Schlozman, Henry Brady, and Norman Nie. 1991. "Resources and Political Participation." Paper prepared for the annual meeting of the American Political Science Association.

————. 1992. "Does Equal Participation Matter: Political Activity and the Dilemmas of Representation." Unpublished.

Washington Post/ABC News poll. October 16–19.

Wattenberg, Martin P. 1990. *The Decline of American Political Parties, 1952–1988.* Harvard University Press.

Williams, Linda F. 1989. "'88 Election Results: Problems and Prospects for Black Politics." Washington: Joint Center for Political Studies.

Wolfinger, Raymond E. 1991. "The Politics of Voter Registration Reform." Paper prepared for the annual meeting of the Western Political Science Association.

————. Forthcoming. "Middle-of-the-Road Facts about Voter Turnout." In J. McGlennon and R. Rapoport, ed., *Picking the President: Is There a Better Way?* Praeger.

Wolfinger, Raymond E., and Steven J. Rosenstone. 1980. *Who Votes?* Yale University Press.

Wolfinger, Raymond E., David P Glass, and Peverill Squire. 1985. "Predictors of Electoral Turnout: An International Comparison." Paper prepared for the International Political Science Association 13th World Congress, Paris.

Index

Abramson, Jeffrey, 144
Absentee voting, 109, 145–46
Advertising. *See* Campaign ads
African-Americans. *See* Race and voting behavior
Age and voting behavior, 37–39, 46, 47, 74–75, 82–83, 85, 104; effect of reforms on, 114, 139
Arterton, F. Christopher, 144
Attitudes toward government. *See* Government, attitudes toward; Politics, attitudes toward
Australia, 7, 8, 14
Austria, 7, 8, 17

Belgium, 7, 8, 14, 136
Benefits and costs analysis. *See* Costs and benefits analysis
Bicameralism and unicameralism, 16, 151–52
Bilingual registration, 29
Blacks. *See* Race and voting behavior
Brady, Henry, 102
Burnham, Walter D., 59
Bush, George, 91, 93

Campaign ads, 158, 160, 161; analyses of, 173–74
Campaign finance, 158, 162, 162–64
Canada, 136
Cavanaugh, Thomas E., 97
Church attendance. *See* Social connectedness
Citizen duty, 17, 55–56, 157. *See also* Political connectedness
Civics courses, 177–78
Class and voting behavior, 58–59, 61–65, 69, 103
Closing dates for registration, 29, 108
Cloward, Richard A., 25, 26, 59
Cohort effect, 75–80
Compulsory voting, 14–15, 151, 154

Costs and benefits analysis: of reforms, 125, 130–33, 135, 154; of voting and nonvoting, 11–13, 14, 17, 20, 21–23, 28–29, 30, 57, 58–59, 143, 157

Demographic factors and voting behavior. *See* Age and voting behavior; Race and voting behavior; Region and voting behavior
Democratic legitimacy, 2, 101–02
Democratic party, 86, 88, 90–94, 98; voting reforms and, 138–41
Deputy registrars, 110
Dewey-Truman election, 24
Dukakis, Michael, 91, 92, 93, 94
Duke, David, 93–94n

Edsall, Thomas B., 59
Education and voting behavior, 18, 20, 65–67, 81, 83–85; effect of reforms on, 114, 139, 141
Election day holidays, 143–44
Elections, 97; competitiveness, 15–16, 20, 23, 53–54, 151; individual concern over, 156; presidential, 6, 9, 15, 24, 90–94, 161; turnout affecting outcomes, 86–87 93–94, 104
Electoral college, 92, 93, 152, 153
Electoral competition, 15–16, 20, 23, 151
Electoral systems, cross-national comparisons, 14–17, 151, 153, 184–85
Electoral and voting reform, 109, 143–46; in campaign financing, 162–64; changing dates and frequency of elections, 14–15, 54–55; costs and benefits, 154; structural, 15–16, 20, 23, 151. *See also* Registration reform
Electronic voting, 144–45

Family: marital status, 37–38, 46–47; wives working, 34–35, 81, 84, 86